WITHDRAWN
PUBLIC LIBRARY
BROOKLINE

D0142100

The American Puritan Imagination

The American Puritan

Imagination

Essays in revaluation

edited by

SACVAN BERCOVITCH

Professor of English and Comparative Literature
Columbia University

CAMBRIDGE UNIVERSITY PRESS

BROOKLINE PUBLIC LIBRARY

EG-TL
70-74

6|86
RA,B.C.L.
4|96

815.1
B48a
Copy1

Published by the Syndics of the Cambridge University Press
Bentley House, 200 Euston Road. London NW1 2DB
American Branch: 32 East 57th Street, New York, N.Y.10022

© Cambridge University Press 1974

Library of Congress Catalogue Card Number: 73-94136

ISBNs:
0 521 20392 9 hard cover
0 521 09841 6 paperback

First published 1974

Photoset in Malta by
St Paul's Press Ltd

Printed in the United States of America

Contents

Acknowledgements

'The veiled vision: the role of aesthetics in early American intellectual history', by Norman S. Grabo, was first printed in *William and Mary Quarterly*, XIX (1962), 493–510, and is reprinted by permission of the Institute of Early American History and Culture.

'Literary consequences of Puritanism', by Larzer Ziff, was first printed in *English Literary History*, XXX (1963), 292–305, and is reprinted by permission of the John Hopkin's University Press. © JHUP.

'The Puritan jeremiad as a literary form', by David Minter, was first printed in David Minter, *The Interpreted Design as a Structural Principle in American Prose* (New Haven, 1969), pp. 50–66, and is reprinted by permission of the Yale University Press. Copyright © 1969 by Yale University.

'Spiritual biography and the "Lords Remembrancers"', by Cecelia Tichi, was first printed in *William and Mary Quarterly*, XXVIII (1971), 64–85 and is reprinted by permission of the Institute of Early American Culture and History.

'"With My Owne Eyes": William Bradford's *Of Plymouth Plantation*', by Jesper Rosenmeier, was first printed in Sacvan Bercovitch (ed.), *Typology and Early American Literature* (Amherst, 1972), pp. 69–105, and is reprinted by permission of the University of Massachusetts Press.

'The Puritan poetry of Anne Bradstreet', by Robert D. Richardson, Jr, was first printed in *Texas Studies in Literature and Language*, IX (1967), 317–31, and is reprinted by permission of the University of Texas Press.

'The example of Edward Taylor', by Karl Keller, was first printed in *Early American Literature*, IV (1969), 5–26, and is reprinted by permission of the University of Massachusetts Press.

'Essays to do good for the glory of God: Cotton Mather's *Boni-*

facius', by David Levin, was first printed in the introduction to Cotton Mather, *Bonifacius: an Essay Upon the Good*, ed. David Levin (Cambridge, Mass., 1966), pp. vii–xxvii, and is reprinted by permission of the President and Fellows of Harvard College. Copyright, 1966, by the President and Fellows of Harvard College.

'The art and instruction of Jonathan Edwards' *Personal Narrative*' by Daniel B. Shea, Jr, from 'Jonathan Edwards' *Personal Narrative*', in Daniel B. Shea, Jr, *Spiritual Autobiography in Early America* (Princeton, 1968), pp. 187–208, was first printed in *American Literature*, XXXVII (1965), 17–32. It is reprinted by permission of the Duke University Press. Copyright 1965, DUP, Durham North Carolina.

'Benjamin Franklin and the choice of a single point of view', by John F. Lynen, was first printed in 'The choice of a single point of view: Edwards and Franklin' in John F. Lynen, *The Design of the Present: Essays on Time and Form in American Literature* (New Haven, 1969), pp. 123–52, and is reprinted by permission of the Yale University Press. Copyright © 1969 by Yale University.

'Christ and Adam as "figures" in American literature', by Ursula Brumm, from Ursula Brumm, *American Thought and Religious Typology*, trans. John Hoaglund (New Brunswick, N. J., 1970), pp. 198–221 (first published in German in 1963), was first printed, in an earlier version, in *Partisan Review*, XXIV (1957), 403–13. It is reprinted by permission of Rutgers University Press.

For help at various stages of preparing this anthology, I would like to thank H. M. Bercovitch, James McIntosh, Roba S. Rush, Peter Shaw and Michael Wood.

I

The American Puritan Imagination:
an Introduction

The New England colonists took pride in the adversities of their locale. America had been Satan's territory, after all, from time immemorial; it was probably the world's last corner to receive the gospel. If we can apply great things to small, the settling of a continent to the errand into an academic wilderness, students of the American Puritan imagination might make similar claims for their own belated labors. That they should have lagged two decades or more behind other Americanists is no surprise. What is astonishing, considering the obstacles, is the vigor and extent of the scholarship. By comparison, the discoverers of 'American romanticism' had an easy time of it. The tradition that relegated *Moby Dick* to children's literature was not nearly so formidable as that which traced to Puritanism whatever seemed repugnant in the culture. Besides, even granted the injustice of the stereotype – the patently inaccurate image of the Puritan as self-serving moral hypocrite, lusting after conspiracy and guilt – granted even the majesty of the Puritans' thought, there was the problem of the aesthetic quality of their work. Thoreau, Whitman speak to us directly; if anything, time has charged their words with greater urgency. But Anne Bradstreet, William Bradford, Cotton Mather — aren't their writings the equivalent in *belles-lettres* for what the emigrants called the howling and barren desert of the New World?

Within the last decade, a growing number of scholars have gone far towards exorcising that misconception as well. A brief glance at the bibliography in this volume will confirm the scope of the enterprise, and this is symptomatic in turn of new directions in college courses, anthologies, reprint series, professional conferences, graduate programs. When I was writing my dissertation, in 1964, I came across the concept of *figura* in Mather's *Magnalia*. I recall the excitement of pursuing typology through seventeenth-century Massachusetts — and my ambivalent feelings, several months later, at learning that Ursula Brumm had already published on the subject. Still later I learned of no less than five dissertations on early New England typology, all of them written at more or less the same time as mine, and all under more or less the same illusion of originality. No doubt a good many other colonialists had similar experiences, as they pursued their different paths through the literature. No doubt, too, they found ample compensation, as I did, in their sense of community. The shock of recognizing a *Zeitgeist* in one's thesis led to the reassurance of shared enthusiasms, the personal and professional pleasures of a common effort.

The effort itself took shape slowly, through a number of heterogeneous influences. One of these was the rise of Puritan intellectual history in the thirties, crowned by the achievement of Perry Miller (1905–63). Much has been written of late about Miller's shortcomings. He did not say everything; he was partial or mistaken about things he did say; and he drastically underrated the aesthetic dimension of the Puritan mind. Nonetheless, the range and brilliance of his work were an inspiration. And the framework he provided not only could accommodate criticism but invited revaluation.[1] For literary scholars, the challenge first took focus in the discovery of Edward Taylor. Miller's view of the New England mind had precluded a poet of real stature, and here, suddenly thrust upon us, was the most talented and impassioned American poet before the mid-nineteenth century. Was Taylor an anomaly? a good poet fallen among Puritans, and unable to repress his calling (though disciplined enough to forbid publication)? Was he a Catholic in disguise? After these predictable initial responses, the criticism set in in earnest. During the early 1960s, Donald Stanford and others defined Taylor's richness of form and substance as the product of Puritan thought. The number of studies on Taylor since then far exceeds that on any other colonial writer.

These studies taught us, first, to understand the poet as Puritan; then, to appreciate the Puritan as poet. Fundamentally, to be sure, the two perspectives are interdependent. We have learned about Taylor's aesthetic by examining his debt to meditational devotion, homiletic techniques, the motifs of folk art, the medieval morality play, the patterns of typological exegesis. We continue to profit in this respect from debates over the relation of his verse to his sermons, explications of his position in colonial ecclesiology and research into the backgrounds of his imagery. At this early stage in our study of Taylor, we cannot say too much about the traditions that nourished his imagination, especially when the analysis brings a variety of issues and influences into clear view, as in Alan Howard's account of Taylor's use of the 'emblem'. Karl Keller's essay in this volume builds on previous research in order to examine the significance of language itself for the poet. Several scholars, notably Kathleen Blake, have outlined the theological framework of the question: the problematic correspondence between words and truth, 'humane' images and transcendent reality. Keller examines Taylor's obsessive concern with the nature and value of poetry as this comes to shape metaphor, theme, and structure in the poems. His approach suggests how far we have come beyond *apologia* towards defining the mind and art of an important American poet.[2]

The recognition of Taylor has helped make us aware of the creative vitality in the colony at large. Gradually we realized, what now seems a statistical truism, that seventeenth-century New England gave rise to more poetry, proportionately, than any other period in our history, and that if most of it was second-rate, as is always the case, some of it had considerable merit. Anne Bradstreet's current reputation rests not upon our surprise that a woman wrote at all in that glacial age, but upon the subtlety, the technical skill, even the relevance of what she wrote. Inevitably, a number of recent critics have studied her as a woman poet – in fact, the first serious woman poet in English literature. But the best of these critics (I think of Ann Stanford in particular) consider her situation as a woman in order to highlight the representative quality of her work: for example, its counterpoint between duty and passion, resignation and assertion, between an orthodoxy that seems too easy at times and a rebelliousness that almost borders on blasphemy. I say 'seems', 'almost', because Anne Bradstreet was neither a conformist nor an individualist, but a Puritan. That is, she felt profoundly involved in this world even as she dedicated herself to the other, and she knew, moreover, that doubt and struggle were part of the road to salvation. One of the merits of Robert Richardson's essay is that it sees Bradstreet's poetic development in the context of her beliefs. Richardson shows that the deepening complexity of her work expressed a search for faith which led her from the natural world to the divine and then back again to man and nature. He shows, too, that the poetry which conveys her search remains a triumph both of faith and of art.

The colonists praised Bradstreet's writings from the start. Why, then, in our own time did she have to wait until past mid-century to receive due tribute? Or more pointedly, seeing that Taylor's manuscripts came to light in the late 1930s, how do we explain the delay in adequate critical response? In part, I think, by something fairly commonplace — 'cultural lag', a period of adjustment, a season of gestation. Matthiessen's *American Renaissance* similarly arrived some twenty years after Lawrence's seminal *Studies in Classic American Literature*. Another reason lies in the shifting climate of literary studies. Scholarship through the forties was polarized between formalism and various types of historicism. When in the next decade the two strains merged — as in the establishment of American Studies — the confluence proved especially fortunate for colonial literature. For, from a New Critical standpoint, the problem was the dearth of well-wrought works of colonial Puritan art. American Studies offered, if not a methodology, then at least a rationale for broadening the definition of art from the unique, extraordinary product to the cultural pattern or artifact. And, so conceived, the harvest of early New England poetry and prose — its innumerable journals, sermons, treatises, jeremiads, histories, polemics, private and public verse, hagiographies and autobiographies — turned out to be extraordinary indeed.

The cultural perspective, if I may call it so, showed up the inadequacy of the standard pejoratives of the thirties. We had been told that the literature was blighted by Ramist logic; now we could examine the relationship between logic and literature in the way Rosemund Tuve examined Ramism in English metaphysical poetry, as lending a particular structure to perception and association. We had heard the Puritans' style condemned for its plainness, and their aesthetic denigrated for its subservience to theology. We felt free now to point out that Dante and Milton were no less subservient; or conversely, that the New England Puritans had recourse as often as Dante and Milton did to poetic licence; or again, that their theology encouraged an intense emotionalism; or once more, that their literary taste was flexible enough to accommodate pagan models, scatology, erotica, ambiguity, and personality. As to the 'plain style', we could assert by authority of the evidence that 'plain' was in no sense synonymous with 'arid' or 'artless'. In keeping with their intellectual outlook, the colonists' writings were highly figurative, abounding in metaphor, parallel, allusion, type and trope, and controlled by a variety of sophisticated rhetorical devices. Their literary theories stressed the virtues of eloquence. Their belief in 'spiritual signification' opened out into a richly symbolic mode of discourse. They conceived of reality, in accordance with their concept of the unity of knowledge, as a system of linked analogies, interlacing every strand of recorded experience, ancient and modern, scientific and humanistic no less than theological. And within that system, they understood their own enterprise, the momentous 'errand' they never wearied of describing, as part of the cosmic drama of redemption.

Needless to say, our insight into these imaginative patterns did not follow simply, or even primarily, from American Studies. American Studies served in the main as an impetus; it was an institutional benediction upon an effort already under way.[3] I would hesitate to categorize any of the essays in this volume as belonging to American Studies, though each of them, in its own way, reflects the tendency towards cultural synthesis. Norman Grabo posits a theory of aesthetics derived from neo-Kantian philosophy; yet as he applies the theory he offers a means of reconciling disparate levels of experience, so that (for example) the relation of expressive form to communication opens new prospects for understanding social history. Larzer Ziff's method is essentially that of intellectual history. Extrapolating from the work of a paradigmatic minor author, he outlines the consequences of Puritanism in terms both of rhetoric and of thought; and on this basis, he proceeds to larger areas of consideration: stylistics, the nature of audience response, modes of behavior and self-definition on the scale of cultural movements. David Levin moves towards similar considerations from the angle of the literary historian. His text, Cotton Mather's *Bonifacius*, is no more a literary document than it is a document in intellectual history or (in Grabo's sense) a particular expressive form. But the insights which Levin draws from it stem from his sensitivity to imaginative substructure and *as such* they elucidate many facets of colonial life, from its millenarianism to its day-by-day pietism, and thence outward to consequences as broad and diverse as those proposed by Grabo and Ziff.

What seems clear from all three approaches — aesthetic, intellectual, and historical — is that each of them reaches towards the others and all towards a method which would grasp the culture in its totality. The study of the Puritan imagination, because the last and most timid of American literary enterprises, has profited most from the recent interest in inter-disciplinary perspectives, and promises most, I believe, to provide a model for comparable efforts in other branches of literature. If so, the model will be exemplary, among other reasons, for the rigor with which these colonialists approach extra-literary disciplines. Cecelia Tichi discusses biographical techniques effectively because she can root the discussion in the pertinent social and theological issues. So also Jesper Rosenmeier's figural reading of Bradford's History shows how a knowledge of hermeneutics can contribute to our understanding of creative process. In both essays, the command of 'extraneous' materials, and the advantages this carries for aesthetic insight, stand as reproof to the parochialism of much of American literary criticism. This holds true as well for David Minter's treatment of the jeremiad. His critique of rhetorical forms gathers substance from his awareness both of the historical factors that undermined the theocracy and of the theocratic vision of corporate destiny which the dwindling latter-day orthodoxy wrung from *de facto* defeat.

The vision of the Puritan Jeremiahs recalls still another reason for the rise of colonial literary studies. I mean the emphasis in the last two or three decades on the crucial role of myth in shaping American history and historiography. This is not the place to explore the phenomenon (which includes developments in psychology, sociology, anthropology, and related fields). It must suffice to note that our consciousness of myth has helped us respond to the tremendous imaginative energy imparted by the Great Migration. Most of the basic elements of the Dream are there: the divine purpose behind America's 'discovery', the teleological distinction of the New World from the Old, the sense of history ascending ineluctably towards the American paradise. Something of all this has long been recognized, but from a hostile or alien point of view. Only recently have we begun to see it in its own terms. To speak as enlightened historians of the 'Puritan myth' is one thing; to enter symbiotically into its modes of expression is something quite different. The former course has served all too often as a vehicle of self-congratulation, reinforcing our own myths of progress at the expense of our appreciation of the Puritans'. The latter course has served perforce to heighten our respect for the dynamics of Puritan thought. In following the development, for instance, of the metaphors of garden and exodus, of errand and trial (on sea, in the settlements, in the heart), we come to feel the visionary force that sustained the venture. What we learn thereby pertains to every aspect of the culture. It has taught us – it promises to teach us a great deal more – about how the settlers adjusted to the new environment, about the nature of their generational crises, about the tensions that ultimately eroded the theocracy. It also reveals, I believe, that the Puritan legacy to subsequent American culture lies not in theology or logic or social institutions, but in the realm of the imagination.

This is by no means to separate the imaginative from the theological or the social, much less to proffer a hierarchy of values. On the contrary, it is to insist on a basic integrity of design. To understand a metaphor we must first know its background and implications. But equally, to know the background, and implications, is to understand the power of the metaphor. Let me offer a familiar instance. The emigrants thought of themselves as a 'new Israel' on an 'errand' to found a 'city on a hill'. To the modern reader (and all too often, to the modern scholar) the terms mean anything – i.e., nothing in particular. To the Puritan their meanings were both precise and complex. 'Errand' implied the believer's journey to God and the communal calling to the New World; 'new Israel' signified the elect, the theocracy as it was prefigured in the Old Testament, and the blessed remnant which, according to prophecy, would usher in the millennium; 'city' meant a social order and the bonds of a true visible church; the concept of 'hill' opened into a series of scriptural landmarks demarcating the march of redemptive history: Ararat, Sinai, Golgotha, and the Holy Mount of New Jerusalem. Each of the terms, then, presents the same constellation of meanings. Each of them tells us that the Puritan impulse was profoundly eschatological; that the eschatology was at once private and public, applicable as it were in the same breath to saint and society; and that the forms of that society expressed the saint's relationship to his church, his fellow-man, the spiritual life to come, and God's grand design for mankind.

The world, the kingdom, and the divine plan! Separately and together, the terms bespeak the comprehensive self-concept that united the colonists (in another of their familiar phrases) 'as One Man with one soul in one body'. To be sure, the terms equally imply the contradictions in Puritanism, the divergent emphases on the spirit and the law, individual experience and social order, self-examination and the commitment to history. Such contradictions fragmented the movement elsewhere, and they surfaced threateningly from time to time in the Bay theocracy. One of the salient effects of exploring the rhetoric is that this requires us to extend the borders of New England studies so as to include the diversity of Puritan sects. Another benefit is that the rhetoric allows us, without losing sight of contradiction, to see the *Gestalt*, the overall coherence of American Puritanism. For the fact is that the theocracy welded together, as did no other Protestant community, the disparate personal and historical thrusts of the Reformation: on the one hand, Luther's pietism and Calvin's 'realized eschatology', centered on the believer's new-birth in Christ; on the other hand, Calvin's disciplinarianism and Luther's 'futuristic eschatology', leading towards chiliasm and the doctrine of national election. Puritanism denotes a large number of groups, most of them (as Cromwell's revolution proved) mutually incompatible. American Puritanism offered the saint a comprehensive identity — as a citizen, as a member of the true church, and as a warrior in the world-redeeming vanguard of the Reformation.

The colonists wrought the synthesis by a gargantuan act of will and imagination. We can trace their effort through all forms of the literature: sermons that integrate the stages of regeneration with communal good works; elegies that render the saint's glorification a preview of New England's destiny; journals that blend mysticism and apocalypse; hagiographies whose subjects are microcosms of the colony; federal exhortations couched in the vocabulary of the covenant of grace. Edward Gallagher has shown how the first history of Massachusetts, Johnson's *Wonder-Working Providence* (1654), is in effect the story of a pilgrim's progress to heaven; Michael Colacurcio has argued that Taylor's apparently atemporal *Gods Determinations* is really an effort to return the colonists to the Good Old Way. In all cases, the inversion of perspective depends on the uses of rhetoric. In all cases, the rhetoric, even as it builds upon broad hermeneutic tenets, affirms the myth within which the colony defined its origins and purpose. And in all cases, the myth devolves upon the meaning of the new continent — 'the ends of the earth', as the emigrant leaders called it, referring to the prophets and the Book of Revelation — the world's fourth and last 'corner' to sound the trumpet of the Son of Man (see Rev. 1, 7).

Nothing more clearly attests to the power of the American Puritan imagination than this mythico-historiography. The emigrants had fled England as from certain destruction. Behind them, they believed, lay the failure of European Protestantism — and before them, as their refuge, what they called 'wilderness', 'desert'. The image speaks for itself of their fear. It also proclaims the means they found to persevere: the daring symbolic pattern which justified their migration by justifying America. The New World, according to that image, was the modern counterpart of the wilderness through which the Israelites reached Canaan, of the desert where Christ overcame the tempter. More than counterpart, it was antitype: the journey then was a foreshadowing of the journey now by a *Christian* Israel to the long-awaited 'new heavens and a new earth'. Why else did God so long conceal America, but to make its discovery the *finale* to His work of redemption? Could mere chance explain the fact that its discovery followed so soon after the Reformation, or that the Book of Revelation found its greatest expositors just before the voyage of the *Arbella*? Was it not by design that a pestilence cleared the land of Indians when the fleet landed? Unmistakably the New World, like Canaan of old, belonged wholly to the history of salvation. Other peoples, the colonists explained, had their land by providence; *they* had it by promise. Others must seek their national origins in secular records and chronicles; the story of America was enclosed in the scriptures, its past postdated and its future antedated in prophecy.

In sum, the emigrants created America in their own image. And having done so, they used the image of America to vindicate their enterprise. Were they in exile? Scripture foretold the hardships in store for the end-time remnant. Did Satan rule the country and its heathen inhabitants? So it had been in the case of the chosen Hebrews, so it would be on the fields of Armageddon: the Puritan errand was an earnest of Christ's hastening deliverance of mankind. The sweep of these and many similar assertions is breath-taking, especially in view of their persistence, *mutatis mutandis*, long after the theocracy faded. Equally striking is the transparent relationship between fear and self-affirmation. As the colonists built up their rationale from one decade to another, the concept of America – and *ipso facto* that of *American* Puritanism – became a barrier against the threat of mutability, a guarantee of success raised by the myth-making imagination upon self-doubt. Significantly, the rhetoric rises to a higher pitch with every setback. It is no accident that King Philip's War elicited a concerted reaffirmation of the cause, or that apocalypticism reached its zenith with the Andros regime and the revocation of the original charter. Perhaps the best known example is the legend of the founding fathers, which dates from 1660, when the English Puritan Revolution failed and when, in New England, the crisis began that issued in the half-way covenant. In these bleak years, barely three decades after the Great Migration, before all its leaders had died, there evolved the saga of a golden age, one which effectually transported all the archetypes of biblical and classical antiquity to the tiny, barren American strand. The rapidity with which it grew amounts to an artistic achievement of a very high order, as well as an amazing, possibly unrivalled cultural maturation. We can see in retrospect that the legend of the fathers marked a decisive victory for American identity. In more immediate terms, the entire process provides a sort of ready-made laboratory for examining the nature and the effects of myth in a modern culture.

American Puritan literature offers itself as a laboratory for still another, related area of study: the transition from medieval and renaissance allegory to modern symbolism. Let me begin with a fairly simple contrast. Allegory originates, as a rule, in an orthodox, absolute design, and proceeds from the abstract to the particular. Symbolism starts in subjective interpretation, and leads from the discrete to the universal. Thus Bunyan's concept of wilderness is allegorical, whereas Eliot's is symbolic. Both *Pilgrim's Progress* and *The Wasteland* may be said to be mythical; but the Puritan work, unlike the other, depends on accepted tradition. The wilderness through which Christian passes assumes meaning for us to the extent that Bunyan persuades us of the 'wilderness of this world' — the world, that is, *sub specie aeternitatis*, at any time, in any place, and hence our time, our place. The significance of Eliot's wasteland, on the contrary, depends on our acceptance of *Eliot's* view. His image works because the evidence he selects elicits a multiple response, serves as 'objective correlative' for a diversity of meanings. The wilderness in *Pilgrim's Progress* restricts us to a particular moral abstraction. We might miss Bunyan's every allusion to seventeenth-century England and still respond as he intended. We might understand them all and still lose the significance, if we did not (on some level) share Bunyan's tradition. Whether or not we agree with Eliot's religious outlook, whether or not we even know he had one, is secondary to the poem, or at any rate to the wasteland as symbol. But we must (on some level) assent to his evidence if we are to feel the wasteland's 'universal' import. Bunyan's wilderness is of this world insofar as we see it first as timeless; Eliot's is spiritual insofar as we first see it as fact.

This contrast bears directly upon how the American Puritans understood *their* wilderness. They shared the allegorical outlook with all Christians. For them as for Bunyan, any believer's life was a journey from the Egypt of sin, across the Red Sea of baptism, and so through the wilderness to the heavenly Canaan. They also thought that for them, as for no others, that spiritual journey had a distinctly historical meaning. Historically, in this world, they had left a sinful land; literally they had crossed a sea to win a new life; they were confronting Satan in a real wilderness; and if their goal was not heaven, it was something no less divine: the thousand-year reign of the saints in glory. They described their undertaking accordingly. Their summons from Europe was an evangelical call, their Atlantic crossing was tantamount to conversion, their hardships in settling the country were the temptations of Satan, the blossoming New World 'garden' made tangible, as it were, the *hortus conclusus* of the redeemed soul. All this they announced in imagery which, we have seen, was thoroughly traditional. Only here they were relying on fact rather than dogma, not on accepted deduction but on willed inference. They were being symbolists, not allegorists.

They themselves would have quarrelled with that distinction. Yet to confirm it we need do no more than recall their contemporaries – the great majority of Puritans, not to say Anglicans and Catholics, for whom, or for the few of them who knew about New England, the whole scheme was at best sheer hyperbole. These sceptics might have noted, further, that the colonists contradicted themselves by using the old form alongside the new. Characteristically, for example, the New England biographer describes his hero, the exemplary emigrant to the American Canaan, as traversing the allegorical wilderness, and speaks of the flight to a 'new world' christologically, as signifying a renunciation of the 'dead world'. Now, to all appearances such statements gave the lie to the very concept of errand. Roger Williams, for one, pointed that out. How, he demanded, could the transit from one part of a dead world to another, or the cultivation of any part of the wilderness of the world, *of itself* have the slightest spiritual meaning, let alone a meaning equivalent to the believer's journey to God? As every Christian child knew, the Hebrews' promised land, figurally understood, meant the blessings of grace, the milk and honey of heaven. What did the Atlantic crossing or the settlement of America have to do with such things? If the allegory was true, the symbol was not; if the symbol was true, the immemorial Christian epic of the soul was a lie. The *significatio* could emanate either from dogma or from experience, but not both.

The theocrats' answer was as simple as it was sweeping. To a deaf or incredulous Europe, they explained that America was *not* 'any' part of the world, precisely as Canaan was not, or Eden, or New Jerusalem to come. And for the benefit of their own flocks, they proceeded to draw out still another, even more astounding, implication of the logic of their symbolism. Having raised America (past, present, and to come) into redemptive history, they imposed upon it the allegory of the saint's life. I have mentioned Johnson's *Wonder-Working Providence* in this respect. By and large, however, the allegory of the New World is the fruit of second- and third-generation works: for example, Samuel Torrey's impassioned jeremiad, *An Exhortation Unto Reformation* (1674); the great election-day orations ˙ on federal destiny by John Norton (1661), John Higginson (1663), Jonathan Mitchel (1667), Samuel Danforth (1670), Urian Oakes (1673), James Allen (1679), Samuel Willard (1682), William Adams (1685), John Whiting (1686), and Nicholas Noyes (1698); Samuel Sewall's visionary tract, *Phaenomena quaedam Apocalyptica, or a Description of the New Heaven as it makes to those who stand upon the New Earth* (1697); Joshua Scottow's neglected minor masterpiece, *A Narrative of the Planting of the Massachusetts Colony* (1694); Increase Mather's *Sermon Shewing That . . . Wonderful Revolutions in the World are near at Hand* (1710); Joseph Morgan's quasi-Bunyanesque *History of the Kingdom of Basaruah* (1715); Cotton Mather's *Theopolis Americana. An Essay . . . of Better Things to be yet seen in the* AMERICAN *World* (1710), and above all his monumental and multifarious New World epic, *Magnalia Christi Americana* (1702).

As these men tell and retell the story, America is not only the destined haven of the saving remnant. It is itself the returned prodigal, the pilgrim redeemed from captivity, the virgin wakened from her long slothful sleep into the light of grace, stirred to new life by Christ, and now preparing to reveal herself for what she always was, *pulcherrima inter mulieres*, the most beautiful of His brides. The emigrant Southerners hoped to live as English gentlemen in utopia; the Spanish Franciscans tried to organize the natives into a model Christian kingdom. The New England Puritans gave America the status of visible sainthood. The importance of their vision to subsequent American thought can hardly be overestimated. Whatever the extent of its influence, it contributes to the differences in cultural development between the various regions of the New World, to the usurpation of American identity by the United States, to the ideal of the True American ('the acme of things accomplished', according to Whitman, 'and encloser of things to be'), and to the anthropomorphic concept of national selfhood — not the secular anthropomorphism of parenthood (Mother Russia, German Fatherland, British Homeland), but the eschatological anthropomorphism of allegory-become-symbol: American dream, manifest destiny, national mission, the promise of a redemptive future which, in Melville's phrase, was 'predestinated at creation'.

But we need not leap ahead to see the imaginative force of the vision. Conceptually and rhetorically, their image of America enabled the settlers more boldly to yoke together the private and the public pilgrimage, to fuse in one configuration the *telos* of the saint, the theocracy, and the country at large. And this in turn encouraged them more broadly to assert the symbolic mode. The aesthetic tensions that resulted between symbolism and allegory are highly instructive in their own right as well as in a larger literary or intellectual framework. For instance, the interpretation of the actual-yet-spiritual wilderness leads out to what might be called the genre of American natural theology — the concern with the New World landscape as a source of higher laws, a key to the golden future, and a proof-by-association of the interpreter's spiritual regeneration. All the benefits of Bunyan's allegory are there, but subjectivized, appropriated by the solitary perceiver and made normative by the authority of *his* voice, *his* experience. The transference issues in a fascinating interplay of traditionally distinct modes of discourse (e.g., typology, metaphor, analogy, 'spiritualization'), all mediating dialectically between allegory and symbolism, and many of them centered, directly or indirectly, on the meaning of America. This is not to say that colonial natural theology never addresses itself to nature in general. It does so frequently, and has its place, accordingly, in the development of Christian naturalism from Augustine through Thomas Browne to Wordsworth. But one cannot help being struck at how frequently, too, the American Puritan interpretation (like that of the American romantics) turns on a unique *national* locale — a 'wilderness', a 'city', a ripening 'garden of God' qualitatively different from all other plots of ground in a fallen world. Or rather, a discovery, not an interpretation, of the locale; for the colonists held that the significance was there from eternity, inscribed in prophecy and promise, like the figural landscape of *Pilgrim's Progress*. Elsewhere, divinity in nature was in the spiritual eye of the beholder. Here the beholder proclaimed his sainthood by identifying the literal—spiritual contours of the land.

At the risk of stating the obvious, I might note at this point that American Puritanism is not monolithic. Variations and discrepancies exist in every form of the literature, and the forms shift with each generation. To the extent that my comments simplify the issues, they are intended heuristically, in the conviction that differences become meaningful by reference to cultural norms. Perhaps my use of 'culture' also needs qualification. Parallel with the rise of colonial literary studies, a quantitative historicism has emerged which challenges the very notion that seventeenth-century Massachusetts was Puritan. Its adherents point out that church-members comprised a small part of the settlement, and that a minority of church-members wrote the literature. Can we generalize from the articulate few? One reason for believing we can lies in our sense of broad-based continuities.[4] Virtually all the essays in this volume express that assumption, from Grabo's specific literary examples to Keller's kaleidoscope of random artifacts of 'process'. The vagueness of terms — 'influence', 'consequences', 'uniquely American', 'national character' — reminds us that we still have no adequate explanations. The connections these writers suggest between art and society give us cause to persist. For instance, they make plain that the Puritan legacy, whatever it is, belongs neither to low culture nor to high. On the one hand, quantitative factors can hardly account for the recurrent figuralism in popular literature (America as the promised land, its leaders as greater Joshuas or Nehemiahs). On the other hand, we have nothing in America like the English line from Milton to Wordsworth to explain the 'Puritanism' of Hawthorne or Melville. It follows that we must seek a synthesis of disparate elements; and the synthesis, I venture to say, lies in the colonists' imaginative response to their experience, where 'imaginative' and 'experience' denote the full gamut of (respectively) creative expression and cultural conditions.

Let me illustrate this by turning briefly to the essays in the section on 'Continuities'. Edwards and Franklin were each in some sense representative of his times, and each had a wide social impact. Yet Daniel Shea and John Lynen do not deal primarily with the popular aspects of their thought — say, with revivalism and moral pragmatism *per se*. Instead, Lynen concentrates on Franklin's view of the self, in a symbolic—epistemological inquiry based upon the tenets of early New England theology. And Shea discusses Edwards' spiritual autobiography in the framework of what he defines as a distinctively colonial approach to personal narrative. Both writers draw very general inferences from their subjects, general enough to make up a composite portrait of the American self in the eighteenth century and beyond. But the inferences are organic to the method. Popular significance emerges from literary structures, and the literary structures derive intellectual significance from an earlier system of belief. Ursula Brumm assumes a similar threefold correspondence in discussing Faulkner's use of the Adamic theme. Her treatment of biblical symbology shows the cultural dimensions of a familiar American 'archetype'; and in doing so, it demonstrates, by implication at least, the effect of social events upon literature. The *donné* of her essay is neither Melville's influence upon Faulkner, nor, strictly speaking, the ironic fate of typology in contemporary fiction. It is the sustained impact of the Great Awakening upon the South.

Now, all this is especially remarkable because of the well-known antagonism between high and low culture in America. Historians have traced that antagonism to the late seventeenth century, when colonial society, they tell us, moved complacently into the Yankee era, as the orthodoxy thundered condemnation in an outmoded rhetoric. No image of American culture in conflict is more common. None is more misleading. It neglects the continuing vitality of the early ideals, as David Levin shows. It distorts the purpose of those jeremiads, which, as Minter and Tichi argue, is primarily to celebrate a past and future glory. Furthermore, it contradicts the effect of the rhetoric. That the vision of the Puritan Jeremiahs was not a mirage, nor merely wish-fulfillment — that metaphor and legend actually triumphed over history — is attested to in numerous writings from the eighteenth century on. Finally, the image obscures the fact that throughout our history the jeremiad has functioned as a ritual mode of social coherence. The conflict itself, that is, between populace and preacher, low and high culture, points to an underlying unity of design. This is made explicit frequently enough, as in the work of Emerson and Whitman. Elsewhere we can follow the dialectic by indirections. The counterpoint in *Walden*, for example, of *imitatio* and parody — spiritual autobiography and the American Way to Wealth — has a major source in what Lynen identifies as Edwards' and Franklin's *complementary* views of the self. Not only complementary, in this case, but mutually sustaining: Thoreau's claim that Walden is 'the only true America' makes sense insofar as Concord shares his belief in a national promise; John Field's dream of economic rebirth gives strength to the prophet's cry that *this* is the land of spiritual rebirth.

Both strains, popular and 'elite', lead back to seventeenth-century Massachusetts. Each of them testifies to the imaginative power of colonial Puritanism and together they argue the viability of a broad cultural approach to the literature. Again, some qualification may be in order. In the first place, the continuities I noted are also an index to change: they involve various combinations of Puritan with decidedly non-Puritan (sometimes anti-Puritan) concepts; they lead us to consider a multiplicity of social and intellectual factors separating one age, one generation, one individual from another; and, as Larzer Ziff and Daniel Shea suggest, they reveal the problems in distinguishing Puritanism in New England from its manifestations elsewhere, in Europe or even in other regions of America. Second, the entire issue of continuities is by no means essential to the study of colonial writing. Jesper Rosenmeier's essay, which limits itself to Bradford's Plymouth History, demonstrates the intrinsic cultural—imaginative value of the literature. Third, and perhaps most important, the cultural approach is one among many. I have stressed it here because it seems to me to epitomize the tendencies that gave rise to colonial literary studies, and most fully to display the potential in colonial literary studies for all Americanists. But I should like to stress, too, that the essays in this volume show a wide diversity of method and approach. I hope I have made this clear in the course of the introduction; and I would add now that that diversity is the most reliable testament we have to the richness of the American Puritan imagination and the most auspicious omen for the future of the scholarship. In 1690, surveying the prospects of his little colony, Cotton Mather was reminded of the many tasks ahead, the promises still unfulfilled; but considering the present, he could not help exclaiming: 'How Goodly are thy Tents, *O New-England*, and thy Tabernacles, *O thou American Israel*!' In all due modesty, and duly mindful of the distance between our academic tabernacles and those of either old Israel or new, we might take similar pride in the achievements of these essays and in the scholarly undertaking they represent.

Approaches, themes and genres

The role of aesthetics NORMAN S. GRABO
Literary consequences LARZER ZIFF
The puritan jeremiad DAVID MINTER
Spiritual biography CECELIA TICHI

2
The veiled vision:
the role of aesthetics in early
American intellectual history

NORMAN S. GRABO

The first publication of Edward Taylor's poetry was heralded as significant enough to bring about a total revaluation of American letters.[1] Twenty-three years later we find that Taylor has indeed shouldered his way into anthologies of American literature but has barely dimpled the still waters of early American intellectual history. This fact raises the problem posed succinctly some years ago by Professor Arthur O. Lovejoy, who wrote that there are instances 'in which the initial specialized interest of investigators in one province has produced a kind of blindness to aspects of the historical material with which they deal that are of great significance in relation to other parts of intellectual history... Learned historians of literature, philosophy, religion, science, or social or political movements, sometimes fall into ... omissions, simply because, knowing only their own subjects, they do not know all that is to be looked for *in* those subjects'.[2] Just such a blindness afflicts historians (literary as well as social, cultural, and intellectual) of the pre-revolutionary period, especially in their use of literary materials. Taylor's poetry only makes the blind spot more obvious because Taylor is unquestionably a fine, if limited, artist, and the usual ways of talking about colonial poets simply cannot account either for his work or for its place in colonial intellectual history.

Modern aesthetics pinpoints the historical problem here by raising a philosophical one. The perennial challenge to philosophers and critics of art has been to find a way of thinking and talking about art that, by transcending the particular limitations of all times and places and personalities, will apply universally — an aesthetic system as valid for the examination of Michael Wigglesworth as for Dylan Thomas, for Edward Johnson as for James Joyce. Behind this attempt lies the conviction that, although the language of literature is identical with that of normal everyday discourse,[3] it somehow functions in a completely different way and has always functioned in that different way, regardless of what either critics or artists thought they were doing in any given historical period. Thus literary statements neither 'mean' the same thing nor mean in the same way that discursive statements do.

Susanne K. Langer's explorations of the nature of art — descending from Immanuel Kant through Ernst Cassirer — offer a case in point.[4] She begins her inquiry by seeking a key concept or problem, the answer to which will raise further, and perhaps unexpected, questions about the nature of art. To begin with, she chooses the concept of *creativity*, supposing that we really mean something when we distinguish between manufactured products and created art. But what is created? The materials of art already exist; the difference must lie in the way they are manipulated or in the end they produce. Give leather, thread, and nails to a shoemaker and he will shape and combine them to produce a shoe — still an object of nails, thread, and leather; give these same materials to a painter and he will arrange them to end up with something quite different, an object wherein the materials as materials disappear into an illusion of space. Given the same materials, a musician might slap the leather, drop the nails, and twang the thread, creating an aural illusion. What distinguishes one art from another, then, is not the materials, but the kind of illusion, appearance, or form created by them. These illusions Langer calls virtual entities to distinguish them from actual entities (the miles depicted in a mountain landscape, for example, are not real miles at all, but only *appear* to be), and each art creates its own special kind of illusion: painting creates virtual space, music creates illusory or virtual time, the dance creates virtual interacting forces, and so on.[5]

These illusions are the result of what Langer calls the *elements* of art. As soon as a painter combines his materials — places a dot, let us say, upon an otherwise blank paper or board or canvas — he makes certain elements of form perceptible — at least the one element of position. Let him extend that dot into a line, and new elements appear: the division of space, direction, balance or imbalance, movement, proportion. The complex combination of these elements makes up the total illusion, the painter's virtual space, the work of art. Likewise the musician in producing a sound simultaneously creates elements of duration and pause, movement and rest, which he combines into a complex structure of virtual time. Literature functions similarly: its materials are words, rhythm, propositions, and grammat-

ical structures which the literary artist combines to create metaphorical elements which are in turn structured into the total illusion
that Langer identifies as virtual life:

Poetry generates its own entire world, as painting generates its entire continuum of space. The relation of poetry to the world of facts is the same as
that of painting to the world of objects: actual events, if they enter its orbit
at all, are *motifs* of poetry, as actual objects are motifs of painting. No
matter how faithful the image, it is a pure image, unmixed with bits of
actuality. It is a created appearance, an expressive form, and there is properly nothing in it that does not enhance its symbolic expression of vitality,
emotion, and consciousness . . . It springs from the power of language to
formulate the appearance of reality, a power fundamentally different from
the communicative function, however involved with it in the evolution
of speech. The pure product of the formulative use of language is verbal
creation, composition, art; not statement, but *poesis*.[6]

This passage poses three major problems for the intellectual historian. First, if the statements of literary art are unmixed with actuality, what degree and what kind of validity can they have for a
historian? For example, when Edward Taylor writes, 'Once at thy
feast, I saw thee pearl-like stand | 'Tween heaven, and earth, where
heaven's bright glory all | In streams fell on thee, as a floodgate',[7]
is he literally describing an actual experience? May we accept Taylor's
seeing a pearl-like Lord as a historical fact, and then infer that a
pearl-like Lord was actually visible to Taylor and his contemporaries?
Or may we conclude that Taylor describes literally what he thought
he saw — even though reason tells us the experience did not very
likely occur in actuality — and so say that he and others like him
suffered from hallucinations? Or may we reason that what is said is
a literal description of an optical illusion, the result of looking into
the sun? Or is the 'fact' of this statement purely psychological, and
valuable only to the historian as biographer? Or did no such event
ever take place and did Taylor not really intend to *communicate*
information about an actual occurrence, but to *formulate* a new experience for his reader?

This consideration raises the second major problem: how can the
historian maintain the distinction between the formulative and communicative functions of language? Because of this dual function,
poetry is the most deceptive of the art forms. More than the sounds
of music or the pigments of the painter, the materials of the poet

impose their own order, their own grammar – the whole symbolism of discourse – upon the artist. Unless the poet eliminates propositions from his materials and writes only jabberwocky or nonsense, he is going to make *apparent* statements as part of his creation of the illusion of virtual life. Langer contends that the formulative function of language assimilates these apparent statements of the communicative function, making them structural elements of the total illusion which she calls an expressive form.

But what does an expressive form express? This is the third problem. Langer suggests that we enjoy such forms – the illusions art presents to us – because we intuit their correspondence with some otherwise inexpressible aspect of our experience. This is certainly no new idea: Jonathan Edwards would have called it the personality or the structure of the will of God; Philip Freneau, the divine plan of Nature; Edgar Allan Poe, supernal beauty; Ralph Waldo Emerson, the oversoul; Carl Jung, the unconscious; and R. W. Gerard suggests that neurobiology will show it to be nothing other than the nerve structure and impulse patterns of the human brain.[8] Langer, like Jung and Gerard, turns inward and concludes that art forms express not ideas as we usually think of ideas – conscious intellectual constructs – but the very nature or form of human feeling itself. Thus she posits a kind of duality in human nature: a rational, discursive, intellectual part traditionally susceptible to the analyses of intellectual history, and a non-rational, affective, or 'feeling' aspect about which so little is known and for which our present vocabulary is so inadequate that intellectual history has mainly avoided contact with it. The hypothesis further contends that just as we speak of the mind's 'elasticity' or the 'shape' of ideas and suppose that they have a kind of reliable form whose structure, patterns, and changes can be described, so we should speak of the form or shape or structure of human feeling, not merely the conscious emotions, desires, and urges for which we possess semi-analytical terms like 'love', 'hate', 'anger', or 'exasperation', but also those feelings trembling vaguely on the threshold of consciousness which we can only communicate through metaphor – butterflies in the stomach, a frog in the throat – and still others so impalpable that we surrender all hope of communicating them through speech and despairingly lump them together under the term 'sentience', the undifferentiated feeling of being alive. And just as the intellectual side of man may be said to have a history, so may human feeling: 'One age shudders and blushes and faints, another swaggers, still another is god-like in a universal indifference. These styles in actual emotion are not insincere. They are largely unconscious — determined by many social causes, but *shaped* by artists, usually popular artists of the screen, the juke-box, the shop window, and the picture magazine.'[9] And we might add such popular foot-tappers as *The Day of Doom*, the lurid confessions of Congregational 'relations', and the long sufferings of the captivity narratives.

To say that '*all art is the creation of perceptible forms expressive of human feeling*'[10] is not to say that a work of art is a symptom of the artist's predominant emotion at the time of creation. One need not be miserable to write a tragedy. The fact that an artist in a foul mood may express his personal malaise by painting entirely in blacks and browns is not what makes his painting a work of art; conversely, the charming correspondence between John and Margaret Winthrop, although it expresses a wide range of personal feelings, remains discourse by only expressing actual emotions symptomatically — it creates no virtual entity, no illusion. On the other hand, some ostensibly discursive works, by virtue of the structural analogy they bear to works of art, may also be expressive of the nature of human feeling as apprehended by their writers. Edwin C. Rozwenc, for example, working from the premise that 'every man's vision is directed by the metaphors which rule his mind', hints at the structural analogy of John Smith's *Generall Historie of Virginia* to the chivalric romance, and William R. Taylor points to the novelistic character of William Wirt's biography of Patrick Henry.[11] The critic's function is to study such symbolic forms; the literary historian's, to examine the changes in these structures through time; and the intellectual historian's, perhaps to speculate upon the changes in the nature or structure of human feeling implied by changes in form.

Langer hinted at another important conception of the nature and function of art when she announced in an informal talk at the Austin Riggs Psychiatric Centre that she was 'scouting the possibility that *rationality arises as an elaboration of feeling*',[12] an idea that would have come as no surprise to Jonathan Edwards or to Edward Taylor, both of whom came to such a notion out of dissatisfaction with the ancient practice of referring to the will, understanding, and affections as separate 'faculties' of the soul.[13] What Langer means is not only that intellectual activity may be a highly specialized and complicated form of basic sentience, but that the mind may be able to function only after the feelings have been conditioned, informed, or, in a sense, structured. The importance of this notion for us lies in the implication that intellectual history must be more than a sequence of ideas, that ideas without emotion would perhaps have no history, that seventeenth-century men and women did *not* feel exactly as we do but worked from a sentient nature somewhat differently structured from ours, and that to ignore the emotional matrix or affective structure from which ideas arise is to fail to see the intellectual process steadily and whole. And if it is art alone that structures and expresses the nature of human feeling, determining both the direction and the extent of intellectual progress, the intellectual historian is going to have to take greater account of the symbolism of artistic form than he yet has.

To the student of the intellectual history of the American colonies, this may appear to be a useless, if not a dangerous, speculation to entertain. Even literary historians ignore the artistic side of colonial literature for its more attractive intellectual sister. But the Puritans found means to satisfy the universal craving for well-wrought mimesis. Having outlawed the satisfactions of high-church ritual (a form of both dance and drama), and fearful of the magnetic attraction of icons and idolatry,[14] they turned to literature. Their style and their taste differed from ours, but the satisfaction we derive from modern literature they undoubtedly found in *exempla*, illustrious providences, tall tales and anecdotes; they explored human character through the popular Thoephrastan 'characters' incorporated in funeral elegies, histories, personal 'relations' of the workings of saving grace, the ubiquitous spiritual autobiographies and saints' lives, and even in intellectual treatises like Edwards's *Treatise Concerning Religious Affections*;[15] they impelled their characters through high adventure in an Indian-infested wilderness in the captivity narratives from Mary Rowlandson to Ethan Allen with no less sense of plot than informs most television westerns; and they learned to shape dialogue into a variety of dramatic forms from the formal debate of Anne Bradstreet's *Quaternions* to the melodramatic scene of parting friends in Captain Johnson's *Wonder-Working Providences*. If this apprentice period of American literary craftsmanship ever is studied seriously as art, aesthetic theory will certainly not be useless.

But it might still be dangerous, especially in light of the fact — or what has long passed for fact — that the colonists themselves positively distrusted art. Poetry, as Perry Miller assures us, was reduced to a branch of rhetoric, becoming a 'dress for great truths, a sugar for the pill' — in short, a decorative varnish for oak-sturdy ideas. To the Puritans, Miller writes, 'poetry existed primarily for its utility, it was foredoomed to didacticism, and because it was the most highly ornate of the arts, it was always in grave danger of overstepping proper limits and becoming pleasing for its own sake'.[16] I do not mean to argue with Miller's description of Puritan poetics; his abundant artillery of quotation would make that futile. But I agree with Alan Simpson that Miller 'has told us too much about the Puritan mind and not enough about the Puritan's feelings. If the seventeenth-century Puritan, with his formal training in scholasticism, usually tries to give a rational account of his faith, it is the stretched passion which makes him what he is'.[17] Moreover, poetic theory in England and on the Continent was in itself hardly more conducive to great poetry. Like the New England soil, the Puritan poetics was flinty and unpromising, yet from an equally hard critical ground flowered an Edmund Spenser and a William Shakespeare, a John Donne and a John Dryden, an Andrew Marvell and a John Milton — the richest ornaments of the English language.[18] To explain the poverty of Puritan poetry, then, by the lowness of its critical esteem is not to explain it at all.

For there is no need to suppose that their practice actually followed their theory. If modern aesthetic philosophers like Susanne Langer really have described a fact about the nature of art for all times, then the question of particular theories or motives becomes irrelevant. And here Edward Taylor offers a case in point, for his comments on poetic theory completely support Miller's description of Puritan poetics, and seem quite unaffected by any profound notions of art. Yet his poems simultaneously betray another, quite sophisticated symbolic sense that might be said to be built into Puritan thought through its theology. I think it is this latter sense that accounts for his art, and not his rhetorical speculations, though he never fully describes either in any systematic way.[19]

Renaissance critics did not share our subtle awareness of symbolic forms and their function in human experience, and they lacked our elaborate vocabulary of symbolism, but we must not therefore suppose that they were not equally subject to the force of symbols. Even if they were not, however, even if the popular explanation Miller defends so ably were valid, certain questions still remain. Why *was* poetry pleasing for its own sake? Why *did* Wigglesworth drop his theology into dramatic form? What impulse accounts for the opening

images of *The Day of Doom*? Or why did Taylor cast his more positive meditations on the same Calvinism into a kind of morality play?
What accounts for Edward Johnson's fictions in his so-called 'history' of the *Wonder-Working Providences of Sion's Saviour*? How
dead *is* the truth in a funeral elegy? I am not sure that these are all
equally significant questions, but if the form an idea takes is important, and if some kinds of 'ideas' representing a major aspect of human
experience can only be observed in the symbolic forms of art and not
at all in discursive statements, then such questions must be answered.
But the common explanations of Puritan art discourage intellectual
historians from even asking them.

Instead historians have fallen into the habit of ignoring belletristic
productions, except when they happen to confirm less esoteric evidence, sometimes with strange results. Vernon L. Parrington, for example, with all the force of a brilliant and powerful style, announces
his choice 'to follow the broad path of our political, economic, and
social development' to the 'germinal ideas that have come to be
reckoned traditionally American ... rather than the narrower belletristic'.[20] Kenneth Murdock and Samuel E. Morison likewise turn
from the belletristic proper to a 'broader' concern for typical native
ideas reflected in Puritan writing. Poetry and fiction are not used to
tell us directly about the Puritan experience, but only to support what
we know from other sources. They are read just as any other documents — proclamations, diaries, church records, or formal histories —
are read, as if words were, as Edward Taylor puts it, 'thoughts
whiffled in the wind' — that is, as if the relationship of words to ideas
were identical in both kinds of document.

Anne Bradstreet, for example, writes, 'Close sat I by a goodly
river's side', and then identifies the river as an emblem of the soul's
progress to the sea of eternal rest. But the historian, in the guise of
editor, soberly corrects her, identifying the river as the Merrimack.[21]
The Tenth Muse thereby becomes one of America's first nature poets,
a sympathetic and genial sketcher of the Massachusetts countryside.
Or again, a Puritan eulogist nails to the hearse of Solomon Stoddard
an elegy in which he incidentally commends the good humor of his
subject. Another eulogist, two full centuries later, accepts his predecessor's hint as gospel and subtly transforms Stoddard into a kind
of jovial and pragmatic Santa Claus, immensely enjoying the clumsy
machinations of his bungling enemies, the Mathers.[22] Still another
historian approaches Johnson's *Wonder-Working Providences* as if

Johnson operated out of the same canons of historical practice as he does, and rejects Johnson's testimony to his times as 'special pleading'.[23]

By rejecting such special pleading, the historian fails to meet the colonial artist on his own terms. Consider, for example, Johnson's treatment of the Hutchinson scandal. Johnson never identifies Mrs Hutchinson by name for some reason. Whatever the reason, the result is that she appears not as a particular woman, but as an omnipresent spirit — the 'Erronist', as he refers to her — sometimes the lady herself, sometimes her disciples, sometimes the devil, and sometimes all together — a much more vigorous and exciting image of this first notable heretic than Winthrop gives us in his journal. Exercising the historian's traditional right to invent speeches, Johnson writes, 'These sectaries had many pretty knacks to delude withal. "Come along with me", says one of them, "I'll bring you to a woman that preaches better gospel than any of your black-coats that have been at the Ninneversity, a woman of another kind of spirit, who hath had many revelations of things to come. And for my part", saith he, "I had rather hear such a one that speaks from the mere motion of the spirit, without any study at all, than any of your learned scholars."' What better term could he have put into the scoffer's mouth than 'Ninneversity' to express the popular scorn for university trained preachers? Johnson also insists that Mrs Hutchinson, that 'masterpiece of women's wit', was 'backed by the sorcery of a second, who had much converse with the devil by her own confession, and did, to the admiration of those that heard her, utter many speeches in the Latin tongue, as it were in a trance. This woman was wonted to give drinks to other women to cause them to conceive; how they wrought I know not, but sure there were monsters born not long after'. Outrageous testimony, of course! But when Johnson says 'Gentle Reader, think not these things feigned because I name not the parties or that there is no witness to prove them',[24] I am willing to take his word for it — even the tall tale of the monstrous births — on the same basis that I accept any fiction. The accuracy of the speech is beside the point. The historical 'fact' Johnson is very consciously and successfully giving form to is the 'spirit of giddiness' that inspired the land. To attempt to explain the intellectual grounds of the Hutchinson episode adequately without careful regard to Johnson's images of spiritual giddiness is impossible; yet rare is the account that reckons with Johnson's art.

Perhaps it is this sin of neglect rather than the positive abuse of literary materials that the intellectual historian commits most damagingly. Assuming that poems are less reliable evidence than other documents, historians refuse to take them on their own ground. Tossing the baby out with the bath water, they reject all the facts poetry offers simply because they happen to be looking for other kinds of facts. John Underhill and John Mason, for instance, both left accounts of their military exploits against the Pequots, and no modern historian dares ignore these vivid first-hand descriptions. Yet the same historian would barely glance at the versified version of the same episode set down ninety years later by Roger Wolcott. In Wolcott's series of stiff tableaux, the blunt and direct descriptions of Mason and Underhill are quite lost. In Wolcott's poem the Indian king — Mononotto — notches an arrow, aims it at the heart of Mason — the hero of the story — relaxes a moment to shoot a prayer to 'his god and fathers' ghosts', and then lets fly at the good captain. 'But wary Mason, with his active spear, | Glanced the prince's arrow in the air'. After this deft gesture, the undaunted captain leaps into Mononotto's 'palace' (a wigwam in Mason's own account), and 'enflamed', sets the Indian village of Mystic afire. Quickly the burning village becomes an emblem of hell, as one might expect, but Wolcott invents some interesting details: he describes an Indian mother who 'Beholds her infant frying at her breast; | Crying and looking on her, as it fries'. Shortly before, he sums up the fate of a romantic Indian couple: 'The fair and beauteous bride, with all her charms, | This night lay melting in her bridegroom's arms'.[25] The pun is grizzly, of course, and the images in both cases ludicrous and bathetic. In their exaggeration they fail, but in their failure they betray Wolcott's emotional understanding of the Pequot campaign. The classical allusion, the artificial elegance of the diction, the heroic proportions of Mason, the sentimental pictures of the frying and melting Indians, even the heroic couplets of the verse itself — all tell the military historian next to nothing about Mason, Mystic and the massacre, but they tell the intellectual historian much about the way such matters were looked at in 1725.

Much the same attitude prevailed in the 1750s, if we may judge from the poems of 'Philo-Bellum', as John Maylem signed himself. Moses Coit Tyler calls Maylem's 'The Conquest of Louisburg' 'tumultuous, gory, and gigantesque';[26] he does not point out that the devices which make the poem so are borrowed from abroad. 'Arms and the hero claim immortal song' betrays Maylem's indebtedness to Dryden's translation of Virgil as well as to the general bombast and pompous heroics of Restoration tragedy. Neither Maylem nor Wolcott could apparently see martial episodes except through the emotional lens of a truly shaping spirit like Dryden's. And this is important. To discount eighteenth-century American verse as weakly imitative of British models may suffice for literary history or even for literary criticism. But intellectual history cannot afford to ignore the fact that the ideas expressed in these poems are as they are because their writers have been conditioned by the forms of others' imaginations, others' feelings. To borrow or inherit a form of verse or a figure of speech may not be significant; to fall heir to a form or figure of thought, however, may have infinite and infinitely subtle consequences.

Let us assume then that the notions about the nature of art with which we began this discussion are valid — that colonial *belles-lettres*, like other arts, are symbolic expressions, often involuntary, of the artist's emotional framework of ideas; that these symbolic forms of thought tell us reliably about Puritan intellectual habits, regardless of what Puritans themselves held about the nature of poetry and the arts; and that the pursuit of such information is not only useful, but essential to understanding the Puritan mind. And let us see if viewing literature in this way adds at all to our knowledge of the intellectual history of New England.

Take, for example, our evaluation of Cotton Mather. Current fashion views Mather with something less than wholehearted favor. Tyler calls his religious devotions a series of 'fanatic pedantries'.[27] Parrington speaks of them as evidence of 'a neurotic temperament', a 'religious exaltation flowered from the root of egoism', which makes Mather 'an attractive subject for the psychoanalyst'. Parrington concludes: 'Intensely emotional, high-strung and nervous, he was oversexed and overwrought, subject to ecstatic exaltations and, especially during his celibate years, given to seeing visions'.[28] Bradley diagnoses the same symptoms as a case of 'advanced hysteria',[29] and Perry Miller reduces the matter to ridicule, making Mather's prostrating himself in the dust of his study floor do no more than call his wife's housekeeping into question.[30] Each of these views springs from the recognition that there is something excessive and unusual in Mather's behavior, which may say more about twentieth-century attitudes than it does about Mather. Given the conventional judgment that Puritans rejected emotionalism and that anything smacking of Catholic or Anglican practice would more likely rouse their ire than their emulation, Mather's spiritual ecstasies do strike one as dangerous or affected or both. Ecstasy and vision came legitimately to the Puritan only in the moment of vocation, Miller says, and so we judge Mather to have been too enthusiastic, too visionary, too mystical. Yet, Miller also writes that 'the more one studies the history of Puritan New England, the more astonished he becomes at the amount of reeling and staggering there was in it'.[31]

Here is where Edward Taylor's poetry makes its point; Miller may have stumbled upon more than he realized. In Taylor's *Preparatory Meditations*, written as part of his devotional duty attending the sacrament of the Lord's Supper, visions (imagined and actual) and sexual images abound, evincing that Taylor reeled and staggered at least as frequently as Mather. Enraptured with the vision that in the bridegroom—Christ God has 'married our manhood, making it its bride', Taylor utters his love as a woman might to her lover:

> My Lovely One, I fain would love thee much,
>   But all my love is none at all, I see;
> Oh! let thy beauty give a glorious touch
>   Upon my heart, and melt to love all me.
>   Lord, melt me all up into love for thee,
>   Whose loveliness excells what love can be.[32]

The striking sensuality and intensity of these lines can be matched from poems anywhere along Taylor's half-century of poetic production. They accost our comfortable conclusions about the Puritans and have led some historians to conclude that Taylor suppressed his poetry because its sensual expressions more properly fit a Roman Catholic than a Congregationalist. Intellectual history resists seeing any connection between a statement like this and eighteenth-century American thought. Yet Taylor gushed like this regularly, ticking off poems like clockwork every six weeks for over forty years — hardly the mark of uncontrolled enthusiasm. The natural question for the aesthetically oriented critic is: why did he express himself this way?

Answering this question leads to the discovery that these poems, with their accompanying sermons, fall into the rigid patterns of the formal meditation — as Taylor's title itself declares — a little-studied but widespread and very popular seventeenth-century literary and devotional genre marked by certain logical and rhetorical conventions. The practice of meditation is ancient, of course, but it was renaissance Catholics like Ignatius Loyola, Francis de Sales, and Luis de Granada who reduced the practice to set forms and who imposed upon the human impulse to communicate with God a method — both the symbols and the logical framework to contain them — for the sake of aiding religious devotion. In the century preceding Taylor's, such meditation had become 'an exercise essential for the ordinary conduct of "good life" and almost indispensable as preparation for the achievement of the highest mystical experience',[33] and so could hardly remain a strictly Catholic indulgence. In fact, the greatest English book in this genre was the Puritan Richard Baxter's *The Saints Everlasting Rest*, published in 1649. Its Catholic tradition seemed nothing to be ashamed of to this Puritan: 'Read this, you Libertines!' he says at one place, 'and learn better the ways of devotion from a Papist!'[34]

New Englanders like Taylor were apparently ready to accept this counsel, for their own books on the Lord's Supper urge the practice of meditation or secret prayer as proper steps to a mystical and sacramental union with the Lord. In these books they fall into the same language as that used by Taylor in his *Meditations* — the language of Marsilio Ficino and Giordano Bruno — the language of renaissance mysticism. Even Samuel Willard, the glory of Congregational orthodoxy, slips at times into the eroticisms of Taylor; he demands: 'Is not this Sacrament appointed to be a Medium of Communion between Christ and his Spouse? Is it not for the expressing of their mutual Conjugal Love to each other? . . . Have I fixed my Choice upon him, and rejected all other Lovers for him? . . . And can I gaze upon him and not be ravished at the Contemplation of his transcendent Excellencies?'[35]

And Taylor's good friend Increase Mather also tried to explain meditation to his congregation, urging them to pursue the exercise till it brought them to a '*Facial Vision*' of God. 'This *Meditation* should make [those who exercise it] *willing to be absent from the Body*, that so they may be present with the Lord', he insists, obviously describing that mystical state called *vacatio*. Therefore the meditation must 'be attended with a *Transforming Power*, changing them into the same Image' as the Lord himself.[36] From his style one could hardly guess that Increase himself ever enjoyed the rapturous vision he described as the fitting end to the meditative process.

Once you become aware of the conventional language of meditation, its use in other contexts gains considerable meaning. For example, at the end of the first stanza of her frequently printed 'Contemplations', Anne Bradstreet records that her autumnal view of 'the trees all richly clad' has moved her deeply: 'Rapt were my senses at this delectable view', she writes. Modern readers — post-romantic if not actually romantics themselves — are likely to find this a statement of calm repose, of engrossed tranquillity. But this is to overlook the greater sinew behind the seventeenth-century use of the word 'rapt'. Closely related through its common root with the words 'rape' and 'rapture', Bradstreet's innocent term functions much more strenuously than modern sentiment usually recognizes. The sexual implications of rapt-ness or of being enraptured are developed in a similar context by Jonathan Edwards, too, with full awareness of their violent suggestions. He compares the justified soul to an opening flower, 'rejoicing as it were in a calm rapture'. But 'calm rapture' is a mild paradox, an experience of 'peacefulness and ravishment' at once. The same erotic language penetrates, with no sense of inappropriateness, Edwards's Theophrastan 'character' of a truly virtuous person, who, like Bradstreet, Taylor, and Willard, 'unmindful of any pain or affliction', looks forward to a time when she will dwell with Christ and 'be ravished with his love and delight forever'.[37] In short, terms proper to mysticism are far more abundant than we ordinarily suppose — abundant enough to warrant calling them common, making Cotton Mather's reeling and staggering far less extraordinary than they formerly appeared.

So the examination of Taylor's love poems (to the supreme lover) goes well beyond qualifying our current evaluation of Cotton Mather. It also makes the 'broader' aims of intellectual historians seeking the native grounds of American ideas look quite narrow by catapulting both Taylor and Mather and an unknown number of their colleagues (there is strangely no history of American devotional practice) into the much broader stream of Western Christianity. This is not to say that all Puritans were minor league mystics, nor to judge Mather's particular brand of mysticism, but to insist that the mystical element cannot be overlooked in discussing the practical developments in American intellectual history. For both Taylor and Mather wrote devotional guides explaining the practice of meditation and its function in preparing for the Lord's Supper. And both books were designed to block or balance Solomon Stoddard's 'Apostasy' regarding the sacrament. Perry Miller properly describes this as New England's most significant intellectual feud between the Halfway Synod of 1662 and the Great Awakening.[38] Taylor certifies Mather's reeling and staggering and so adds a dimension to that debate for which Miller cannot account and which might need no accounting for were it not for its pervasiveness in the New England temperament, part of the shape of human feeling in the seventeenth century. This is what Taylor's poetry makes so clear.

His poems directly express the influence of a vital emotional tradition on the thought and expression of American Puritans – a tradition that explains Cotton Mather's devotional habits in his own terms and not those of post-Freudian critics. Taylor and Mather could no more see man's communion with God apart from the shaping vision of renaissance mystical writers like Loyola and de Sales than Wolcott and Maylem could view war without the palliative spectacles of John Dryden's poetry. Parrington's derogatory analysis of Mather's visions could only have come from an emotionally unsympathetic and religiously sentimental point of view, ignorant of the devotional methods and vocabulary of the late seventeenth century. This practice is clearly manifest in the lyrics of Taylor and others – symbols of ideas held not in the head alone, but in the heart, which both Taylor and Susanne Langer make the proper seat of knowledge.

Of course it may finally prove to be that Langer's philosophy really enunciates no valid principle of the nature of art. It is weak at several points, especially with poetry, and indeed it may break exactly at the point where it tries to account for later seventeenth- and early eighteenth-century literature, where the language of discourse and the symbolic constructs of art seem indistinguishable. But that is a matter only time can determine. Meanwhile intellectual history has an obligation to see where the assumptions and skills of aesthetics may lead it; it especially needs to find new ways to use colonial literary materials. Renaissance writers were fond of describing the difficulty of getting at truth in the image of a veiled oracle. The artistic debility of colonial literature often seems a dense veil, but it may be that the obscurity lies, as Lovejoy suggests, in the eye of the beholder.

The literary consequences of Puritanism

LARZER ZIFF

Two great obstacles to the use of the word Puritan must be removed before it will serve as a meaningful term in literary discussion. First, it can be argued that the religious tradition which insists upon the Spirit at the expense of the laws, which reserves the term Christian for a far smaller number of people than those regularly in attendance at the parish church, and which considers a relatively grave deport-ment to be the appropriate outward sign of inward gifts is, among users of English, at least as old as Wyclif, and as recent as any American election campaign. To say this, I believe, is to maintain that the Anglo-American Christian tradition, not to speak of other cultures and other religions, exists in a tension between legalism and antinomianism, between the belief that religion, taking its impetus from revelation, through reason achieves forms and laws which are essential to the aiding of weak human nature and to the continuity of divine law upon earth; and the belief that since man's relation to God is super-rational, consisting as it does of the Lord's gift of grace to the individual believer, laws and rituals are dead except insofar as they are directly informed by the Holy Spirit acting through the individual believer.

That this latter, antinomian, belief is at the core of Puritanism cannot be doubted, nor can one reasonably claim that it does not well antedate Elizabeth's day. Accepting this, however, I would still maintain that Puritanism is not the antinomian pole itself but the political movement which, in the late sixteenth and early seventeenth centuries, brought into being institutions which adjusted the tension in favor of that pole.

At this point, the second objection may well be taken; it is the nominalistic one. Can a term be meaningful, it asks, if that term is meant to cover Thomas Cartwright and Andrew Marvell, Arch-bishop Ussher and Roger Williams, John Winthrop and John Milton?

In short, if one applies the term Puritan to all who in the late sixteenth and early seventeenth centuries were disatisfied by the degree of reform represented by the established church and who, therefore, supported the Millenary Petition and temporarily achieved a major goal with the establishment of the Commonwealth, what ideology can they be said to have shared in common? No generalization can be established which will not fail to cover a sizeable portion of this group.

Appreciating this point of view and granting that any definition of Puritanism is condemned to having a misty margin, I would, nevertheless, maintain that Puritanism is that political movement which arose in England in the second half of the sixteenth century and which, accepting the basic assumptions of the Christian doctrine of John Calvin (but not necessarily his ecclesiastical polity), strove to establish the institutional consequences of that doctrine. The Puritanism about which I speak came to an end at the Restoration when it lost the political motive.[1]

In offering this definition, I do not mean to assert that the core of Puritan ideology did not exist in earlier centuries, nor do I mean to deny that it lives on in our own day. I confine the term to, roughly, a one-hundred-year period, 1560—1660, not for the sake of arbitrary precision but because I believe that these were the one hundred years during which what was latent in English Christianity achieved so strong a social as well as ideological dominance that even after the tension had once again been adjusted with greater power for the legal pole, its effect was felt as a constant public factor in ecclesiastical and civil polity, in economics, in social institutions, and in literature.

At the height of the Puritan movement, loyal Anglicans were too disturbed at the total political and theological drift of the times to take arms against Puritan literary style in itself, for the style was, after all, a seemingly minor symptom of a much greater ailment. During the Commonwealth period, however, one minor loyalist clergyman, Abraham Wright, gained everlasting if small distinction by amusing himself with considerations of what was happening to style under the Puritans, rather than, as his more illustrious colleagues were doing, taking the more oppressive aspects of the movement as his topic. He is a perceptive commentator on a shift in the imagination which was to have vast literary consequences, and is, therefore, an excellent guide into the problem.[2]

Son of a silk-dyer and warden of the Merchant-Taylor Company,

Abraham Wright was born in London in 1611 and underwent the typical career of the loyal Anglican clergyman of the mid-seventeenth century. He was educated at the Merchant-Taylor's School, and he benefitted from that institution's close connection with St John's College, Oxford, going on to a fellowship there where he found favor with the college president, William Laud. As St John's, Wright was foremost among the undergraduate wits, and was, as an example, the composer of a rag initiation for new freshmen which had brief but great vogue. His list of oaths began, 'Yee are to sweare as yee hope/ to drinke ale out of a tenpenny bottle', and concluded, 'Sworn and delivered and sealed wth/a kisse on ye sacro-sanctitudinicall slipper'.[3] Wright was a fellow at the college when Laud attained the height of his glory as president by playing host to the royal family in August 1636, and one of the principal events in the festivities was the presentation of Wright's play, *Love's Hospital or The Hospital of Love*. The contemporary report is that 'It was merry and without offence and so gave a great deal of content'.[4]

Witty, graceful, and shrewd, finding no paradox in being at once worldly and a divine, Abraham Wright was a fair type of the ministerial generation which had grown up experiencing no other ecclesiastical polity but that defended so ably by Richard Hooker. An eloquent preacher, he had every reason to look forward to a snug vicarage, a modest career as an occasional poet, and, most probably, a series of ecclesiastical preferments.

But the year in which Wright was called to the comfortable vicarage of Oakham, Rutland was 1645, a covenanting year, and Wright, who insisted on principle that he would avoid oaths and obligations, had to relinquish the post to a Presbyterian and enter into a life which but ten years before had been typical of the Puritan who would not take oaths: a bit of tutoring in a great man's family; a bit of preaching to a small but loyal London congregation from which he received some income but where, technically, he was not in office. Like the Puritans who had run through the pattern earlier, he looked for political events to restore his rights, and with moderate bitterness whiled away his time in minor literary activities. At the Restoration, he declined a reward for his loyalty, the chaplaincy to Elizabeth of Bohemia, preferring to assume the Oakham vicarage where he lived from 1659 to his death in 1690, refusing preferments in favor of devoting himself to his parish and his garden.

Change the school to Charterhouse, change the college to Emmanuel, change the date back some fifteen years, all of these are immense changes and yet, from one point of view, not very fanciful, for a similar pattern would emerge : a college reputation as a preacher, a vicarage closed by the inability to subscribe to an oath, a meager income tutoring in private families, some unofficial preaching to city congregations, and, finally, thanks to political reversals, a comfortable pulpit — these were the particulars of the career of many a Puritan preacher.

Not at all typical of the Puritan, however, are Wright's literary activities during his own dark days in the 1650s. Like his fellow loyalists and like the Puritans before him, to be sure, he did his share of reflecting on the viciousness of the times and of recording the 'true' as apposed to the officially pronounced interpretation of one or another political or ecclesiastical event. But Wright felt more keenly than most that one of the chief evils of the Puritan reign was literary, that a great tradition of letters, both sacred and profane, was being destroyed. In a period of great personal and political upheaval he attempted, nevertheless, to separate the manner from the matter, the style from the content, and to talk of the baneful influence of Puritan style as part of, but yet distinguishable from, Puritan policies. His two pertinent books on the subject are an anthology of poems, advisedly entitled *Parnassus Biceps*, and a set of sermons, *Five Sermons in Five Several Styles*. Both were published in 1656.

Four of the five sermons in Wright's collection he himself had preached : the first in the manner of Bishop Andrewes before Charles I on an Ash Wednesday ; the second, in the manner of Bishop Hall, before the clergy on the occasion of Wright's ordination ; the third, in the manner of Cartwright, before a mixed group at Oxford ; and the fourth, in the manner of the Presbyterians, at St Paul's before a city group. The fifth sermon, in the Independent manner, was composed for the purpose of illustration in the volume and was what Wright thought typical of the Smithfield lay-preacher in the 1650s.

Wright said in his preface that he published his book to offer a view not of the doctrines but of the style and manner of their presentation in order to drive home the need for one versed in human learning to serve as preacher, 'especially forasmuch as it is too clear and evident since these *TIMES*, that all men will not be brought by the same way of preaching to heaven : some are well satisfied with the plain easie way of *Doctrine* and *Use*; others are not taken with any sermons, but what is fill'd with depth of Matter, height of Fancie, and good Language'.[5]

From our perspective, Wright in his skillful parody of the Independent sermon is tilting at windmills, and while he includes two examples of his own handling of the plain, easy way, it is clear that he prefers 'depth of Matter, height of Fancie and good Language'. Still, in his Cartwright and his Presbyterian style sermons he does not load his argument; they are creditable performances, quite representative of, for example, the American Puritan sermon. Bitter as was his situation, Wright did not as too many have since done, confuse the enthusiasms of the sectarians with the mainstream of the Puritan movement, nor did he claim that learning resided with the loyal Anglicans alone.

But he did demonstrate different uses of learning. In both of the Anglican-style sermons, the text is approached primarily as a set of meaningful words, but words, nevertheless, which must, then, have their function identified through syntactical analysis and their meaning revealed through rhetorical analysis. Literary example is used as an aid in the process, and once the words have been split into their parts and made to stand in revealing relations to one another the task is completed.

These Anglican-style sermons are extremely verbal performances in which even transitional sentences glitter with puns. The plain-style sermons show up by contrast not because they are plain in the sense of having no conceits – Wright does fortify them with some sturdy and effective similes drawn from the London trades – but because in their steady movement from doctrine to reason to uses back to another numbered doctrine and numbered reasons and numbered uses, a sense of the concrete behind the word emerges, a sense that the words themselves are artificial vehicles but that the truth they are intended to carry is absolute and independent of them.

Another striking difference between the sets of sermons is that in the Anglican-style pair, classical, rabbinical, medieval and modern texts are cited, but as we move through the Cartwright and Presbyterian style to the Independent style sermon the allusive context shrinks almost to nothing. The active ingredients in the Anglican sermon are: an I, a speaker of learning, wit, and eloquence; a you, an audience which, it is assumed, is capable of following the learning, appreciating the wit, and savoring the eloquence; and a subject-matter, which, biblical as it may be, since it is set in words is susceptible of treatment in the way that all great writings are, as a set of words which can be made to yield up their meaning through the application of conventional analytic techniques. On the level of the

Independent sermon, the active ingredients are an urgent I, a speaker with non-verbal access to the meaning of his text; you, an audience which is seeking with his aid to penetrate through the words of the text and the words used in the sermon in order to share that non-verbal meaning; and the meaning itself, imperfectly captured in any set of words but capable of breaking through a sufficiently inspired presentation — one which will not be deluded by words themselves.

What we can infer from Abraham Wright we can validate, I believe, from a general knowledge of the sermon literature of the period and we can, furthermore, explain it in terms of Puritan ideology. Since, for the Puritans, salvation was effected by the Holy Ghost providing the saved believer with grace, the sermon was completely aside from the conversion process unless the preacher were regarded as an instrument of the Holy Ghost, as a speaker of the saving word. And this saving word was something different from any particular words he might use, but was, rather, the force which hovered behind them. For the majority of Puritan preachers, the fact that they were instruments of the Holy Ghost meant that they had to prepare themselves to be as serviceable as possible, and their preparation consisted, in large part, of their performing prodigious feats of scholarship. But the learning was for the sake of their refining themselves as instruments and was not necessarily to be the context or even the manner of their utterance. The non-Puritan represented by Wright, however, did not so much see himself as a step in the conversion process but rather as one who was addressing Christians in need of instruction, moral leadership, or reprovement, so that the particular nature of the congregation — court, university, city, or rural — dictated his content to a great extent. Learning was necessary because it provided materials in variety to prepare the preacher for any kind of audience. Wright himself indulged in Puritan styles when he thought he had this sort of audience; indeed, as was noted, he himself had preached the Cartwright and Presbyterian sermons he included in the collection.

George Herbert further confirms the point. In *A Priest to the Temple*, he appears to be advancing a Puritan point of view and confounding the distinction just made when he urges his priest to give 'a plain and evident declaration of the meaning of the text', and not to crumble it into 'small parts, as, the Person speaking, or spoken to, the subject, and object, and the like'.[6] But we must bear in mind that Herbert's subtitle is *The Country Parson*, and that he recognizes a group of 'Reverend Prelates of the Church, to whom this discourse ariseth not',[7] such as those in the universities, in noble houses, and in non-rural parishes. Recognizing this, we see that, like Abraham Wright, he is asserting the relativity of content and manner to audience, as opposed to the Puritan plain style advocate who, in effect, maintains the plain style as the absolutely good one, applicable at Cambridge, at St Paul's, at the parish church in Northamptonshire, and in the meeting house in the New England wilderness.

A major contradiction appears to develop, however, when having established the nature of plain style and related it to Puritanism we note that a significant seventeenth-century body of opposition to Puritan style was based on the irresponsible flood of passion and the wild allegorizing to be found in Puritan expression. This opposition, it may further be argued, led even dramatists in the Stuart period to a greater simplicity of diction so as to assert their dissociation from Puritan excess. If passion and allegory were also Puritan traits, what becomes of plain style as a meaningful characteristic?

The contradiction is not, I believe, a real one, which is to say that plain style and passionate allegorizing are related elements of Puritanism.

Abraham Wright can again help us to a distinction. His *Parnassus Biceps* (Oxford and Cambridge being the two heads of modern Parnassus) appeared in the same year as *Five Sermons* and is a collection of poems by Wright and others, all of them, he said, drops from an ocean of wit. The year, 1656, was a good time to publish them, he claimed, because England could well use such water, the fountains of poetry having been dried. Wright claimed that the authors of the poems, whom he did not identify — Jonson and Herrick were among them — were priests as well as poets and while subsequent investigation has somewhat reduced the number of ordained clergymen contributing to the volume, Wright is still left with a goodly number including four bishops. Moreover, Wright's chief use of the term priest is metaphoric: 'Your Authors then of these few sheets are Priests, as well as Poets; who can teach you to pray in verse, and (if there were not already too much phantasticknes in that Trade) to Preach likewise: while they turn Scripture-chapters into Odes, and both the Testaments into one book of Psalmes: making *Parnassus* as sacred as *Mount Olivet*, and the nine Muses no lesse religious then a Cloyster of Nuns'.[8] What he wants to bring to the arid England of Cromwell is the sense of the day just passed when 'it was held no sin for the same man to be both a Poet, and a Prophet; and to draw predictions no lesse from his Verse, then his Text'.[9] Wright believed, as he said in the preface to his other book, that 'the same man may be both a *Poet* & a *Prophet, Philosopher* and an *Apostle. Virgil's* fancie was as high as the *Magi's* star, and might lead Wisemen in the West as clearly to their *Saviour*, as that light did those *Eastern Sages*'.[10]

Wright was not merely asserting the value of poetry – the Puritans, too, he knew, made verses – but was insisting that since poetry was the most skillful and considered combining of words of which man was capable, it should be regarded as divine even if the framer of the words, like Virgil, happened to be a pagan. He opposed this tradition, one which measured the divinity of inspiration by the success of the artifact in which it was embodied, to the lack of tradition of 'our new-enlightened and inspired men, who are as bold with the Majesty and glory of that Light that is unaprochable, as with their own *ignes fatui*; and account of the third Person in the blessed Trinity for no more then their Fellow-Ghost; thinking him as much bound to them for their vertiginous blasts and whirlewinds, as they to him for his own most holy Spirit'.[11]

Puritanism, Wright is saying, shifts the glory of literature from the form and content of the work which, of necessity, speaks through respected conventions, to the alleged inspiration of the writer who insists that the glory of his work is that it is the product of the Holy Ghost speaking through him. The Puritan notion of inspiration as proceeding from the Holy Ghost's relationship to the true believer is consistent, as we have seen, with the plain style, for this is what leads the sermonizer to disregard the beauty of words in favor of *the* word. To some extent in poetry, sermons, and polemics, and especially in history, this belief justifies the passionate outburst, the long exclamation of a writer seized with a supernatural transport and committed to setting it loose where it can work as it will among other men. It will not, in itself, save them, for salvation can come only when they establish their own relationship with the Holy Ghost, but it may serve as an important step toward that establishment. Passion and plainness are not contradictory.

Nor are plainness and allegory. Believing, as they did, that reformation of the Church of England was a necessary step toward the establishment of the holy commonwealth on earth, the Puritans were intensely aware of human history, of the history of political institutions and of religions, and saw such as part of the pattern of

Christian history. While they as renaissance men, had abandoned theories of cyclical history and saw the history of God's rule on earth as linear, proceeding with total continuity from the day of creation through their time to the day of general resurrection, and though they differed as to the Lord's time-table, some feeling that they were as far along as the pouring of the fifth vial described by John, still the Puritans had a lingering sense of the cyclical, inherent in their belief that the Bible contained archetypal patterns of collective human experience as well as of individual human behavior. As is well known, they tended, in varying degrees, to substitute the Bible for a great deal of human learning and in so doing, as such as Abraham Wright point out, they lost, in their literary productions, a very rich allusive context. Their language, accordingly, was drained of meaning.

Even while they distrusted wit and metaphorical elaboration, however, they could quite consistently leap to metaphor so intense as to be allegorical for in so doing they were relating their experiences to the patterns in the Bible. The meaning which had been drained by their dismissal of words in favor of *the* word was, in a sense, to be regained by making the most of biblical patterns and their relation to modern experience. In leaping from the literal over a vast range of expression to arrive at the allegorical, they were, in effect, dismissing a whole dimension of what we might today call external reality. A Puritan history of the migration to New England, for instance, may be as literal and detailed as Winthrop's *Journal*, or, overleaping other forms, may be as allegorical as Edward Johnson, who gives us little sense of specifically who, did specifically what, specifically when, but feels he has told about the migration when he describes an idealized band of stout Christians setting forth on the Lord's work. Here, for instance, is one of the New England settlers, nameless of course, after listening to his friend's pleas that he remain in England: 'But as Paul to his beloved flock, the other replies, "What doe you weeping and breaking my heart? I am now prest for the service of our Lord Christ, to re-build the most glorious Edifice of Mount Sion in a Wildernesse, and as John Baptist, I must cry, Prepare yee the way of the Lord, make his paths strait, for behold hee is comming againe, hee is comming to destroy Antichrist, and give the whore double to drinke the very dregs of his wrath. Then my deare friend unfold thy hands, for thou and I have much worke to doe, I [ay] and all Christian Souldiers the World throughout." '[12]

A non-Puritan in the period can, understandably, be irked at the excessiveness of the account and its distortion of reality while, at the same time, he maintains that Puritanism also errs in its plainness – for the distortion proceeds on the assumption that reality is secondary to the absolute message behind it.

Just as the Puritan movement is antedated by what we may choose to call Puritan ideology, for instance in the time of Wyclif, so, certainly, plainness, passion, and allegory did not await that movement to make their presence felt in the English literature. But as I have maintained that the political and social movement known as Puritanism gathered together one aspect of what was latent in Christianity and made it so dominant for a brief period that it has ever since been prominent in the Anglo-American tradition, so I would maintain that its characteristic combination of plainness, passion, and allegory crystallized in the century 1560–1660 and has ever since been a strong feature if not a separate tradition in our literature. Because of the historical accident which permitted Puritanism to gain dominance in America at the outset of its settlement and to maintain that dominance for a longer period than it did in the homeland, I would further maintain that the much debated matter of the difference between English and American literature could very well be illuminated by a consideration of the literary consequences of Puritanism, which is to say that American literature seems strongly marked by the characteristics I have described. The word behind the words appears strongly in Emerson, for instance, and is surely the basis for his inconsistency. And Henry James seems a modern Abraham Wright when he poses an Englishman, very like Wright's loyal Anglican, and an American, very like Wright's Puritan, in the following manner:

Both the men had the signs of character and ability. The American was thin, dry, fine, with something in his face which seemed to say that there was more in him of the spirit than of the letter. He looked unfinished and yet somehow he looked mature, though he was not advanced in life. The Englishman had more detail about him, something stippled and re-touched, an air of having been more artfully fashioned, in conformity with traditions and models. He wore old clothes which looked new, while his transatlantic brother wore new clothes which looked old.[13]

Henry James's distinction is one of the social consequences of Puritanism and yet it has point-by-point co-relatives in the literary consequences. James's contemporary, William Dean Howells, however, dealt with the actual problem of Puritanism in American fiction with no concern for such niceties but with a simple concern which is typical of all but recent studies. Puritanism, Howells said, made itself felt most prominently in the way of life described by fictionists like Mary Wilkins and Sarah Orne Jewett so that the literary consequence of Puritanism was the quite obvious one of providing a considerable subject-matter for the local-colorist.[14] Such a view dominated literary history until quite recently.[15] Now Professor R. W. B. Lewis has refined Howells's gross point into a study of the thematic consequences of Puritanism,[16] and Professor Charles Feidelson has related the Puritan sensibility to symbolic technique in American literature, so that the *literary* consequences, in a more responsible sense, are receiving consideration. Most recently, Professor Roy Harvey Pearce has attempted the difficult task of identifying the Puritan literary imagination and tracing its ascent (are there yet some who would argue descent?) through the history of American poetry,[18] while elsewhere I have attempted to show how Puritan millennial theory affected even point of view in Puritan literary works.[19]

The recent work is encouraging because, surely, revolutionary cultural movements like Puritanism affect literature by changing the way men perceive and describe reality rather than by simply providing a different set of customs to serve as subject-matter. The characteristics I have here described — plain style, passion, allegory — appear to me to be the literary signs of this great shift in the imagination and to be compatible with the recent scholarship I have cited as well as to apply to such descriptions of the typically American form of fiction as that of the late Richard Chase.[20]

Although I have here chiefly discussed the American consequences because of the 'laboratory' nature of American Puritanism, I believe the combination of characteristics to be applicable to an important and identifiable strain of English literature. In this area, however, the distinction between Puritan, specifically, and Dissenter, generally, has, I feel, too quickly led literary historians to abandon their attempt to trace a Puritan tradition in modern English letters. What I have said about Puritanism I have said about an English movement, and although the literary consequences are more muddied in the home isle, what with the violent literary reaction at the Restoration, they are no less present than in America and are deserving of detailed study.

4

The Puritan jeremiad as a literary form

DAVID MINTER

> Still warble, dying swan! still tell the tale,
> The enchanting tale, the tale of pleasing woe.
>
> John Keats, 'To Byron'

Long after the finest hours of the Puritan experiment, Americans continued to echo the rhetoric of design: they invoked the 'wise and glorious purposes' for which men had been 'placed' in the New World; they praised the 'new order' America had created 'to teach old nations'; and they celebrated the 'blessings' she was destined to 'shed . . . round the world'.[1] In fact, however, life in both New England and Georgia proved confusing. Before the end of the seventeenth century the Puritans were forced to redefine their errand and revise their experiment; and within twenty years of its launching the Georgia project had gone so badly that its authors and trustees were forced to surrender their colony to the crown. Developments in both places forced men to acknowledge that the products of their actions failed to meet the specifications of their designs. By mid-century the builders of Massachusetts knew that they had met with considerable success — that they had established a strong plantation. Yet they found in apparent success what the Georgians found in obvious failure: that they had missed their grand self-designation.

Soon after the fate of the Georgia enterprise became apparent, men began to tell its story. The most interesting of the Georgia stories is the so-called 'Tailfer Book' — *A True and Historical Narrative of the Colony of Georgia* (1740), by Patrick Tailfer, David Douglass, and Hugh Anderson, with comments by the Earl of Egmont. The work is deliberately satirical. As spokesmen for 'the few surviving Remains of the Colony of *Georgia*', as members of a small group that managed to escape back 'to a LAND OF LIBERTY', the authors offer their narrative as 'a true and impartial account' of Georgia 'from its first settlement, to its present period'. Their sole purpose is to recount and explain the 'shipwreck' met by the 'Plan' of the 'Projectors' of that 'unhappy colony'.[2]

In prosperous Massachusetts, where failure took subtler, more disturbing form, and where loyalty precluded satire, spokesmen for the community followed a less direct path to a more thoroughly interpretive genre. By 1650 the Puritan model had been established in Massachusetts. The 'foundation', Peter Bulkeley asserted in 1651, has been 'laid, by many skilfull builders'. What accordingly was required of later Puritans was that they hold fast, keeping 'the foundation ... the same'.[3] As defined by William Stoughton in 1668, 'the solemn work' of the children and grandchildren was 'not to lay a new Foundation, but to continue and strengthen, and beautifie, and build upon that which hath been laid'.[4]

The work of caretaking and maintaining proved, of course, less heroic and more domestic than the work of designing and constructing a grand model. It also proved more confining and confusing. For New England the decisive event in the middle seventeenth century was England's official refusal to attend the New England model – her official decision to go her profligate way, whoring after toleration, ignoring the model city built specifically for her redemption. Then, to make bad matters almost unbearable, piety in the promised wilderness began to wane. 'O', Stoughton said, Election Day, April 1668, 'what a sad *Metamorphosis* hath there of later years passed upon us in these Churches and Plantations.' 'O *New-England*', he continued, 'thy God did expect better things from thee and thy Children'.[5]

By smashing the New England dream of being a city upon a hill, England made the Puritan voice, in an unsought, unsettling sense, a voice crying alone in a wilderness. The already tame and domestic task of maintaining the celestial city became provincial as well. It was not as an isolated colony, nor as a tarnished model in a 'far remote, and vast Wildernesse', that New England could hope to fulfill her high self-designation.[6] As the century progressed, bringing 'Ruine upon Ruine, Destruction upon Destruction' – as it became increasingly apparent that both the Puritan design and the Puritan understanding of 'Divine Expectations' were being 'frustrated' – the whole New England enterprise became problematical.[7] Too much had failed to go according to plan. The sons and grandsons of the builders continued to celebrate the beauty of their fathers' vision – a vision of such '*Divine Original* and *Native Beauty*' that it 'would dazzle the Eyes of

Angels, daunt the Hearts of Devils, ravish and chain fast the Affections of all the Saints'; and they continued to praise the dedication of their fathers' action – the trials they had passed through, the tribulations they had overcome. But they did so in knowledge that men and events on both sides of the Atlantic were saying no to the Puritan design.[8]

It was not merely that the second and third generations found it a sad fate 'to be styled *Children that are corrupters*'.[9] It was also that they were compelled to wonder whether New England were doomed to stand, not 'as a Citie upon an hill, [but] ... desolate and forsaken'.[10] Again and again they were forced to ask whether what they represented, what they had become, meant that their fathers had come 'flying from the depravations of Europe, to the American Strand' only to fail and fall short.[11] Finding themselves in a changing world curiously in conspiracy against the original Puritan aim, later Puritans were forced, again and again, to seek some way to reshape their heritage and redefine what they were about.

The steady purpose and free enthusiasm of the builders depended upon unrepeatable experience, and it died when they died. 'The first generation', Stoughton said, 'have been ripened time after time ... But we who rise up to tread out the footsteps of them that are gone before us, alas! what are we?' The second- and third-generation Puritans wanted to fulfill their caretaking assignment. But that assignment was theirs by accident of birth, not by decision to voyage, and they were in fact ill suited to it. They wanted to be about heroic tasks of their own, and that meant, within the historical context in which they found themselves, giving up being a model for England and becoming a strong and prosperous society. If their still young society could not be made the revealing, transforming model their fathers had said it must be, if New England could not renew the old, perhaps she could be significant simply as a thriving, dedicated land.[12]

The initial difficulty the second- and third-generation Puritans faced in seeking out their own heroic course was a matter of loyalty. They could never bring themselves simply to ignore the task their fathers had bequeathed them; nor could they ever admit that in fact they were not keeping the foundations the same. But the subtler, potentially more divisive difficulty they faced derived from the very character of their fathers' experience. By teaching that 'the Successes and Events of [human] Undertakings and Affairs are not determined' by man's intent, that man's effort may be frustrated and disappointed despite 'the greatest Sufficiency' and the highest resolve, their fathers' experience questioned the wisdom of all heroic activity.[13]

It was through strangely turned interpretation of their fathers' design that the Puritans sought first to remain loyal sons without remaining captive to their inherited task and second to master their problematical heritage. In tracing the course of their fathers' action – in telling their fathers' story – they sought not only to revise the logic of their own situation but also to redefine the fate of their fathers' design. They wanted to save their fathers as well as themselves from an inadequate fate. Interpretation became for them a way of taming 'a time and season of eminent trial'.[14] Through it they attempted to master failure – to deliver themselves from an inadequate fate; through it they attempted to salvage one of the failed 'Designs of men' and thereby move beyond human 'Defeat and Disappointment'.[15]

The 'jeremiad' was the form Puritan interpretation took. On designated fast-days New Englanders congregated to repent that they had erred and strayed. Neither the theory – that sin was linked with judgment, judgment with repentance, repentance with forgiveness, forgiveness with hope, and hope with reform – nor the practice of public lamentation represented Puritan improvization. But the role such lamentation played in New England was special because the covenant the Puritans had made with God was special. Unlike the covenant of grace (with which it was, of course, not coextensive), their communal covenant had to do not with eternal salvation of the elect of God but with a pledge to perform a mission within the world. Faithful performance of this mission would lead to victory, and victory would be rewarded on earth, not in heaven: God specifically would bless New England, giving her peace and prosperity within, influence and praise without. Concomitantly, however, betrayal of the agreement would be met not with eternal fire but with present visitations of God's wrath – with plagues and droughts, wars and rumors of wars, with scorn and laughter, derision and infamy.[16]

The jeremiad became, increasingly after 1650 and especially after 1660, the characteristic utterance of the Puritans. Again and again, as Perry Miller has shown, they told and retold the story of 'God's Controversy with New-England'.[17] The original intention of the jeremiad was to inspire reform. After cataloging calamities – droughts and plagues and savage raids – Puritan spokesmen label them tokens of God's displeasure with His people's failure faithfully to run their errand. Various 'sad affliction [s]' – 'epidemical sickness' and 'Pekoat furies' – function within jeremiads as signs of providential chastisement of a recalcitrant and inconstant people.[18] Having been reminded that only 'the singular pity and mercies' of their God can shield them from deserved annihilation, suffering them to live, the people are called to repent and reform.[19]

In its classic form, as defined by Perry Miller, the jeremiad was rooted in immediate difficulties. In July 1646, John Winthrop noted that great harm had been visited on grain crops by an invasion of caterpillars. 'In divers places', he said, churches observed a day of humiliation, whereupon 'presently after the caterpillars' disappeared.[20] Later Puritans continued to link 'tokens of God's displeasure' with their having become 'a people so unworthy, so sinfull, that by murmurings of many, unfaithfulness in promises, oppressions, and other evils' they had 'dishonoured [God's] Majesty, expos[ing] his worke here to much scandall and obloquie'. Year after year election sermons reminded the folk that they had 'cause for ever to bee ashamed', and cause also to call upon God 'rather [to] correct us in mercy, then [sic] cast us off in displeasure, and scatter us in this Wildernesse'.[21]

The Puritans tended, however, increasingly to blur the rationale of the jeremiad. More specifically, in a distinctly anthropocentric turn they began to treat consciousness of failure as the chief visitation of God's wrath. The burden of sensed defeat and faithlessness gradually displaced 'Pekoat furies' as a token of punishment for defeat and faithlessness. Distinctions between human acts of betrayal, divine judgment of betrayal, and human consciousness of both betrayal and judgment lost their sharpness. The Puritans continued of course to be disturbed by acts that rendered their city a defective model and by calamities that disclosed divine displeasure. But what most distressed them was knowledge that, despite careful and ostensibly successful building, they and their fathers had fallen short. At times, as a result, they appear most to lament the necessity of lamentation. But they were moved by more than longing to have that cup pass from them. They needed new assurance, yet were compelled – because their design had failed – to seek it surreptitiously.[22]

There was accordingly, coincident with the generalizing and blurring of the logic of the jeremiad, a tendency to use it to relativize God's judgment. Early Puritans assumed that they must either keep and fulfill their commission or become not a dimmer beacon on a lower hill but a byword for infamous failure. Later Puritans found themselves in a situation defined by the curious intermingling of three elements: the crumbling of their design, the waning of their piety, and the waxing of their prosperity. And in an effort to overcome the incongruity of obvious prosperity amid felt declension, they not only defined consciousness of failure as punishment for failure; they also decided that to fail in a designation sublime was after all to fail with a difference. If the Puritans would but continue to gaze from their present peak to the serene summit of their ancestors' desire, and if they would but condemn their failure, New England still could be truly new. In lamenting their sad decline, New Englanders subtly thanked their God and notified the world that they yet were not as other men, that they, despite all, were a chosen people dedicated to perfection. Our churches are not perfect, Cotton Mather admitted, but they 'are very like unto those that were in the first ages of Christianity', which even Quakers and Roman Catholics knew better than lightly to criticize. We have failed, Mather also acknowledged, but we 'Nevertheless . . . have given great examples of the methods and measures wherein an Evangelical Reformation is to be prosecuted'.[23]

The Puritans thus used careful dissection rather to minimize than to stress the importance of their failings. By emphasizing the heights from which they had fallen, they underscored the height at which they yet stood. But this strange logic did not alone suffice. The Puritans also used the jeremiad to move completely beyond caretaking and correction. They continued, to be sure, to lament their failure. And they sought to avoid as well as repent 'sins against the purpose and Covenant' of their community; they felt, after all, no desire to adorn the Puritan edifice with 'hay and stubble, in stead of gold and precious stones'. But what they most needed – and what they finally found in the jeremiad – was a way of skirting the requirement that they persevere in what they called the 'old way' of New England.[24]

That the caretaking generations had been left to make their way with 'a fixed unalterable' design through an era characterized by drastic change and seemingly dedicated to undermining their design – that they, in the name of all they held dear and holy, were required to remain loyal to a design that had failed – proved more than curious and perplexing. It constituted the most troublesome problem the second and third generations had to confront.[25] And though they tried to avoid the implications of their failure, those implications became the elements of their characteristic nightmare. Why had the God who had sent His chosen few into a wilderness to build a model society, through them to give to the world a model for ordered and meaningful society, so soon permitted England to intensify her flirtation with social and religious pluralism? Why should New England be forced to suffer the knowledge that nothing had made her more anachronistic within the world she wanted to save, that nothing did more to chafe her relationship with that world, than her efforts – efforts prescribed by her covenant with her Lord God – to stem the tide of toleration? Why had her God bound her to a design so unalterable that it defined all adjustment and accommodation as betrayal? And why had her God sent her into a land that demanded and rewarded preoccupation, not with building and maintaining a model city and living model lives, but with hard work and close trading? The Puritans knew, of course, that trial, temptation, and uncertainty were the appointed lot of man: that it was not given man to know '*what* Afflictions shall come upon him' or what shall be 'the Time of his Death'; that he was called to 'follow the Lord, as it were blind-fold[ed]'. But the wilderness they knew, placed against an English backdrop, seemed to confront them not with trial but with insoluble dilemma: with choice between the disloyalty of compromise and revision and the failure of scorn and irrelevance.[26]

Puritan orthodoxy possessed, it should be noted, one direct solution to the dilemma of the caretaking generations – that of radically applying to the pursuits of the first generation the wisdom set forth in Urian Oakes' sermon of 1677. Puritans knew, almost by right of birth, that mere men were never able 'infallibly' to determine the issue of their plans and activities; that God alone governed time and ordered history, and that God's ways were to man inscrutable. 'God is the Lord of Time, and Orderer, and Governour of all Contingences', Oakes insisted, including the 'Time and Chance that further or hinder the Designs of men'. Men accordingly should labor, Oakes continued, 'to be prepared and provided for Disappointments', for 'Changes and Chances', for 'Occurrents and Emergencies that may blast' their 'Undertakings'; for only with sound preparation could they hope in the face of 'such Frustrations' to keep 'Faith and Prayer . . . a going' and to avoid either flying 'out against God' or fainting and sinking 'in Discouragements'.[27]

Radical application of this 'good Counsel to men of projecting Heads' would have permitted explanation of the failure of the Puritan design, which would in turn have justified revising or abandoning it. Indeed, such a step would have undone even the need of using the jeremiad to generalize and relativize judgment. But Puritans were no less the children of their fathers than of their God: they were no more capable of asserting that their fathers had misread God's commission than they were capable of flying out against the God who had placed them in their trying land. They used Oakes' good counsel to explain their own false starts. But in their effort to move beyond their appointed tasks and yet remain loyal to their fathers, they extended in two ways their already revised jeremiad.[28]

On one side they used it to substitute tribute for action. They made humiliation a form of homage, lamentation a mode of loyalty. By decrying their failure, by contemning their disloyalty, they defined themselves as a dedicated people. Preaching, hearing, and reading jeremiads became tests of loyalty and acts of heroism. The ingenuity and eloquence the clergy could muster in detailing declension, the openness and remorse the people could summon in accepting judgment — these were strange tests of fortitude, courage, and devotion. But to the Puritans they were altogether necessary. For it was only by substituting formal repentance for active reform and loyal discourse for loyal action that the Puritans managed in good conscience slowly to move beyond caretaking and enter their changing world.[29]

On the other side, however, they made the jeremiad a work of celebration. In it they not only confronted their 'great and dangerous *Declensions*'; they also celebrated, and in celebrating reclaimed, the great work of their fathers. Had the second and third generations been concerned solely with their own freedom, had they been less loyal sons, they should have felt no further need of the jeremiad. But because they wanted also to free their fathers' design from disappointment and defeat, they made their works of complex lamentation works of praise and celebration.[30] In 1648 Thomas Shepard called 'all the Godly wise' to the task of celebratory interpretation: 'let us . . . consider and look back', he said, 'upon the season of this great enterprise'. In 1669, John Davenport, one of the last survivors of the first generation, extended the recitative jeremiad. But the form belonged to the second and third generations, who used it to re-order the entire New England experience.[31]

By recalling 'the Considerable Matters, that produced and attended the First Settlement of Colonies', by telling of the 'more exemplary' among 'the *Actors*' in the settlement story, and by relating 'Memorable Occurrences, and amazing Judgments and Mercies', the makers of the jeremiads established a standard and defined the genius of dedicated action. Quoting Virgil's *Aeneid*, Cotton Mather stressed the importance of understanding what drove men eminent in piety to endure so many calamities and to undertake so many hardships. The explanation he offered was dedication to the Puritan design. The '*Actions*' that 'signalized' Puritan settlement and construction were authored by men so dedicated that they withstood 'temptations', overcame 'Disturbances', and confuted 'enemies'; their 'Methods' and their dedication together enabled them to weather 'out each horrible tempest'.[32]

For latter-day Puritans, however, dedicated action took a different form. Deprived of the tasks of radical social and theological construction, they turned to construction of another sort. They reconstructed 'the Beginning' of the 'remarkable' work of their fathers.[33] They defined 'the End and Design' that had inspired and informed that work.[34] And they recounted and praised those of their fathers' '*Actions*' that seemed to them 'of a more eminent importance'.[35] In short, they substituted the dedicated action of telling and retelling their inherited story for the dedicated action of pursuing their inherited task. Through their lamenting—recounting—celebrating jeremiads, they hoped to 'preserve and secure the interest of Religion in the Churches of . . . New-England'.[36] But beyond renewing life at home, they sought to complete their fathers' 'Great Design'. They saw in their jeremiads analogues and extensions of the grand action from which they had derived. Having redefined action, and having moved to new unity by tracing grand action, the makers of jeremiads were able to proffer their works not as mere lament but rather as a mode of constructive activity, a form of creative endeavor.[37]

The jeremiad accordingly became not simply a way of reviving 'religion' in New England, but more strangely a way of spreading 'abroad in the world, some small Memorials' of the New England story.[38] The Puritan interpreters thus would salvage a design that had failed. Beyond 'Defeat and Disappointment', beyond the death of a dream, they reconstructed the story of New England.[39] Whether that story would '*live* any where else or no', at least it would '*live*' in and through interpretations of her 'History'.[40] By this indirection the Puritans were able to approximate the perfection they had missed. In

1730, a century after the inauguration of the Great Migration, Thomas Prince composed a sermon in which all things are duly ordered: New England is 'a Countrey' of 'Religion, good Order, Liberty, Learning and flourishing Towns and Churches'; wherefore it possesses 'a destinguishing Name in the World' and reflects 'singular Honour to the Persons and Principles of it's [sic] original Setlers' and the 'very grievous Trials . . . Hardship and Affliction' they endured. Echoing biblical passages of promise that had all along provided the model of Puritan hope, Prince envisaged and recorded perfection achieved only in vision and record.

And now the WILDERNESS and the solitary Place is Glad for them: The Desart rejoices and blossoms as a Rose . . . The Glory of LEBANON is given to it, the Excellency of CARMEL and SHARON; they see the Glory of the LORD and the Excellency of our GOD. The Waters of the Divine Influence break out in the Wilderness, and the Streams in the Desart: The parched Ground becomes a Pool; and the thirsty Land, Springs of Water: In the Habitations of Dragons where they lay, there grows up the Grass; and an High Way now is there, which is call'd the *Way of Holiness*, over which the Unclean do not pass, and the Wayfaring Men do not err therein.[41]

Despite the 'great and dangerous *Declensions*' of 'transcendently guilty' men, both the Puritans' original design and the action to which it led are preserved and completed in the story that the jeremiads tell.[42] Through poetic rendering, the work of the Puritan builders is redeemed: the wayfaring men within no longer err; those without now see the glory of the Lord; within the New England Way has become and without it is acknowledged as the Way of Holiness. And further, should 'the Plantation . . . soon after this, *come to nothing*', as another interpreter put it, its story nonetheless would survive in the lamentation and celebration of its telling.[43]

The jeremiad thus became, to borrow from Wallace Stevens, a 'poem that took the place of a mountain', an interpretation that embodied a failed design and so preserved and, in one sense, realized and perfected it. Through the jeremiad second- and third-generation Puritans 'recomposed' their heritage. Through it they were able to 'discover, at last, the view toward which they had edged', and to find, at last, 'A place to go in [their] own direction'. With it they became 'complete in an unexplained completion', and were able to accept their 'unique and solitary home'.[44]

That the jeremiad became imaginative interpretation does not mean, of course, that any jeremiad is a literary masterpiece. None is. In their own way, however, the latter-day Puritans were true, though very imperfect and partial, poets: they followed, if not to the bottom, at least into the darkness of their night, there to order words of themselves and of their origins, there to seek a basis of renewal; in their tales of pleasing woe, they sang, as best they could, 'of human unsuccess | In a rapture of distress'.[45] Their characteristic decision was, to be sure, rather to skirt than fully to explore the incongruity, first between the intent of the design and the result of the actions of their fathers, and second between the purposes to which they had been dedicated as children and the causes to which they were giving themselves as men. But in their jeremiads they acknowledge and, in their most interesting moments, attempt even to master these incongruities: they attempt, that is, to reconcile, by proclaiming them one, the intent and the achievement of their fathers and they attempt, while going about other business, to remain loyal to the purposes to which their fathers had dedicated them.

5
Spiritual biography and the 'Lords Remembrancers'

CECELIA TICHI

Contemporary discussions of the New England Puritan 'Lords Remembrancers' — a term by which Puritan minister Urian Oakes designated the Puritan historians recording God's mercifulness to a New England people[1] — have generally focused on the Puritan conception of history as an ethical and belletristic discipline thematically concerned with the all-encompassing man—God relationship in its myriad manifestations through time. Scholarship has further revealed what models and traditions the Puritan historians worked from, enabling students of the period to understand how and why historical evidence was marshaled to evince God's providential signaling of the imminent apocalypse regarded by Puritans as the logical culmination of the Reformation.[2] Although some of the Puritan historians might take vigorous exception to twentieth-century charges of aesthetic failings, their own statements of intention and purpose correlate in the main with contemporary scholars' findings.

Yet if it is true that the sensibilities of an age are best comprehended by other generations temporally removed, then perhaps the Puritans for all their discursive remarks about history were unable to comprehend fully the nature of their works. Indeed they appear unconscious of the conjunction of factors contributing to a generic specialness evident in their work from the time of William Bradford to that of Cotton Mather.[3] For to explore the spiritually biographical strain in New England Puritan histories — a strain of which the historians themselves seemed unaware — is to discover new thematic and rhetorical grounds on which to evaluate those works. It might further explain why New England readers, long grown accustomed to being comforted by their historians' spiritual biographies of their tribe, should in the early eighteenth century cancel book subscriptions in dramatic repudiation of Thomas Prince's austere timetable of their region's development, his *Chronological History of New-England*.[4]

It was while traveling extensively in early eighteenth-century England that Prince 'found the want of a regular History of this Country every where complain'd of'.[5] Prince might have squelched complaints by referring Englishmen to Nathaniel Morton's *New Englands Memoriall*, a work which in his 'early Youth instructed [him] in the History of this Country'.[6] Or he might have informed his English friends that Edward Johnson's *Wonder-Working Providence of Sions Saviour* had been in their midst since 1654, though dismal sales had led its enterprising publisher to rid himself of surplus copies by binding the work as Part III of a quite different volume. Aside from these, Prince could have recommended Cotton Mather's *Magnalia Christi Americana* (London, 1702), for Prince himself said the work advanced his knowledge considerably. Yet he was evidently unsatisfied with it since he began to entertain thoughts of writing the 'regular history' his English cousins found wanting on their bookshelves. Back in New England his perusal of the unpublished manuscripts of William Bradford and William Hubbard strengthened his determination to compile a 'naked Register, comprizing only Facts in a Chronological Epitome'.[7] Thomas Prince thus determined to depart from the historiographical tradition of Bradford, implicitly of John Winthrop, of Morton, Johnson, and Hubbard, and even of his acknowledged mentor, Cotton Mather. In so doing, he broke a tradition unique in seventeenth-century literature: spiritual biography of a tribe.

Several writers have explored the Puritans' tribalism, a term more functional than rhetorical, since extraordinary social cohesion affected the entire fabric of Puritan life — including their writing of history. Perry Miller observes that 'the Puritan philosophy demanded that in society all men, at least all regenerate men, be marshaled into one united array'.[8] That unity was, of course, non-democratic, for their vestigially medieval concept was one of fixed social degree and order in which, as John Winthrop said, 'some must be rich some poore, some highe and eminent in power and dignitie; others meane and in subjeccion', all of it 'for the preservacion and good of the whole'.[9] Nearly one half-century later Hubbard echoed Winthrop's sentiments, asserting that variance in social station was 'the beauty and strength' of such a society.[10] Expectedly, the pattern of Puritan settlement was of 'groups and towns, settled in whole communities', with maintenance of 'firm government over all units'.[11]

The Puritan disposition toward clustered settlements with initially

fixed social strata was combined with events in Scripture to give New
Englanders a sense of themselves as a tribe. That is, 'the basic reality
in their life was the analogy with the Children of Israel. They conceived that by going out into the Wilderness, they were reliving the
story of Exodus and not merely obeying an explicit command to go
into the wilderness. For them the Bible was less a body of legislation
than a set of binding precedents.'[12] Aboard the *Arbella* in transit to
America, Winthrop had drawn a parallel between himself and Moses
leading his Tribe into the Wilderness, saying he would 'shut upp this
discourse with the exhortacion of Moses that faithfull servant of the
Lord in his last farewell to Irsaell [Israel].'[13] Winthrop's reference
is not singular in New England literature, for ministers and historians
delighted to place the biblical Canaan in apposition to the New
England one.

It is possible that the metaphor of the Mosaic tribe gave the
Puritans expression for a tribal cohesion already ingrained in them.
Perry Miller writes that their acceptance of government as an unavoidable fact of earthly life occurred 'because they, just emerging
from feudalism, were still a folk rather than an aggregation of disparate individuals, still possessed by a deep, an ingrained sense of the
community that sometimes seems atavistic'. Yet Miller adds that the
'situation in New England at first did everything to accentuate this
primitive tribal instinct, to underline the analogy with the people of
Israel'.[14] Whatever the sequence of influences leading to the Puritans'
tribal self-identification, their concept of society, their pattern of
settlement, and their interpretation of Scripture all coalesced to make
them a self-professed tribe from the very beginning.

Other events reinforced that tribal sense as they passed their first
decade in the Bay, for within ten years after their arrival the Puritans
had institutionalized that most rigorous test for membership into their
saintly tribe: the personal narration of saving grace.[15] Without that
testimony of salvation revealed to an individual through long, ard-
uous, and agonizing introspection, he could not partake of baptism or
the Lord's Supper. In short, he could not be a church, or tribe,
member. The importance of this membership, apart from its theological and political ramifications, was that it set off certain men as quite
publicly holier than thou. Those persons not only had a private relationship with their God, but a social one through fellow church
members with whom they were in covenant. 'The basic fact about
congregationalism was its emphasis on the going relationship among

men'.[16] And the church covenant was the 'basis of their public lives as well as the solace of their private moments'.[17] In delineating Puritans of saving grace from their less holy New England neighbors not in covenant, the Puritans increased the strength of their tribal cohesion.

Expectedly, there were certain outward manifestations of this social bond. Those in covenant called each other 'Brother' and were not wont to let their fellows drift from them even when geographical distance impeded.[18] In addition, Edmund S. Morgan finds that the Puritans' high regard for family structure made sufficient impress on their religion to intensify their tribalism. He concludes that in Puritan churches 'God tended to become not merely a husband or father but the husband or father only of families that belonged to orthodox New England churches', adding that 'they made him so much their own, in the guise of making themselves his, that eventually and at times he took on the character of a tribal deity'.[19]

The Puritan penchant for tribalism, coupled with their historians' prominent membership in the tribe, made its due impress on New England Puritan historiography. The 'Lords Remembrancers' were not merely recording the stories of randomly holy lives, nor compiling a miscellany of God's providence affecting disparate individuals who happened to collect into towns for convenience. Moreover, they were not atomizing the Puritans as singular men whose relation with God was unconnected to that of their fellows. Puritan tribal membership made each man part of a social and spiritual organism. One could not help but view the journey of his soul in the wilderness as linked firmly with the soul-journeys of his fellows. In this light it is not surprising that a recent writer, reading the Town Book of Sudbury, Connecticut, is 'impressed that the selectmen were aware of the precise "condition" of every inhabitant'.[20] One need only leaf through Samuel Sewall's diary, with its fastidious recording of the state of numerous individuals at all times, to become aware of this encompassing human concern, that is, of Puritan tribalism operating.

Thus the Puritan historians wrote narratives of a New England tribe organically unified and spiritually journeying in an atmosphere of frequent indifference and hostility. In so doing, and evidently un-known to them, they were heavily influenced by a Puritan literary genre developed in England and carried on in the New World.[21] That is, in writing their histories they expanded the spiritual bio-graphy to include not only the individual but the tribal society. In this their works are unique in seventeenth-century literature.

The Puritans had splendid biographical precedents, with Plutarch's *Lives* pre-eminent because of its 'conception of biography based, like the "character", on ethical principles'.[22] For this quality Cotton Mather called the Roman historian 'incomparable', although long before Mather's birth and preceding the migration of the Bradford and Winthrop parties, English Puritans came to espouse a quite different biographical model, that of Augustine's *Confessions*. The Church Father's purpose was not to record dramatic deeds, but to 'show his spiritual evolution, the coming-into-being of his full personality'.[23] Thus in the *Confessions* 'deeds are not recounted simply because they occurred, but because they represent stages of spiritual growth'.[24] Although Augustine's work had no comparable successor for over 1000 years and no spiritually sympathetic heir until John Bunyan wrote the best-known of all spiritual biographies, *Grace Abounding*, still the Church Father set the tenor for the kind of biographical writing the Puritans favored. In a genre whose practitioners write 'chiefly of deeds' or 'chiefly of psychic states', the Puritans were unmistakably prone to the latter.[25] With their proclivities for spiritual diagnostics it could hardly be otherwise.

William Haller, among others, has traced the development of spiritual biography from its place as sermon adjunct to that of independent literary form, principally in the eighty years before the Civil War.[26] Its salient premise lay in the importance of the individual's spiritual welfare, ascertained by the introspective self responsible for it and thus obliged to 'mark with care each event or stage in its development', duly noting 'every symptom of progress or relapse'.[27] Since the symptoms pointed toward central themes in the biography, the reader encountered no soul long fixed in any one state of grace or torpor. The Christian's earthly life 'was seen as in constant movement; progress or deterioration was always taking place. . . Growth in grace continued throughout the lifetime of the believer in a manner comparable to organic growth; it was therefore possible to trace its progress and to plot the symptoms of regeneration'.[28] Understandably, since the soul, Satan, and God were parties in the action, there was no need for genealogical prominence or earthly eminence to justify the writing of spiritual biography. Its subjects came from all social classes since their souls were equally precious before God.

The Puritans put these writings of individual spiritual wayfaring to a social use. The 'virtue [of the form] would be that it might teach other men, also engaged in the fight for godliness, something of the way in which that fight was apt to go. If every good man was a pilgrim toward blessedness, the best guidebooks might be accounts of how others had fared on the road toward Heaven'.[29] In other words, the spiritual biography emphasized a unity of Christian experiences, a 'belief that spiritual life varies little from man to man'.[30] Since there were similarities in the morphology of salvation, as well as in the indices of damnation, 'a reader might recognize and rejoice in his own tokens of grace and election by reading of them in others; or, through the writings of others, he might be startled out of reprobate habits by discovering their symptoms and aftermath'.[31]

Just as the form of spiritual biography varied little from writer to writer, so its diction tended to be repetitive. Spiritual biography was not to point up its subject's singular interior experiences, or to emphasize his eccentricities of soul, for the biographer's theme 'attaches significance to what all Christians have felt and undergone, and disregards or suppresses idiosyncrasies except as they illustrate typical stages or predicaments in the soul's development'.[32] The stylistic result of such thematic reinforcement of Christian unity was a 'conventional phraseology' which could 'enhance the description of feelings or experiences noteworthy for their universality rather than their uniqueness'.[33] George Starr suggests that 'in this light, the traditional idiom seems entirely appropriate: it amplifies the rendering of individual experience by associating it with the experience of all Christians. In short, the spiritual autobiographer naturally found himself thinking "what oft was thought", and since he felt that it had been "ne'er so well express'd" as in the Bible, he was content to employ the same imagery and turns of phrase'.[34]

Before discussing the Puritan historians in this light, one further point needs to be made about the language of spiritual biography: it was fraught with the technique of spiritualizing. Starr reminds us that it was incumbent upon the Puritan to be mindful of worldly minutiae, lest he suffer the grave consequences of important details unheeded. Meaningful texts were everywhere, and 'one could attach as much significance to a tradesman's annual inventory as to the Christian soldier's shield, helmet, and sword'.[35] Spiritualizing worked two ways, however, since 'a number of Biblical people and things which were repeatedly subjected to this sort of interpretation took on well-defined spiritual values'.[36] Moreover, the 'mere mention of them would suggest the spiritual import of whatever one happened to be describing', so that there developed an 'allusive shorthand' in which 'strange and uncommon experiences could be made familiar, singular and exotic episodes could be made meaningful, by even the most casual reference to Biblical precedents or analogues'.[37] Spiritualizing underwent a further refinement, for one 'result of the tendency to regard everything in life and literature as amenable to spiritual interpretation' was that 'certain ordinary objects and activities acquired distinct symbolic significance'.[38] In other words, there evolved a group of objects, persons, and situations from life and from the Bible, each appropriately meaningful in connotation to the reader. It appears especially likely that the New England Puritans' tribalism solidified their conditioned spiritual response to utterance of a cluster of repeated terms. Starr mentions spiritual wayfaring, or journeying, as a favored figure in English spiritual biography. Understandably, the figure was doubly important for those New England Puritans whose ocean crossings committed journeys of the flesh to congruent soul journeys.

The spiritually biographical intent of unifying Christians' experiences in language replete with lessons drawn from life and from literature makes it understandable why the Puritan colonists, so familiar with the genre of spiritual biography, did not write the kind of travelogues or territorial histories they knew from English precedent. In tracing the journey of their tribe in New England, the heritage they followed was not mainly that of renaissance travel narratives or regional history, but of spiritual biography. To be sure the Puritans did, some of them, write of New England's topography and natural resources, and how men were faring with them. Francis Higginson has plenty to say about 'fat black earth' around the Charles River, about production of 'a quart of milk for a penny', about flying squirrels and air 'of a most healing nature to all of a cold, melancholy, phlegmatic, rheumatic temper of body'.[39] And William Wood (whose Puritanism must be asserted tenuously) has considerable maritime advice about Massachusetts for his 'mind-travelling Readers'.[40] But this sort of vicarious tour is not what the Puritans had in mind when they set down the story of the Holy Commonwealth. Nathaniel Morton makes this quite clear. 'I shall not insist', he says, 'upon the Clime nor Soyle of the Country, its Commodities of Discommodities; nor at large on the Natives, or their Customes and Manners: all of which have been already declared by Captain *Smith*, Mr. *Higginson*, Mr. *Williams*, Mr. *Wood*, and others'.[41] Nor is Morton merely denying a duplication of effort, for he freely acknowledges his debt to

Bradford, his uncle, and to Edward Winslow, both of whom concerned themselves more with things of the spirit than of the soil.[42]
Morton's purpose is best indicated in his statement of hope that his
New Englands Memoriall may *'be a help to thee in thy journey through
the wilderness of this world, to that Eternal Rest which is onely to be found
in the Heavenly* Canaan'.[43] Here the influence of spiritual biography
is evident, for the work can be a guidebook for its reader, himself a
wayfarer in the world. Morton's 'world' is obviously one larger than
New England, and the desired end of the life journey is no rocky
coast reached after an Atlantic crossing, but heaven.

The spiritually biographical strain in New England histories may
help to explain the frequent 'wilderness' or 'American desert' metaphors found in those works. The biographers' propensity for spiritualizing possibly clarifies the meaning of the Puritan wilderness as the
'Lords Remembrancers' understood it. For it was initially a link more
with the biblical wilderness into which Moses led his tribe (and therefore a reinforcement of Christian similarity of experience) than it was
physical, palpable environment. 'The seventeenth-century New
Englanders were more concerned with analyzing the changes in their
communal state of soul than in recording their reaction to the unique
American environment'.[44] Critics who have condemned the Puritans
for their initial failure to paint verbal landscapes of the American
wilds may have misunderstood the colonists' use of the figure, as well
as their initial understanding of America.[45] The New World furnish-
ed a setting for the Puritan communal quest for salvation; in working
out the pattern of that quest under the aegis of historiography, the
'Lords Remembrancers' shaped the spiritual biography of a people.
They continued to do so as long as New England remained tribal.

Limitations of space make it here impossible to examine closely the
Puritan historians' interpretations of tribal successes and failings in
the communal struggle for salvation. Their common touchstone include establishment and maintenance of government (stated in
spiritualizing similes of buildings), the antinomian crisis (expressed in
terms of insidious sickness debilitating the spiritual body, itself
moving from back-sliding darkness forward into saving light), the
Indians (regarded as a going indication of God's disposition toward
the tribe whose mettle was being tested), and the wilderness (treated
initially as a spiritualizing metaphor, but whose palpable nature the
later historians found to be ineluctable). Yet since this discussion has

already broached at several points the spiritualizing figure of the journey, it is well to pursue that image in works of the 'Lords Remembrancers'. For to observe its various uses in the context of spiritual biography is to absolve the Puritan historians of a most frequent criticism: that either because of sloth or imaginative incapacity, they tended to copy from Winthrop and Bradford.[46]

Couched midway in Edward Johnson's *Wonder-Working Providence* is this succinct evocation of the spirit of Puritan mission in New England: 'So here behold the Lord Christ, having egged a small handfull of his people forth in a forlorne wilderness, stripping them naked from all human helps, plunging them in a gulph of miseries, that they may swim for their lives through the Ocean of his Mercies, and land themselves safe in the armes of his Compassion'.[47] Johnson's lines summarize vividly the thematic constructs of the 'Lords Remembrancers' and indicate somewhat the rhetoric of harrowing journey by which the historians express themes of salvation sought against grim worldly odds. The wayfaring motif of spiritual biography pervades the histories, not only in the literal sense of Atlantic crossings enumerated but in a widely metaphorical one. Between the historians' careful telling of ships remarkably delivered from peril and their imaginative extension to New England itself as a ship, there is varied play on the theme of journeying. Winthrop, with characteristic verbal economy, concludes after marking thirteen years of notably safe ocean passages, that 'indeed such preservations and deliverances have been so frequent, to such ships as have carried those of the Lord's family between the two Englands, as would fill a perfect volume to report them all'.[48]

Winthrop never filled the volume, but Edward Johnson, whose editor feels he was likely with the Winthrop party aboard the *Arbella*, does offer a dramatic portrait of the sea voyage so fraught with spiritual import. Johnson's emphasis is on a people being tried as they 'betooke them to the protection of the Lord on the wide Ocean'.[49] The trials consist of an impending Spanish ambush (thankfully unrealized), a storm so vicious as to send cattle and horses overboard (interpreted as God's settling of purposeful hearts by paring away materialistic excess), and disease (by godly design instilling in the Puritans grave reservations about facing a return voyage to sin-ridden England).

Johnson's care to show every ostensible misfortune of the ocean voyage as a divinely designed advantage reveals his belief that the ocean crossing was a tribal response to God's call. The new land – respite from English deprivations and godly arena for continuance of the Reformation – could be claimed only by communal commitment to a terrible sea voyage. Johnson pointedly observes that many of these emigrants 'never before had made any path through the Waters' and that others were 'so tenderly brought up that they had little hope of their Lives continuance under such hardships'.[50] He further remarks that the advanced ages of some more invited a 'quiet Couch' than a 'pinching Cabbin' and that among the lot were 'weakly Women . . . now imboldened to venture through these tempestuous Seas'.[51] The circumstantial unsuitedness to the voyage of those willing to make it gives Johnson room to 'magnify the grace of Christ'. In addition, it gives his reader a close view of prodigious social assent to God's will.

The profound impact of the Atlantic voyage is revealed in the New England historians' metaphorical use of the ocean. William Bradford quite simply describes Plymouth's thankfulness to God who 'had brought them over the vast and furious ocean, and delivered them from all the perils and miseries therof', and he pauses, 'half amazed at this poor people's present condition', before immediately envisioning their 'sea of troubles' on a shore without welcoming friends, public inns, or houses for shelter.[52] His nephew, Nathaniel Morton, avers the integrity of his uncle's recollection by including the passage in *New Englands Memoriall*.[53] Edward Johnson, too, applies the ocean metaphorically to the colonists' impending terrestrial trials, suggesting the Puritans must 'wade through the Ocean in steddy resolution'.[54] Ever one to see strengthening virtue in adversity, Johnson asserts that Christ 'were not to be injoyed, but by passing through an Ocean of troubles, Voyaging night and day upon the great deep'.[55]

Viewing the world as vast ocean, the historians people it with a colonial band of travelers or pilgrims whose every step is marked with danger. William Bradford, using the biblical parallels so characteristic of his writing, states that Plymouth may say 'with the Apostle, 2 Corinthians xi.26, 27, that they were "in journeyings often, in perils of waters, in perils of robbers, in perils of their own nation, in perils among the heathen, in perils in the wilderness, in perils in the sea, in perils among false brethren; in weariness and painfulness, in watching often, in hunger and thirst, in fasting often, in cold and nakedness"'.[56] Nathaniel Morton assents to the aptness for Plymouth of the biblical journeying by including the entire passage in his work. Edward Johnson, too, cites the treacherous snares awaiting this pilgrim people. Assigning to an Englishman a speech incredulous in tone as he sees a friend depart for the New England wilderness, Johnson writes that 'now after two, three, or foure moneths spent with daily expectation of swallowing Waves and cruell Pirates, you are to be Landed among barbarous Indians, famous for nothing but cruelty, where you are like to spend your days in a famishing condition for a long space'.[57] Sympathetically, Cotton Mather remarks that the colonists landed in a world 'in which they found they must live like strangers and pilgrims'.[58]

In part the historians justify the pitiful wayfaring of their tribe as God's intention that they remain humble. Summarizing a discussion of New England's early afflictions, William Hubbard suggests that 'such were the solemn trials that God was pleased to acquaint them with in their first adventure, the more to exercise their faith and patience, and daily to remind them that they were pilgrims and strangers upon the earth, and must not seek great things for themselves'.[59] Cotton Mather concurs that ''twas a most heavy trial of their patience, whereto they were called the first winter of this their *pilgrimage*, and enough to convince them and remind them that they were but Pilgrims'.[60]

Yet even with proper humility and watchfulness, the wayfarers are warned that death or destruction can meet them at any turn. William Hubbard's warnings are appropriately couched in metaphors of journey. 'Many that go forth', he says, 'know not that they shall return, and the mariner that is ready to let fall his anchor knows not but it may be that fatal one which shall put an end to the navigation of his life.'[61] Recounting several incidents resulting in death, Hubbard concludes that 'such examples left upon record, may serve as buoys to give notice of the dangerous temptations, that like rocks which lie unseen, are found in discontented minds, on which they often shipwreck their souls forever, as well as lives'.[62]

The New Englanders did not feel their pilgrimage was a desolate one. God had, after all, sifted them as choice grain to be sent abroad, ultimately under his care. The historians are accordingly not remiss in fixing the source of the wayfarers' strength and guidance. Hubbard, remarking that their first New England landing 'entertained [them] with no other sight than that of the withered grass on the surface of the cold earth; and the grim looks of the savage enemies', then asserts that 'surely such passengers or pilgrims, had need of some other more inward support and comfort the world is not acquainted with'.[63] He suggests that a good conscience coupled with the faith of Abraham was the basis for that support. Cotton Mather concurs that 'the passage of these our *pilgrims* was attended with many smiles of Heaven upon them'.[64] Later singling out John Cotton as particularly favored of God, Mather writes that 'there have been few that have seen so many and mighty effects given to the "travels of their souls"'.[65] Even when at the death of Plymouth's patriarchs Nathaniel Morton remarks that the colony was 'poor' and 'tottering', he can yet say that 'God was pleased to minde it, even in its low estate', since 'he hath not hitherto left us without a *Joshua* to lead us in the remaining part of our pilgrimage'.[66]

The historians extend the spiritually biographical terms of pilgrim wayfaring to individuals. Frequently the metaphor is a euphemistic reference to death. Nathaniel Morton, writing that Pastor John Robinson had succumbed to the plague, says that 'now the Lord had appointed him to go a greater journey, at less charge, to a better place'.[67] And William Hubbard notes that, among others, President Henry Dunster of Harvard 'ended his pilgrimage' in Scituate.[68] Cotton Mather records the demise of such worthies as Thomas Hooker and John Eliot as concluded pilgrimages, applying the figure somewhat differently when describing the death of Theophilus Eaton's son, since that death 'was counted the sorest of all the trials that ever befel [Eaton] in the "days of the years of his pilgrimage"'.[69] Mather's use of the figure is not always so blatant, for at least twice he invokes the metaphor of a journeying ship now come to the end of its voyage. Of John Eliot's last days on earth, Mather writes that 'when he was become a sort of Miles Emeritus, and began to draw near his *end*, he grew still more heavenly, more savoury, more divine, and scented more of the spicy country at which he was ready to put ashore'.[70]

The figure of New England itself as a ship underway is the historians' furthest imaginative extension of the wayfaring theme. Significantly, only the later historians Hubbard and Mather fully realize the metaphor, for in retrospect they could see not only the quality of spiritual journey, but the social structure that ordered it. The ship figure became appropriate to a society in godly transit, one whose prominent members might be designated as such key parts of the vessel as the mast or helm, or such leading mariners as captain or helmsman. Hubbard, citing the reasons for William Bradford's gubernatorial longevity despite availability of others well qualified for the position, says the Plymouth colonists were 'like mariners in a storm or dangerous channel, that having experience of a skilful and able pilot are loath to change the helm till the storm be over, or the haven obtained'.[71] He inserts a short anagrammatic elegy on Thomas Dudley, in which the figure of Dudley as a ship's mast is central:

HOLD, MAST, WE DY

When swelling gusts of antinomian breath
Had well nigh wreck'd this little bark to death,
When oars'gan crack, and anchors, then we cry,
Hold firm, brave mast, thy stand, or else we die.
Our orth'dox mast did hold, we did not die;
Our mast now roll'd by th' board, (poor bark) we cry.
Courage, our pilot lives, who stills the waves,
Or midst the surges still his bark he saves.[72]

Hubbard did not write the lines, but his belief in the appropriateness of the metaphor is indicated by readiness to include the elegy in a narrative where verse stanzas are most infrequent. At another point he is gratified that a fractious General Court ended in 'much love', since, 'if the tackling had been loosed, so as they could not have strengthened their mast, the lame would at that time easily have taken the prey'.[73]

Just as Hubbard applies the helmsman figure to Bradford, so Cotton Mather makes the same application to Winthrop. After presenting Winthrop's 1645 vindication of some charges General Court deputies had leveled at him, Mather notes that 'the people would not afterwards entrust the helm of the weather-beaten bark in any other hands but Mr. Winthrop's until he died'.[74] Previously, at the beginning of the *Magnalia*, Mather had invoked the figure of New England as a ship, stating his intention to describe colonial 'temptations and enemies tempestuated; and the Methods by which they have still weathered out each horrible tempest'.[75] He subsequently links his diction to that of classical antiquity, writing that 'the word GOVERNMENT, properly signifies the *guidance of a ship*', and adding that Cicero and Plutarch so used it.[76] He goes on, 'New England is a little *ship*, which hath weathered many a terrible storm; and it is but reasonable that they who have sat at the helm of the ship, should be remembered in the *history* of its deliverances.'[77] Among those remembered is Francis Higginson, New England's Noah landing his ship in the new world.[78]

Evidence indicates, in sum, the Puritan historians' readiness to express variously the broadened wayfaring theme of spiritual biography now inclusive of an entire people. Seemingly, the necessity of that people to commit both spirit and flesh to an ocean voyage heightened their feelings of communal soul in quest. It further induced their historians to use diction reflective of that quest. But that diction was not ploddingly copied one from another. Together in their spiritualizing intent to use a figure binding New Englanders in unity of Christian experience with Old Testament antecedents, the 'Lords Remembrancers' nonetheless work the figure variously. It seems more accurate to suggest that their common rhetoric is based in the 'allusive shorthand' of spiritual biography than that it stems from laziness or failure of imagination.

Now it is quite possible that the influence of spiritual biography had at times a rhetorically deleterious effect on the Puritan historians. Their frequent use of figures connotatively freighted to assure their audiences of unity in Christian experience seems in places to have lulled them (or perhaps trapped them) into a phraseology lacking freshness or vitality by current standards. The journeys, pilgrimages, ships, etc., become metaphoric clichés to readers not so happily conditioned to the rhetoric of spiritual biography. Even the most imaginative of the historians is guilty at times of spiritualizing his audience to ennui. For example, Edward Johnson's soldiers of Christ and Mather's continuous ministerial arrows piercing hearts of the elect are annoying in frequency and wearing in sameness of expression. The figures are all appropriate, but had the historians not been so strongly influenced by techniques of spiritual biography, they might have worked harder for a fresh use of language which could yet have comforted an audience seeking assurances of Christian unity of experience and wary of spiritual eccentricities.

Indeed, neglect by subsequent generations of a form once so popular as to be anthologized probably indicates how little attuned have been post-seventeenth-century sensibilities to the rigid formula of spiritual biography. But aesthetic alienation ought not to prevent an intellectual understanding of the generic grounds from which the 'Lords Remembrancers' worked, albeit unconsciously. Important as it is to know the Puritans' view of history as cosmic drama and their belief that Providence guided the affairs of men, it is equally significant to recognize their literary antecedents. Without that recognition the histories of the 'Lords Remembrancers' cannot be justly evaluated.

Awareness of the spiritually biographical strain in New England historiography might further make Cotton Mather's *Magnalia* seem less anomalous in structure than it appears to be when viewed alongside the straightforwardly chronological narratives of Mather's predecessors. They, except for Hubbard, could energetically build upwardly spiraling suspense pointing toward apocalyptic climax. Yet late in the century when the apocalypse began to seem doubtful, the chronological narrative methods of Bradford, Morton, Winthrop, and Johnson became infeasible for Puritan historiographers, since the climax had been stripped away. The remaining historians were left to cast about for new ways to shape events they felt meaningful. William Hubbard's work suffered from his failure to find appropriate new forms, for after his solid accounts of early lustres of growth, he trails off into a cliché-ridden, perfunctory narrative.

Yet Cotton Mather, writing in the throes of the Puritan declension in New England, nonetheless believed that religion infused history with a superlative symmetry of form.[79] And this conviction freed him from the confines of chronology, which he abandoned in favor of a spatial structuring. His introductory '*Bill* of *Fare*' promises passages 'deserving . . . a room in History'.[80] John Cotton 'claims a room in [his] pages', and Mather regrets that insufficient biographical data make it impossible to 'give much breadth to the room which we dedicate in this our history unto the memory of our [Zachariah] Symmes'.[81] Mather constructs a memorial temple into whose rooms the reader may enter and relive a segment of the New England past. Thus he exasperates those such as his protégé Thomas Prince who insist upon historical writing as a scheduled tour through time.

Yet the *Magnalia*'s formal aberrance from the histories of Mather's predecessors does not deny its spiritually biographial link with works of the 'Lords Remembrancers'. For while Mather offers many exemplary *Lives* of prominent New Englanders as models for emulation, they are *in toto* the quintessence of the Puritan tribe.[82] Nor is Mather's copious use of individual biography in the *Magnalia* lacking in precedent in earlier Puritan histories. In their concern for the tribal journey, the 'Lords Remembrancers' sometimes used the spiritual states of individuals to reflect on the health of the social body. For example Bradford records how reprobate John Oldham 'did make a free and large confession of the wrongs and hurt he had done to the people and church here, in many particulars, that as he had sought their ruin, so God had now met with him and might destroy him; yea, he feared they all fared the worse for his sake. He prayed God to forgive him and made vows that if the Lord spared his life he would become otherwise.'[83] Winthrop similarly narrates John Underhill's public penitentials, when he 'came in his worst clothes, . . . in a foul linen cap pulled close to his eyes' to declare 'what power Satan had of him since [his] casting out of the church'.[84] In humility he 'besought the church to have compassion of him', and Winthrop observes that 'accordingly he was received into the church again'.[85]

Similarly, Edward Johnson devotes an entire chapter to the redemption of an individual arriving in New England at the time of the antinomian controversy. The soul is lost, confused, despairing, and finally rescued by Thomas Shepard's preaching. 'The man was metamorphosed', Johnson writes.[86] And although the author may have based the story on his own experiences, the character is too generalized to be pinpointed as Edward Johnson. He is, instead, a spiritually questing Puritan Everyman in New England, and in describing his redemption Johnson constructs a paradigm of the briefer spiritual biographies recorded by his fellow historians. It appears likely that such little stories as those of Oldham, Underhill, and Johnson's character are cameo spiritual biographies of individuals whose states of soul bear on those of their fellows. The confessions and redemptive resolutions must have had a cathartic effect on Puritan society, and once included in the histories they provided a person believing himself sunk in sin and error with some pattern for redemption and the encouragement that society would love him all the better for his free acknowledgment of spiritual travail.

Connecting the foregoing spiritually biographical vignettes to the full-length lives in the *Magnalia* is the generic stricture of spiritual biography that its subjects' worldly station is irrelevant, that state of soul is pre-eminent thematically. Thus, while Mather engages himself at great length with such a worldly, active man as William Phips, many of his lives deal with spiritual self-realization unenhanced by worldly activity. Mather's portrait of young Thomas Shepard agonizing in a cornfield over the state of his soul includes no mention of the prestigious brick Boston house which Phips so aspired to as a mark of the world's grace. Rather, the spiritual wayfaring of such men as Shepard abounds in the *Magnalia*, having precedent in the brief narratives included by the earlier 'Lords Remembrancers'. To be sure, Mather's subjects remain in mind because their names are those of New England genealogical avatars of the seventeenth century. But it is state of soul and not social eminence that motivates the writing of spiritual biography, and to know this is to fix Mather's affinity to his predecessors in theme as well as rhetoric.

The spiritually biographical strain in New England Puritan historiography halted abruptly with the publication of Thomas Prince's *Chronological History of New England*. Depending for its vitality on the tribal cohesion that molded Puritan society into an organic whole, the spiritual biography of the tribe necessarily succumbed in a society no longer tribal. Thomas Prince's own comment, 'I am for leaving every one to the freedom of worshipping according to the light of his conscience', indicates in the early eighteenth century a supreme assertion of the individual moral will over accession to the aggregate social conscience.[87]

Yet though spiritual biography was no longer a valid component of historical writing in New England, its deep impress remained evident even in so tonally secular a historian as Thomas Prince. For all Prince's purposive departure from the literary effulgence of the *Magnalia* and his espousal of historiography as clustered facts hung from a timeline of dates, still he did not reject the usable past shaped by the 'Lords Remembrancers'.

On the contrary, in the 1730 centennial year of the arrival of the Winthrop party in America, Prince displaced the spiritual biography of the tribe from history into that socially wide-reaching New England oration, the election sermon.[88] Before his prestigious Boston audience he retold with eloquent succinctness of the spiritual wayfaring of the Puritan tribe. There is no condescension, no preciousness, no patronizing tone in Prince's recapitulation of the familiar story. His recent editor remarks that Prince 'creates a work with the American sense of epic destiny to appear later in the *Vision of Columbus, The Rising Glory of America, The Ages, Passage to India*, and *The Bridge*. He uses history to ask the question, "What is an American Puritan?" He uses history ... to see again the utopian opportunities which the New World can afford.'[89] For quite possibly Prince understood in his time what future American men of letters would discover again and again: that if one literary mode had become inappropriate to convey the spiritual biography of an increasingly heterogeneous people, still there remained in Americans something of the tenor of that quest for societal self-realization. Though various literary forms came later to embody this socially-questing spirit, its tradition in American literature was founded in the spiritual biographies of the 'Lords Remembrancers'.

Four major figures

William Bradford JESPER ROSENMEIER
Anne Bradstreet ROBERT D. RICHARDSON, Jr
Edward Taylor KARL KELLER
Cotton Mather DAVID LEVIN

6

'With my owne eyes': William Bradford's
of Plymouth Plantation

JESPER ROSENMEIER

In the year 1650, when he had ceased recording the role of Christ's
New Plymouth plantation in the great and ancient warfare between
God and Satan, William Bradford took up the study of Hebrew.
As a notebook for his painstaking exercises he used some pages in the
manuscript of his History, copying more than 1000 Old Testament
words and 25 phrases, together with their English translations.[1]
The particular words seem to have been chosen at random, but of the
25 phrases, almost half deal with family relationships, especially
that of fathers and sons. Having translated about 200 words (the first
is translated as 'to walk before him') Bradford explains why he was
trying to learn Hebrew:

> Though I am growne aged, yet I have had a longing
>   desire to see, with my owne eyes, somthing of that most
>   ancient language, and holy tongue, in which the Law
>   and Oracles of God were write; and in which God
>   and angels spake to the holy patriarks of old
>   time; and what names were given to things
>   from the creation. And though I cannot
>   attaine to much herein, yet I am refresh-
>   ed to have seen some glimpse hereof;
>   (as Moyses saw the land of Ca-
>   nan a farr off.) My aime and
>   desire is, to see how the words
>   and phrases lye in the
>   holy texte; and to
>   discerne somewhat
>   of the same,
>   for my owne
>   contente.[2]

As we see in the 'hourglass', Bradford did not begin the study of Hebrew merely to learn another language or to keep active in his later years. He was possessed by a 'longing desire' to realize as literally as he could the most ancient holiness, the holiness manifest in creation and the first people of God; he felt compelled to return to that glorious language in which the Spirit of God had spoken the world into being and the angels had conversed with the holy patriarchs. Of course, Bradford believed that the Bible in any language would speak about judgment and salvation with power and authority, but the Hebrew contributes a vividness lacking in other versions. Hearing God speak in his original tongue, as, for example, in Psalm 29, when his voice divides the flames of fire and shakes the wilderness, might bring Bradford directly back to the moment when the voice was first heard; he would be permitted to be present in the past.

Bradford's remarkably strong yearning for the resurrection of the past suggests, as I hope to show, more than mere nostalgia; he tenaciously insisted that the holiness of the ancient moments still stood as the perfect image for the present and future. The more carefully and precisely the ancient moments are unearthed, the more fully, he seems to have believed, would they mirror the divine. By learning the most ancient and holiest of tongues, Bradford hoped to see with his 'owne eyes' something of the coming kingdom, of the time when the holiness first revealed in creation would again be fully visible.[3]

Yet, at the same time, we recognize that the Hebrew studies were done for Bradford's 'owne contente'. In addition to demonstrating his longing for the past and his dream of a future glory, they are a very private work and disclose his isolation from the outside world. We do not see Bradford looking into Canaan as the confident leader of a chosen people. Behind him the ranks of a nation do not close in support and anticipation; the people of Plymouth are looking toward other lands.

The effort to resurrect the literal language of some original perfection is not unique to Bradford; it can be found in the writings of many other Separatists, most notably in Henry Ainsworth's *Annotations on the Pentateuch, or the Five Books of Moses; the Psalms of David; and the Song of Solomon*.[4] In the *Annotations*, Ainsworth presents extended commentaries on Deut. 3: 25–7, 34: 1, and Num. 27: 12, where Moses' view of Canaan from the top of Mt Pisgah is described. In Deut. 3 : 2 5—7, God denies Moses' supplication to pass over Jordan 'and see the good land . . . beyond', and orders Moses instead to 'speak no more unto me of this matter. Get thee up into the top of Pisgah, and lift up thine eyes westward, and northward, and southward, and eastward, and behold *it* with thine eyes: for thou shalt not go over this Jordan.' In Deut. 34 : 1, Moses obeys God's command, and goes 'up from the plains of Moab unto the mountain of Nebo, to the top of Pisgah, this *is* over against Jericho', where God tells him that the Canaan he sees before him is the land promised to the ancient fathers, 'unto Abraham, unto Isaac, and unto Jacob'.

In his commentary on these texts, Ainsworth takes great care to draw a picture of Canaan rich in physical detail; he wants the reader to have as literal a view of Canaan as Moses had when he stood on Mt Pisgah. On Moses' looking toward Jericho and Zoar, Ainsworth comments:

JERICHO,] In Gr. *Jericho*, a city within the land of Canaan, which the Israelites first conquered, by faith causing the wall to fall down. . . CITY OF PALM-TREES,] So Jericho is called here . . . of them and other fragrant fruits there growing, as balsam and the like; the city had the name of Jericho, by interpretation 'odoriferous', or 'fragrant'. UNTO ZOAR,] In Gr. *Segor*. Thus the last part which Moses viewed was nearest unto him and the pleasantest of all the land of Canaan: for 'all the plain of Jordan, was well watered, it was as the garden of the Lord'.[5]

And interpreting the phrase 'this good mountain and Lebanon', Ainsworth writes:

MOUNTAIN,] That is, *mountain country*: See Exod. 15 : 17. LE-BANON,] In Gr. *Antilibanon*; in Chald. *the house of the sanctuary*, because the temple was built of the cedars that grew on mount Lebanon . . . So the temple is called Lebanon . . . But that seemeth not to be meant here; but rather the mount Lebanon in the north part of the land, which was both an high and fragrant mountain, with sweet and goodly trees growing thereon . . . This great desire Moses had, because of the promises which God had made to Israel, to be accomplished in that land, the figure of our heavenly heritage.[6]

Living in Holland several thousand years after Moses, Ainsworth did not expect to write a commentary on the Old Testament that would be 'scientifically' exact. Rather, the quality he sought was the fullness of God's revelation to Moses. The Canaan Moses sees before him is the fulfillment of the promises given to Abraham and his seed. If, Ainsworth believes, the reader is to see what Moses saw, he must be transported back and stand with Moses on the high and fragrant mountain and look at the pleasant Jordan flowing toward Jericho and Zoar. The more directly he can see with Moses' eyes, the more vividly and graphically the past will live. For Ainsworth, the ancient facts are figures and types, and the more vividly the past lives, the more effective as prophecy it may become. Made real to our senses, Mt Nebo, planted with sweet and goodly trees, more fully prophesied the time when '"John from an high mountain was showed the holy Jerusalem", Rev. 21: 10'. Moses' Canaan is 'a figure of our heavenly inheritance, proposed to them that do the law, but given to them that are of the faith of Christ, John 1:17'. And God 'showeth Moses all the kingdoms and glory of Canaan, from an high mountain, for his comfort and strengthening of his faith, who saw the promises afar off, saluted them and died, as did his godly forefathers, Heb. 11: 9, 13'.[7] In God's denial of Moses' request to cross into the promised land and in his death are 'foreshowed the end and abrogation of Moses' law, when men are come to the gospel of Christ: for, "after that faith is come, we are no longer under the schoolmaster", Gal. 3: 25'.[8] What Moses saw — and, Ainsworth hopes, later men will see — from the top of Mt Pisgah is the fulfillment of the Old Testament quest for the promised land. But Moses sees something more and other: for his 'comfort and faith', God shows him the future promised land, of which the Canaan before him is the figure and type.

The fusion of graphic detail and prophetic vision in these passages is remarkable in seventeenth-century typology. Few other exegetes bring past and future, detail and dream, so unselfconsciously and richly together. Others who interpret the history of redemption may be profoundly familiar with the meanings of the types; and in their preaching and writings they may demonstrate their skill at finding deep connections between the old and new dispensations, as well as their knowledge of the spiritual values emblemized in the ancient people and events. Yet most typologists do not endeavor to realize so sensuously the land that Moses saw. They explicate the typological meanings of Canaan, but the land itself remains distant and unresurrected. By means of his rich literalness Ainsworth brings Moses resurrected into the world of seventeenth-century Englishmen and makes him walk before them. The vividness of his exegesis has its source in Ainsworth's experience of Christ's incarnation. Like Luther, who believed that Christ was the sun who lights up the Old Testament figures and types, Ainsworth sees all of the Bible as the revelation of the same divine light. It is the presence of Christ that illuminates facts and transforms them into prophecy. Therefore, the more fully Ainsworth can share Moses' view of Canaan, the profounder, he expects, will be his description of Christ's incarnation. Ainsworth cannot rest merely knowing that Moses saw Canaan afar off; he must himself see the living land. For Ainsworth, the ancient facts are ripe with Christ.

In his commentaries on Num. 2 7 : 1 2 and on the two texts from Deuteronomy, Ainsworth refers repeatedly to ch.1 1 of the Epistle to the Hebrews, where Paul writes about the nature of faith and its relationship to the promised lands, both Moses' Canaan and Christ's kingdom on earth. 'Faith', Paul says, 'is the substance of things hoped for, the evidence of things not seen'. It was by believing in God's promises that the Old Testament saints were given eyes to see into the future promised land. 'By faith', he writes, Abraham 'sojourned in the land of promise, as *in* a strange country . . . for he looked for a city which has foundations, whose builder and maker *is* God'. Abraham, Abel, Noah, and Sara all died before the promises had been fulfilled. Yet though they 'died in faith, not having received the promises, but having seen them afar off', they were 'persuaded of *them* and embraced *them*, and confessed that they were strangers and pilgrims on earth' who desired 'a better country, that is, a heavenly: wherefore God is not ashamed to be called their God: for he hath prepared for them a city'.

The city that God had prepared for his New Testament saints differs from that prepared for Abraham and the ancients. By Christ's kingdom is not meant the land between the Jordan and the Mediterranean. Nevertheless, it was possible for Ainsworth to identify so profoundly with Moses because the life and object of faith were the same for Old and New Testament believers. Though outwardly the promised lands are very different manifestations, they are, Ainsworth thought, incarnations of the same Christ.[9] And because he found Christ present in the entire history of redemption, Ainsworth trusted that the New Testament promises of the New Jerusalem would flower into fact in the same way Abraham had faith that the Old Testament prophecies of Canaan would be fulfilled in visible form. Furthermore, the oneness of old and new believers would extend to their earthly lives. As the Old Testament faithful chose to suffer

affliction rather than 'enjoy the pleasures of sin', so Christ's chosen
who have come 'unto the city of the living God, the heavenly Jerusalem' must serve him with 'reverence and godly fear' whatever
their sufferings.

The country the Separatists sought was, as Paul writes, heavenly,
not earthly.[10] The New Jerusalem, though in this world, would not
be of it. The Separatists were indifferent to the specific, physical
place they settled. As people of faith, they believed that they had
received the promises, and they considered themselves to be strangers
and pilgrims on earth. The land they wanted to leave behind as they
went to Holland and America was the land of spiritual darkness and
corruption which knew no physical boundaries but could be found in
most of Europe's nations. Their task, John Robinson explained in
A Justification of Separation from the Church of England, was to build
the temple anew:

The apostle writing unto the Galatians ... calls the church of the new
testament, 'Jerusalem which is above, and the mother' of the faithful:
and John in the book of the Revelation ... opposeth unto Babylon
spiritual, the new Jerusalem coming from God down out of heaven: and
the tabernacle of God, where he dwelleth with men, making them his
people, and himself their God. Now as the people of God in old time,
were called out of Babylon civil, the place of their bodily bondage; and
were to come to Jerusalem, and there to build the Lord's temple, or
tabernacle, leaving Babylon to that destruction, which the Lord by his
servants, the prophets, had denounced against it ... so are the people of
God, now to go out of Babylon spiritual to Jerusalem ... and to build
up themselves as lively stones into a spiritual house, or temple for the Lord
to dwell in, leaving Babylon to that destruction and desolation, yea
furthering the same, to which she is devoted by the Lord.[11]

How much more significant the spiritual journey was to the Separatists than their physical circumstances Bradford expresses in the
climactic passage in ch. 9 of *Of Plymouth Plantation* where he contrasts his own standing on the dunes of Cape Cod with Moses
standing on Mt Pisgah. The Pilgrims, Bradford writes, could not
'as it were, goe up to the tope of Pisgah, to vew from this wildernes
a more goodly cuntrie to feed their hopes; for which way soever
they turned their eyes (save upward to the heavens) they could have
little solace or content in respecte of any outward objects. For summer

being done, all things stand upon them with a wetherbeaten face; and the whole countrie, full of woods and thickets, represented a wild and savage heiw'.[12] The heavenly kingdom above that Bradford so dramatically contrasts with the savage wilderness of New England in November is the city of eternal light, the New Jerusalem described in ch. 21 of the Book of Revelation. The Pilgrims believed that in the not-too-distant future, John's vision would become reality; a glorious society would be gathered where God would dwell so fully in all that 'no temple' would be 'therein, for the Lord God Almighty and the Lamb are the temple of it', and 'the city' would have 'no need of the sun, neither of the moon, to shine in it: for the glory of God did lighten it, and the Lamb *is* the light thereof'. Yet until the day of the city's descent to earth, the chosen cannot do without temples. They must, as Paul wrote to the people of Corinth, come out of uncleanness, for they are the temple of the living God; 'a holy priesthood', Peter calls them, 'lively stones', joining together to build a spiritual house in love and affection.[13] Though each soul experiences salvation in its own unique and separate way, the central experience is the same for all, and in the new light, the wall between private and public is broken down.

The blueprints for the Separatists' spiritual house can be seen in two of John Robinson's letters, the first written at the 'parting' in 1620, the second sent in 1621 to 'the Church of God, at Plymouth, in New England'. Writing as their shepherd, Robinson, 'in love and dutie', laid down the rules the Church must follow if it hoped to be a living temple. First, all brothers and sisters in Christ must daily 'renew . . . repentance with God', for sins both known and unknown. In their precarious situation with a dangerous voyage before them, repentance for sins unknown became especially important. If, like the Ninevites, they repented sincerely, they might, though under judgment, avert God's wrath; if they did not, they would suffer the fate of Jonah. If he earnestly repented, a man would be pardoned; and 'great', Robinson promised each Pilgrim, 'shall be his securitie and peace in all dangers, sweete his comforts in all distresses, with hapie deliverance from all evill, whether in life or in death'. When, after repentance, 'heavenly peace' rules in each man's heart, the next task is to make the peace live among all hearts. Robinson warned them to take special care 'that with your commone imployments you joyne commone affections truly bente upon the generall good, avoyding as a deadly plague of your both commone and spetiall comfort all retirednes of minde for proper advantage, and all singularly affected ... maner of way'. It was crucial that 'every man represe in him selfe and the whol body in each person, as so many rebels against the commone good, all private respects of mens selves'. 'Be ... I besheech you, brethern', Robinson pleaded, 'careful that the house of God which you are, and are to be, be not shaken with unnecessarie novelties or other oppositions at the first setling thereof'.[14] In the second letter, written almost a year after the first, Robinson insistently echoes his earlier call for 'heavenly peace'. 'God forbid', he writes, 'I should need to exhort you to peace, which is the bond of perfection, and by which all good is tied together, and without which it is scattered. Have peace with God first, by faith in his promises, good conscience kept in all things, and oft renewed by repentance: and so one with another, ... for Christ's sake'.[15] Of all the corruptions threatening their peace, none turned out to be more destructive of their spiritual house in Plymouth than the 'deadly plague' of private affection. Late in life, as Bradford reviewed the past, it was the rebellion against the common good that he judged the cause of Plymouth's failure to fulfill its early promise. In his sly warfare against God, Satan had entered Plymouth disguised as 'necessitie' and 'insensibly by degrees'[16] destroyed the people's love for each other. It was by pleading 'necessitie' that some people had managed to break away from Marshfield in 1632; an act of encouragement to others, Bradford thought, who wanted to move 'under one pretense or other, thinking their owne conceived necessitie, and the example of others, a warrante sufficiente for them'. The result, he feared, would be New England's 'ruine'.[17]

That, even in the first years, Robinson's fear of private affection was well founded is indicated by Robert Cushman's *A Sermon Preached at Plimmoth in New-England, December 9, 1621 ... Wherein Is Shewed the danger of self loue, and the sweetnesse of true friendship*.[18] The Plymouth community already is plagued by self-love; the people are succumbing to temptation. Taking his text from I Cor. 10: 24, 'Let no man seek his own, but every man, another's wealth', Cushman called his audience 'belly-gods' who sought riches, ease, 'new doctrines and deuices', outward honor, and their own wills. Instead of seeking 'their owne bellies', Cushman told them to concede their need of each other, for 'it is here yet but the first dayes, and (as it were), the dawning of this new world'. It was time 'to looke to present necessities ... to open the doores, the chests, and vessels, and say, brother, neighbour, friend, what want yee?"[19] If each gave to all, Cushman promised them that they would be translated from 'this wandering wildernesse vnto that ioyfull and heauenly *Canaan*'.[20]

The harder the Separatists strove to bring their new world into being, and the more they suffered for its sake, the intenser grew their speculation about the time when they might expect the promises to be fulfilled in the incorruptible inheritance. Increasingly they became convinced that the inheritance would not be passed to them in England or on the Continent. Three years after the beginning of the Thirty Years Wars, Cushman wrote of the terrible judgment God was about to let loose on 'his people in the Christian countries of *Europe* (for their coldnesse, carnality, wanton abuse of the Gospel, contention, etc.), either by Turkish slavery, or by Popish tyrannie',[21] and Robinson not only expected Babylon in Europe to be destroyed but considered it his obligation to further its destruction. Of course, this profound sense of impending disaster was general among English Puritans. For example, in 1629, John Winthrop stated in his *Reasons to be considered for iustifieinge the undertakers of the intended Plantation in New England, & for incouraginge such whose hartes God shall move to ioyne wth them in it*[22] that the 'churches of Europe are brought to desolation, & our sinnes, for which the Lord beginnes allreaddy to frowne upon us & to cutte us short, doe threatne evill times to be comminge upon us'. In this 'generall calamity', God had provided New England as a place of 'refuge', where the church could be served by spreading the gospel among the Indians, by raising a 'Bulworke' against the Jesuits who were busy building Antichrist's kingdom, and by helping 'on the comminge of the fullnesse of the Gentiles'.

As the day of darkness descended on Europe, the light of the heavenly kingdom began to dawn in the American wilderness. As more and more true Christians came to New England, 'a light', Cushman wrote, would 'rise up in the dark'. He could not 'thinke but that there is some judgement not farre off, and that God will shortly, euen of stones, rayse up children vnto *Abraham*'.[23] Likewise, Robinson, in his farewell sermon to the Pilgrims, told them of a great glory awaiting them on the other side of the ocean. Surveying the state of the Protestant churches in Europe, Robinson could not but 'bewail' their 'condition'. He acknowledged that Luther and Calvin had been 'precious shining lights in their times', but clearly

God had still much grace to reveal. Robinson, Edward Winslow wrote in *Hypocrisie Unmasked*, told the church 'he was very confident the Lord had more truth and light yet to break forth out of his holy word', for it was 'not possible the Christian world should come so lately out of such Antichristian darkness, and that full perfection of knowledge should break forth at once'.[24] The moment of 'full perfection' would, of course, be the millennium, and no Separatist preacher dared predict the precise year of Christ's coming; but for many years, Robinson had been stating his belief in a glorious harvest of souls to take place about the year 1700. Thus, in *A Justification*, he writes, ten years before the Pilgrims left Holland: 'And the many that are already gathered by the mercy of God into the kingdom of his Son Jesus, and the nearness of many more through the whole land, for the regions are white unto the harvest, do promise within less than a hundred years, if our sins and theirs make not us and them unworthy of this mercy, a very plenteous harvest'. For this great harvest – Robinson envisaged it as another reformation – the Separatists were to act as forerunners, as sowers seeding the fields with future Luthers and Calvins in the same way 'John Huss and Jerome of Prague finished their testimony in Bohemia and at Constance, a hundred years before Luther; and Wickliffe in England well nigh as long before them, and yet neither the one nor the other with the like success unto Luther'. 'It must be ... considered', Robinson wrote, 'that religion is not always sown and reaped in one age: "one soweth and another reapeth!"'[25]

Throughout his life, Bradford shared Robinson's belief in the Separatists as sowers of the imminent reformation. Thus in ch. 4 of *Of Plymouth Plantation* he gives as one of the four major reasons for the Pilgrims' decision to move to New England their 'great hope ... for the propagating, and advancing the gospell of the Kingdom of Christ in the remote parts of the world; yea though they should be but even as stepping-stones, unto others for the performing of so great a work'.[26] It was not simply a desire to save the souls of the Indians that made the advancing of the gospel crucial for the Pilgrims; equally important, perhaps more so, was their conviction that the Indians must be converted if the marriage of Jew and Gentile that heralded the coming of Christ's Kingdom were to be consummated.[27] Later, in the annal for 1629, Bradford expresses his hope that the arrival of more members from Leyden signifies 'the beginning of a larger harvest unto the Lord, in the increase of his churches and people in these parts, to the admiration of many, and

allmost wonder of the world'.[28] As the seventeenth century progressed, Bradford began to wonder if the fields of the Lord had not
ripened much earlier than Robinson had foretold. In 1648, he had
'Ancient Men' of the *First Dialogue* tell 'Young Men', that it seemed
'as if' Robinson 'had prophesied of these times'[29] — of 1648 rather
than of 1700. Four years later, when he composed the *Third
Dialogue*, he was less certain that these were the promised times,
but he did not relinquish his faith in being part of a great cycle of
redemption. 'In the beginning of the Protestant reformation,
"Ancient-Men" ask "Young-Men", how could they so clearly see in
the dawning, as we may now in the meridian, if we will but open our
eyes?'[30]

No passage more convincingly demonstrates the fierceness of
Bradford's millennial expectations than the long 'A late observation,
as it were by the way, worthy to be noted', that Bradford adds to
Of Plymouth Plantation in 1646. 'A late observation' opens with
Bradford's acknowledgment that the English Puritans' victory over
spiritual Babylon has caught him by surprise. 'Full little did I thinke',
he writes, 'that the downfall of the Bishops, with their courts, can-
nons, and ceremonies, &c. had been so neare when I first began these
scribled writings (which was aboute the year 1630, and so peeced up
at times of leasure afterward) or that I should have lived, to have
seene, or heard of the same; but it is the lords doing, and ought to
be marvelous in our eyes!' As Bradford celebrates the destruction of
the Anglican bishops, 'Babell', he strings together texts from the
Old and New Testaments proclaiming the triumph of God's saints
over the satanic forces of Babylon. Like the Jews conquering the
promised land from the giant Anakims, and like David, newly
crowned king of Israel, routing the Jebusites from Jerusalem, the
Puritans have slain the forces of evil and taken possession of their
heavenly Jerusalem. Addressing the saints at Plymouth, Bradford
asks them:

Doe you not now see the fruits of your labours, O all yee servants of the
lord? that have suffered for his truth, and have been faithfull witnesses
of the same, and yee little handfull amongst the rest, the least amongst the
thousands of Israll? You have not only had a seede time, but many of
you have seene the joyefull Harvest. Should you not then rejoyse? yea,
and again rejoyce, and say Hallelu-iah, salvation, and glorie, and honour,
and power, be to the lord our God; for true, and righteous are his Judge-
ments. Rev. 19: 1, 2.

As he continues, Bradford's fervor rises to a pitch, and he reaches for the text from Revelation where John sees the heavens open and Christ on a white horse leading the heavenly hosts to the glorious victory that ushers in the reign of peace for 1000 years. 'Who hath done it?' Bradford asks rhetorically, 'who, even he that siteth on the white horse, who is caled faithfull, and true, and judgeth, and fighteth righteously . . . Whose garments are dipte in blood, and his name was caled the word of God . . . For he shall rule them with a rode of Iron; for it is he that treadeth the winepress of the feircenes, and wrath of god almighty! And he hath upon his garmente, and upon his thigh, a name writen, The King of Kings, and Lord of Lords . . . HAL-LELU-IAH. Anno Dom: 1646'.[31] The long-awaited moment had finally arrived. For decades, the Separatists had identified the Anglican episcopacy with the antitypical Babylon that must be destroyed if the heavenly city were to be built. The more the bishops persecuted them by imprisonment, exile, and death, the deeper the Separatists' conviction grew, and when the longed-for downfall finally did happen, Bradford could see its momentous significance only by relating it to John's vision of Christ's descent.

Bradford's joy at the bishops' downfall is deep and genuine; it is also shrill, almost desperate. God has poured his blessing on England; New England is not the chosen place. What role than for the church at Plymouth, that 'little handfull amongst the rest', who had been among the sowers and now were witnessing the 'joyefull Harvest' in God's English fields? Twenty-five years earlier they had crossed into the wilderness, confident that, as Robinson had promised them, 'the Lord had more truth and light to break out of his holy word'. But now, in 1646, Bradford had to admit that the light had broken out first in the very land they had left behind. Still, Bradford by no means thought all was lost for Plymouth. The New England churches remained within the universal Israel, the true church. What he and his people must do was to accept God's judgment, repent, and reform.

Bradford apparently responded to the downfall of the bishops' Babel by writing most, if not all of Book Two of *Of Plymouth Plantation*. Just as, in 1630, the planting of true churches elsewhere in America had been one reason for his writing Book One, so in 1644–5, events in England prompted him to make a formal history of the notes he had been keeping for fifteen years. In these two periods, one beginning in 1630, the other probably in 1644–5, Bradford's feelings of joy at the spreading light and his fear of God's judgment on Plymouth grew so acute that he felt compelled to picture the glorious past, so that the younger generation might see and emulate their ancestors. About the date of composition for Book One there is no question. Bradford himself said that he began it in 1630. Probably it did not take long to write; it fills only 52 of 270 pages in the manuscript, and, in contrast to Book Two with its 26 separate annals, Book One stands a sustained and continuous narrative divided into 11 chapters. With regard to the composition of Book Two, we can say with great certainty that Bradford wrote all the post-1631 annals, about one-third of the history, after 1639. In the 1631 annal, Bradford includes a passage about Isaac Allerton taking an 'oath . . . concerning this ship, the *Whit-Angell,* before the Governor and Deputie, the *7 of September,* 1639'.[32] However, more crucial for a precise dating of the writing of *Of Plymouth Plantation* are two passages, one in the annal for 1620, the other in the annal for 1621. In the 1620 annal, Bradford writes that the peace treaty with Massasoit has lasted for twenty-four years, thus indicating that the 1620 annal was composed in 1644. The other passage is Bradford's description of the first marriage in Plymouth, which, 'according to the laudable custome of the Low-cuntries, in which they had lived, was thought most requisite to be performed by the magistrate, as being a civill thing . . . and most consonate to the scriptures, Ruth .4. and no wher found in the gospell to be layed on the ministers as a part of their office . . . And this practiss hath continued amongst, not only them, but hath been followed by all the famous churches of Christ in these parts to this time, Anno: 1646'.[33] There is nothing in the manuscript that indicates the date 'Anno: 1646' was not written at the same time as the rest of the passage. On the contrary, the color of the ink, the uniform handwriting, even the evident flaw in the pen, all indicate strongly that the larger part of the 1621 annal and all the subsequent history were written twenty-five years after the events had taken place. In other words, very likely, all of *Of Plymouth Plantation* is a work of retrospection. The writing of Book Two took about four years. The last annal, that of 1646, was finished in 1650; Bradford comments on Edward Winslow's trip to England, that he 'was detained longer than was expected . . . and so he hath now been absente this ·4· years'.[34]

Identifying the likely dates for the composition of *Of Plymouth*

Plantation makes it possible for us to draw two general conclusions about Bradford's decision to turn historian. First, that Bradford wrote his History in the two relatively short periods points to his unspoken assumption that history written is less vital than history lived. Second, in the exultant, anxious moments when Christ's kingdom seemed to be advancing elsewhere in the world his need to write his notes into formal history became pressing. His note-taking indicates that from the beginning he may not have been entirely satisfied with the way Plymouth was acting its role in the history of redemption, but his dissatisfaction did not become sufficiently strong to urge him to write formally until 1630 and 1644. For the first decade and for the years between 1630 and 1645, Bradford judged the life of the Plymouth church to be, in some measure at least, the living fulfillment of the ancient promises. Like many of his contemporaries, Bradford believed history would be fulfilled, not in another book, another written word, but in a new state of being. History, he thought, was not something that just happened *to* him and his fellow Separatists; it lived *in* and *through* them. Of course, they did not regard themselves as the ultimate anti-types; but they did firmly believe that their lives were divine synecdoches, minute but vital parts in the great arch of grace spanning from Abraham to the New Jerusalem. As long as they could be reasonably confident that they stood under God's special providence, that they were growing in brotherly affection and evolving toward the future glory, what need to record past events? As long as Christ the Word lived within as love and affection, what more would history offer? Surely mere words could not equal a living body as an expression of power. To be history transcended writing history.

The Pilgrims believed God had chosen them to be his synecdoches in history because their religious experience had convinced them they could be no other. In their present life, they had, they felt, tasted and seen the life of the future. Describing the setting up of the first Separatist churches, Bradford writes that God had touched the people's 'harts . . . with heavenly zeale for his trueth',[35] by which he meant that they had experienced a new life within them; out of death, of void and nothingness, another man had emerged. Not Adam, but Christ now lived within them. This divine touch altered not only the way they felt about the world but the way they acted in the world. To be one with the Spirit made the body into a temple of God. The flesh became the means for testifying or making manifest the new man within. And what was true of the individual was true also of the community; in its outward life, its body, a society of faithful declared that God dwelled in its midst. Further, in both individual and community, the religious experience created an assurance of redemption as a never-ending process. The new birth within had been so momentous that what had sprung to life must, it seemed, continue to grow until its ultimate union with the divine, a union consummated in silence, in, as Bradford wrote, quoting Zechariah, the stillness of flesh before the Lord.[36]

In 1630 and 1644 when the living stones of Plymouth seemed to be hardening into dead walls, when private interests were threatening the common good, and God was signifying his displeasure by choosing other men and places to receive his blessings, the time had come to hold up a mirror of past glory wherein the people might see their ancestors' former holiness. In his mirror, Bradford hoped, the ancient virtues would be so literally and brightly reflected that they would act as an irresistible model for imitation. Consequently, Bradford fashioned *Of Plymouth Plantation* to make the strongest possible impression on the younger generation. Undoubtedly, he wanted to demonstrate to the whole world what great deeds Christ had performed in New England but, more immediately, he wanted to assist the children at home as they carried on their warfare against Satan. Throughout *Of Plymouth Plantation*, certain episodes are related and others ignored; some letters are quoted fully and some not at all. Bradford wrote biographies of his personal heroes while neglecting other important figures. Clearly he weighed which episode, letter, or biography would make the greatest impact on his spiritual heirs. As historian, Bradford's aim is not to portray the past with the fullest possible objectivity but to resurrect a bygone holiness; a holiness that, he knows and never loses sight of, must be resurrected by and in his audience.[37]

Sometimes Bradford's exhortation is explicit, at other times implicit, but it is always present. For example, in the passage from ch. 9 in Book One, 'But hear I cannot but stay and make a pause . . .', Bradford emphasizes the first planters' sole reliance on 'the spirite of God and his grace' to make their children

rightly say: our faithers were English men which came over this great ocean, and were ready to perish in this willdernes, but they cried unto the Lord, and he heard their voyce, and looked on their adversitie, etc. Let them therefore praise the Lord, because he is good, and his mercies endure for ever . . . Let them confess before the Lord his loving kindnes, and his wonderfull works before the sons of men.[38]

If, in the most desperate circumstances, your fathers had such a faith in the Lord, what, Bradford seems to be asking the young, '"may and ought" you not believe who have received so many more outward evidences of his grace?' 'What great work of the spirit is not in store for you if you return to trusting in the Lord as they did?'

Again, in ch. 4, Bradford's purpose is more complex than simply to give the reasons for 'removall'. Indirectly, he is inviting the young in New England to measure their actions against their fathers' unselfish devotion to the common good. Were they, he wondered, those 'others' who would advance the great work of redemption in the wilderness? At a time when they were moving away from Plymouth,[39] Bradford wanted them to measure their 'necessity' against the hardships the older generation had endured to preserve the sacred bond of their fellowship. Was it worth tearing it asunder for a little more land? Did they want to leave Plymouth, as their elders had left Holland, 'not out of any new fanglednes, or other shuch like giddie humor, by which men are oftentimes transported to their great hurt, and danger. But for sundrie weightie and solid reasons'?[40] From his description of their fathers' heated debate about moving, did the young not see how deeply people could disagree without destroying the covenant? Had they considered the cost, the 'great hurt'?

Bradford's exhortations are stated more directly in the brief comments accompanying many of the letters he inserted throughout *Of Plymouth Plantation*. For example, in ch. 6, having quoted letters and documents extensively, Bradford concludes by explaining that he has 'bene the larger in these things, and so shal crave leave in some like passages following, (thoug in other things I shall labour to be more contracte,) that their children may see with what difficulties their fathers wrastled in going throug these things in their first beginnings, and how God brought them along notwithstanding all their weaknesses and infirmities. As allso that some use may be made hereof in after times by others in shuch like waightie imployments'.[41] Bradford quoted so many letters because, he said, he wanted to show no prejudice. He would relate some events more fully than others, but he desired rather 'to manefest things' in other people's own 'words and apprehentions, then in my owne, as much as may be, without tediousness'.[42] However, Bradford's impartiality is not the same as disinterest. He would let people speak their own pieces; and in their deceiving or loving words, they would show more clearly than Bradford could on whose side they had fought in the great war between God and Satan. Tedious it might be to quote letters full of details about obscure financial matters, but the minutest of details was supremely important for the faith or the betrayal it manifested. As Bradford would later turn to the literal language of creation to see for himself the ancient holiness, so he inserted the literal facts of Plymouth's past in order that the young might see the naked truth with their own eyes. Letters were the means whereby the truth could be literally drawn out of the past to live again in the present; letters, Bradford agreed, 'were the better parte of histories'.[43]

If letters were the most important way Bradford chose to bring the past into the present in *Of Plymouth Plantation*, the second most important way to realize the original state was biography. In letters, a man's nature could speak for itself, but in biography, the historian could inject his own views and create a memorial, a paean and an exhortation. In biography, the virtues of the dead had not died but spoke to their children. Bradford wrote two major biographies in *Of Plymouth Plantation*, one of Robinson in ch. 3 of Book One and one of Brewster in the 1643 annal. In his picture of Robinson, Bradford emphasized the Leyden pastor's love of his flock and his devotion to the common good. He was, Bradford writes, in 'every way . . . a commone father unto them', and when he died, it was as hard for the Pilgrims to find another leader as it had been for 'ye Taborits to find another Ziska'.[44] The biography of Brewster is very different. Where in 1630 Bradford is content to stress Robinson's devotion to the fellowship, his attitude fifteen years later is much more violent and apocalyptic. He portrays Brewster as a man of great faith and courage who patiently suffered poverty, persecution, exile, and other tribulations. As elder of the Church, Brewster was careful 'to preserve good order . . . and puritie . . ., and to suppress any error or contention that might begine to rise up amongst them'.[45] His most 'singuler good gift' was in prayer, in 'ripping up the hart and conscience before God'.[46] As evidence of God's special blessing and 'marvelous providence' on Brewster, Bradford singles out his long life. Exposed more than ordinary men to dangers that could easily have killed him, Brewster lived to be almost eighty—a clear testimony that he and his fellow believers were 'upheld' by God in the same

manner the Old Testament patriarchs Daniel and Jacob were preserved by special providence. 'Daniell', Bradford writes, 'could be
better liking with pulse then others were with the kings dainties', and
'Jacob though he wente from one nation to another people, and
passed thorow famine, fears, and many afflictions, yet he lived till old
age, and dyed sweetly and rested in the Lord, as infinite others of
Gods servants have done, and still shall doe'.[47]

These parallels between the old and modern heroes are interesting
examples of Bradford's use of the Old Testament, but even more
remarkable is the framework of threat and damnation within which
the whole biography is set. After a brief description of Brewster's
dying moments, Bradford asks if he 'was the worse for any former
sufferings? What doe I say, worse? Nay, sure he was the better, and
they now added to his honour.'[48] And Bradford, then, in the manner
of 'A late observation' quotes several Bible texts that, on the one
hand, promise the just that their sufferings will be rewarded in the
imminent kingdom, and, on the other, warn the wicked that they
'shall rott (with their marble monuments)'.[49] In other words, in the
beginning of the biography, Bradford implicitly asks the reader where
he wants to be: in the field of the saints ripening for the harvest, or
rotting with the wicked? This implicit question is renewed in the end
when he quotes two texts from Job and Psalms where the destruction
of 'bloody and deceitfull men', and the cutting off 'ye branch of ye
wicked'[50] are threatened. This attitude, at once promising the greatest of delights and threatening the ultimate rejection, can be found
throughout *Of Plymouth Plantation*; but it emerges sharply in the later
annals, indicating Bradford's increasing uneasiness with the spiritual
state of Plymouth. It also demonstrates the tenacity with which he
clung to his belief in the promises. Though events might have gone
counter to his expectations for the future, he could not possibly give
up his faith in the New Jerusalem. Like Ainsworth, having had a
profound experience of fulfillment within himself, Bradford could not
conceive of the promises as false or irrelevant. On the contrary, the
further Plymouth seemed to fall from grace, the more Bradford felt
the need to assert the validity of the promises. And the more adamant
his insistence, the more violent his threat of destruction, the fiercer his
call for repentance and sacrifice.

How profoundly Bradford and the Pilgrims conceived their lives
in terms of this double attitude is seen in Robinson's *New Essays*;
or, Observations Divine and Moral, especially ch. 3, 'Of God's

Promises', ch. 28, 'Of Afflictions', and ch. 19, 'Of Examples'. Following conventional covenant theology, Robinson defines 'the promises of God' as 'a kind of middle thing between [God's] purpose, and performance of good unto them, whom he loveth'. Because of his love, God has revealed the promises as signs of his willingness to be 'a debtor' to man, 'though not by receiving from us, yet by promising unto us; promise being as we say, due debt'. In order that God's love may 'satisfy itself in a gracious purpose of good towards us in his heart, and actual performance of it accordingly, in due time', God makes the promise

known unto us beforehand, both for our present comfort in the knowledge thereof, and for the ground of our hope and expectation of the good things promised, and accordingly to be received at his hands, in their time: he having by his promise bound over unto us both his love, and truth, and other attributes for performance. And herein, the Lord provides very graciously for his poor servants, who are oft times brought into that distressed state both outward and inward, as they have very little else, save the promises of God, wherewith to comfort themselves. Which yet are sufficient, if we improve them, as we ought.[51]

Most significantly, Robinson links afflictions with the promises and interprets sufferings as prophetic of the New Jerusalem. A man, Robinson thinks, first experiences the suffering as punishment for sin, but, as he begins to mourn and repent, he perceives that God has both dealt justly with him in punishing his sin and led him to a new realization of mercy. 'It is most necessary', Robinson writes, 'for all his people ever to hold this general conclusion; that in all their afflictions the justice and mercy of God meet together; and that he begins in justice, and will end in mercy'.[52] The believer comes to see that God does not sanctify crosses to men, but men to crosses 'in giving us grace to make a right use of them', and right use is 'to thank God, that makes afflictions bittersweet, by turning deserved curses into fatherly corrections to us'.[53] As the repentant heart's experience of affliction changes from justice to mercy, the sufferings become harbingers of the New Jerusalem, prophecies peculiarly fitted to typify the second coming. Robinson writes in a crucially important passage:

God hath, in a peculiar manner, entailed afflictions to the sincere profession of the gospel, above that of the law before Christ. The law was given by Moses, whose ministry began with killing the Egyptian, that oppressed the Israelite; and was prosecuted with leading the people out of Egypt, through the sea, and wilderness, with great might, and a strong hand; and lastly was finished with bloody victory over Sihon, and Og the kings of Canaan. But Christ's dispensation was all of another kind: his birth mean; his life sorrowful; and his death shameful. And albeit the love of God towards his people be always the same in itself, yet is the manifestation thereof very diverse. Before Christ's coming in the flesh, in whom the grace of God appeared, God showed his love more fully in earthly blessings, and peace; and more sparingly in spiritual, and heavenly: but now, on the other side, he dealeth forth temporal blessings more sparingly; and spiritual with a fuller hand. It is not improbably gathered that, after the destruction of the dragon, and beast, and recalling of the Jews after their long divorce from the Lord, and the blessings of both kinds shall meet together, and the Church enjoy, for a time, a very graceful state upon the earth both in regard of spiritual, and bodily good things.[54]

The afflictions, the 'crosses of Christ' that are prophetic of the 'very graceful state' are threefold. The first cross is persecution for Christ's sake; and the Pilgrims knew persecution directly and fully. The second cross is the evil men inflict when the faithful speak out 'Christ's truth'. The last cross is the sufferings that occur 'in the course of godliness, though human, and as they do all other men; as bodily sickness, death of friends, crosses, losses by sea, and land, and the like'.[55] When these afflictions are suffered for Christ's sake – but only then – they prefigure his kingdom. In such times, the repentant believer can rest assured that God will provide all the strength necessary to meet and overcome the trial. And if he makes the cross heavier, he will increase the strength and bring about 'full deliverance in due time. "He will redeem Israel from all his trouble."'[56]

In light of Robinson's writings on justice and mercy mixed in the afflictions, *Of Plymouth Plantation* becomes a deeply and deliberately prophetic book. The union of justice and mercy is present in little providences (the salvation of a man fallen overboard), and in great events (the journey of the entire company toward the heavenly Canaan); whether minor or major, the Pilgrims' sufferings foreshadow their 'deliverance in due time'. Bradford did not include so many remarkable and special providences simply to record the many times he had witnessed the hand of God intervening on behalf of the saints or to eulogize the steadfastness of the first planters; above all, he wanted to portray the affliction so that the promise of the New Jerusalem would be set clearly before the next generation. For example, in ch. 2, when the Pilgrims leave England to go to Holland, Bradford, having struck the motif of the search for another country, shapes the voyage in imitation of Christ's crucifixion and resurrection. Like Christ, the Pilgrims were 'often times betrayed',[57] persecuted, and imprisoned: clearly an example of affliction suffered for Christ's sake. Because of persecution, the men became separated from their wives and children and almost lost their lives in a terrible storm. However, at the point when they had given up all hope of reaching land and had resigned themselves to death, 'the ship rose againe', Bradford writes,

If modestie would suffer me, I might declare with what fervente prayres they cried unto the lord in this great distres, (espetialy some of them) even without any great distraction when the water rane into their mouthes and ears: and the mariners cried out we sinke, we sinke; they cried (if not with mirakelous, yet with a great hight or degree of devine faith) yet Lord thou canst save; yet Lord thou canst save... Upon which the ship did not only recover, but shortly after the violence of the storme begane to abate; and the lord filed their afflicted minds with shuch comforts as every one cannot understand. And in the end brought them to their desired Haven, wher the people came flockeing admiring their deliverance, the storme having ben so longe and sore, in which much hurt had been don.[58]

For Bradford, the deliverance from the terrors of the storm is a remarkable instance of God's special providence whereby he saves men and gives them a life of faith more vivid than they had ever known before. But more than that, the deliverance is a prophecy of the time when the church, the ship of God's chosen, voyaging toward the promised land, has weathered the storms of history and reached its final 'haven'. It promises that those who are persecuted, imprisoned, separated, and exiled, all shall be delivered and united as the Pilgrims were after 'these first conflicts, and sharp beginings', when 'all gat over at length, some at one time, and some at an other, and some in one place, and some in an other, And mete togeather againe according to their desires, with no small rejoycing'.[59] On the other shore, the people who have gone before stand waiting.

In this passage, as throughout Book One, Bradford's tone is quietly, even joyously triumphant. Writing ten years after the crossing, he knew that the outcome of all his and the other Pilgrims' sufferings had been a most magnificent and merciful deliverance. From the setting up of the first Separatist Churches in England to the raising of the first house 'for common use' in Plymouth in the very season that Israel had begun the building of the temple in Jerusalem thousands of years before, the Pilgrims' lives had been an example of the way God brought his chosen peoples out of death into new life. This certitude that all of their early history was analogous to Christ's passion is reflected in the structure of Book One. The eleven chapters – and they are chapters, not annals – tell of remarkable providences that re-enact Christ's death and resurrection, but each providential event is not an isolated episode; it is one further stage in the larger and continuous movement toward the building of the new temple. Book Two, on the other hand, is very different. Where each chapter in Book One deals with the events of more than one year, the twenty-five annals in Book Two describe what happened in each of the years between 1620 and 1646.[60] The annals are filled with extraordinary scenes from the history of Plymouth's salvation; but they do not stand as parts of a great and coherent whole, as actions in an evolving drama. The years are shining but isolated moments, beads of revelation that remain unstrung. In Book One, Bradford's primary concern is with action; in Book Two his preoccupation is with time. The difference between the two books is the distance between the voice of 1630 calmly and confidently exhorting the reader to pause and consider the people in the wilderness, and the voice of 1646 leaping to its recitation of the verses from the Book of Revelation.

However, the fact that the tone of Book One is joyous and triumphant does not mean that Bradford felt only joy and triumph about Plymouth when he began to write. The confidence of his first narrative draws its strength from being a relation of past actions; the present is not directly dealt with. Indeed, much that was happening in New England in 1630 seemed to Bradford to necessitate repentance. Most important, the people were forsaking the common good. And what did God mean to signify to Plymouth by planting so many new churches in the Bay? And what did he mean to signify by the first murder, when John Billington killed John Newcomen? Bradford may have been pleased to see so many pure and primitive churches being planted in the wilderness. So, at least, he appears to be when, in the 1630 annal, he lauds the Plymouth church for having been that 'one small candle' whose 'light here kindled hath shone to many, yea in some sort to our whole nation; let the glorious name of Jehova have all the praise'.[61] Proud he may have been, but also, we sense, sad and wistful. Writing in retrospect fifteen years later, Bradford seems regretful and apprehensive about the consequences that the settling of Boston had had and would have on Plymouth.

Still, the situation in 1630 was a far cry from that of 1644. In 1644, the longed-for reformation was taking place 3000 miles away, in the very place the Pilgrims so deliberately and at such great cost had left behind. As Bradford confronted these events and their meaning, it seemed that God had told the people in New England that they must look inward and acknowledge their spiritual failures. And repent quickly, for though they had 'full little' expected the joyful harvest to begin so soon, it was now very clear that God was reaping all around them. The enormous tension Bradford must have felt in the late 1640s and 1650s shows itself in the way he uses the afflictions in the annals. As in Book One, he continues to see events as analogous to Christ's death and resurrection. Whether it be a terrible drought that is broken by 'sweete and gentle showers', resulting in a 'fruitfull and liberall harvest',[62] or famines eased by providential arrivals of relief ships or by rich catches from the sea, Bradford aims to demonstrate the myriad ways God lets life sprout out of death.

To looke humanly on the state of things as they presented them selves at this time [he writes in the 1626 annal], it is a marvell it did not wholy discourage them, and sinck them. But they gathered up their spirits, and the Lord so helped them, whose worke they had in hand, as now when they were at lowest they begane to rise againe, and being striped (in a maner) of all humane helps and hopes, he brought things aboute other wise, in his devine providence, as they were not only upheld and sustained, but their proceedings both honoured and imitated by others; as by the sequel will more appeare, if the Lord spare me life and time to declare the same.[63]

Clearly the basic pattern remains the same throughout *Of Plymouth Plantation*; what is greatly diminished is the delighted assurance that in bringing them into the wilderness, God is bringing them home to himself. The presence of mercy, of 'good in the later end', is strenuously asserted; but the deliverance does not seem vividly or joyously experienced. Instead, the dominant tone becomes a mixed one of damnation and reward. The union of justice and mercy within the same experience no longer holds, and Bradford confronts Plymouth with an increasingly absolute and cataclysmic choice.

The more events did not conform to his expectations, to his knowledge of the end God has in mind in history, the deeper grew Bradford's sense of sinfulness, both personal and communal. The less liberty, order, and beauty that emerged from his sufferings, the more punished he felt, the greater failure he judged himself to be. In his pain, he responded with an angry but tightly controlled demonstration of the betrayal perpetuated on Plymouth by all those men, especially the merchant-adventurers and agents, who had put their own interests above the common good. It was not God's promises that had failed, but men who had not carried his promises along toward their fulfillment. Thus, commenting on Thomas Weston, who deserted the Pilgrims though he had promised to stand by them forever, Bradford paraphrases Psalm 146: '*Put not your trust in princes* (much less in merchants) *not in the sone of man, for there is no help in them*'.[64] Not only does Bradford thus bring Weston under God's judgment, but in a moment of outrage, he drops his mask of objectivity and passes his own sentence on the betrayer. 'See', he cries indignantly 'how his promise is fulfild'.[65]

In most of the annals, Bradford, writing retrospectively, seems intent on showing what might have been if a deeper devotion of all to all had prevailed. In the 1628 annal, for example, he describes what looks like a promising turn of events. Isaac Allerton, Brewster's son-in-law and agent for the Plantation, had paid off a large part of the debt owed to the English merchants and had begun to make arrangements for the people from Leyden to come across. Having drawn this picture of promise, Bradford, in the next three annals, records how the promise failed through Allerton's rashness, deceit, and greed, and how, by 1631, Plymouth, instead of being free, was £5000 in debt. So it was with Ashley, who put private over public interests — Ashley, who walked naked among the Indians, slept with their women, learned their language, and sold them weapons. Allerton got his just reward; he was ostracized, moved to Connecticut, and died bankrupt. Ashley met his deserved end by falling overboard on a return trip from Russia, where he had been trading for beaver.[66] In these cases, Bradford's way of anticipating the future day of righteousness when God will call men to stand before him is to put down every penny and every beaverpelt that people have used to further their own ends rather than those of God's plantation at Plymouth. He will gather all the naked facts and make the judgment certain.

In his use of afflictions, Bradford, we have seen, concentrates on the relationship between present suffering and future freedom, between crucifixion and resurrection. However, he believes that Christ's passion is more than the key to the future; it is also the experience through which to view the past. Of course, the Separatists accepted the traditional typological view of the Old Testament as prophetic of Christ and his church. Thus Robinson writes that 'the whole priesthood of Aaron, under which the law was established . . . was a type of Christ's priesthood, though the high priests in a special manner, and their sacrifices . . . and being a part of the law, which was a shadow or first draught . . . whereof the gospel is the lively portraiture . . . it must needs be ceremonial, and so a type'.[67] Yet, for Robinson and Bradford, it was more important to see the Old Testament figures as people who in their afflictions knew death and rebirth. Abraham's willingness to sacrifice Isaac may well be prophetic of Christ's sacrifice, but the experience precedes the prophecy. As a living reality, Christ, Bradford believed, was present to Abraham. It was this belief, similar to Ainsworth's faith in Christ's presence in both Old and New Canaans, that made it possible for the Separatists to identify closely with the holy patriarchs. Brewster's life re-enacts Jacob's and Daniel's; the Pilgrims' wanderings retrace Israel's exile and search for the promised land. Arrived in New England, Bradford stands as Moses stood on Mt Pisgah, and the downfall of the bishops brings to life once more the defeat of Jebusites and Anakims. The Old Testament events and people are, as Bradford calls them, 'examples'.[68] Yet they are more than exemplary, more than static emblems of virtue, courage, longevity, or faith. Between Israel and Plymouth exists more than a parallel, more than an analogy; for when God's chosen peoples go in search of Canaans, the ancient lives are re-enacted. The past lives again in the present. 'We are', Robinson maintained, 'the sons and daughters of Abraham by faith'.[69] The later re-enactments differ from the first drama only in fullness; the light breaking out of the Word in 1620 shines more clearly than the light breaking in on Abraham or Moses.

This sense of being one more, perhaps the final, re-enactment of the primitive state extends to the Separatists' view of their church and its place in the history of redemption.[70] 'As we do believe by the Word of God', Robinson wrote, 'that the things we teach are not new, but old truths renewed; so are we no less fully persuaded that the church constitution in which we are set, is cast in the Apostolic and primitive mould, and not one day nor hour younger, in the nature or form of it, than the first church of the New Testament'.[71] 'In essence', the church 'is one and the same . . . from the beginning to the end of the world'.[72] In fact, Robinson believed the ideal Separatist church to be not an hour younger than the moment when 'the Lord created a church of angels in heaven, which were all good and holy without mixture, till some by sin fell from their first and original estate'.[73] In his writings about a church forever old, forever new, Robinson establishes a view of the history of redemption in which the moments that become crucial are other than those traditionally regarded as the apexes of the covenant of grace. Robinson accepts — almost offhandedly — the usual division of sacred history into four periods, 'the first whereof is from the beginning of the world, till the giving of the law: the second from the law, till Christ's coming: the third from Christ, till the end of the history of the New Testament: the fourth, and last from that time, hitherto'.[74] But for Robinson, as for Bradford, the turning-points have been the moments of separation when the primitive church once more has emerged out of darkness into light. Such moments are the first gathering of the angels in heaven, the church of Adam and Eve, Israel in her exodus out of Egypt, her leaving Babylon, and the establishment of the Apostolic church. Yet another time was, as Bradford describes it in the opening sentence of *Of Plymouth Plantation*, 'the first breakinge out of the light of the gospell, in our Honourable Nation of England'.[75] For Robinson and Bradford, those circles of light were related to each other, not as static repetitions but as interweaving cycles of ever-growing redemption. Robinson's vision was of a world with churches on every hilltop. 'Men', he wrote, 'are not to come out of Babylon, and there to stand still, and remember the Lord afar off, but must resort to the place where he hath put his name, for which they need not go either to Jerusalem, or to Rome, or beyond the seas; they may find Sion the Lord's mountain prepared for them on the top of every hill'.[76]

Given the intensity and scope of his endeavor, it is most remarkable that Bradford abruptly stopped writing his History in 1650 with the annal for 1646. He adds the dates 1647 and 1648, but no further divine events and remarkable providences are recorded. Since his purpose as late as 1654 remained the same as in 1630, why did he shift to other forms? Why did history seem less and less an adequate means of expression? His later writings consist of three dialogues, one now lost; several poems; letters; the Hebrew exercises; and a list of 'the names of those which came over first, in the year • 1620• and were by the blessing of God the first beginers and (in a sort) the foundation of all the Plantations and Colonies in New England; and their families'.[77] This shift to other modes was begun already in 1648 while Bradford was working intensely on the annals; but though the forms differ, Bradford's purpose and attitudes seem essentially not to have changed since he first began *Of Plymouth Plantation*. He still wants the children to return to an imitation of the fathers. As in the History, he depicts a prior glorious state, its subsequent loss, assertion of God's continued mercy if men will repent, and threat of damnation if they do not. Thus, in the first *Dialogue*, Bradford relates the noble lives of the first Separatists, men like Barrow, Jacob, Brown, Smith, Ainsworth, Robinson, and Clifton who were 'precious in the eyes of the Lord, and also in the eyes of such as knew them, whose virtues we with such as you as are their children do follow and imitate'.[78] Again, in the third *Dialogue*, 'Ancient-Men', having proven the superiority of Congregationalism over the Catholic, Anglican, and Presbyterian Churches, tell 'Young-Men' that 'we have the rather noted these thinges, that you may see the worth of these things and not necligently loose what your fathers haue obtained with so much hardshipe'. The young are exhorted to 'stand fast in the libertie . . . wherwith Christ hath made vs free', to obey rulers, and to help 'propagate' the truth to 'generations to come, till the coming of the Lord'.[79]

His increasing concern for his children's future caused Bradford to change from history to dialogue. He must, he felt, make the generations confront each other more immediately than in the muted way of *Of Plymouth Plantation*. Face to face with 'Ancient-Men', 'Young-Men' could hear the truth more directly and become more deeply convinced of the righteousness of the past. Though he exhorts, threatens, and promises, he nevertheless portrays the relationship between fathers and sons as remarkably harmonious in the Dialogues. The severe discord and disappointments in Plymouth are vague echoes as the ancients describe the saints in the light and the glory of primitive churches. In fact, in his desire for harmony between the generations, Bradford makes it appear as if the young are imploring the old to instruct them about the past rather than the old men feeling the necessity to teach the young. Thus, the third *Dialogue* does not open with the old summoning the young but with 'Young-Men' asking 'Ancient-Men' 'to pardon our bouldnes, in that we have importuned you to giue vs meeting once more in this kind, for our instruction & establishmente in the truth'. They have been, they say, troubled and confused by the claims of so many churches to be the one true church, and 'humbly craue,' their elders' 'best judgment and advice'.[80] Throughout the *Dialogue*, they express repeatedly their gratitude for answers to disturbing questions; and when they leave, they are apparently much relieved to know who are the true church. As they leave, 'Ancient-Men' remain on the stage, serene and confident, ever ready to lend stability to their troubled children's lives.

The shift in the narrator's identity from the 'I' of the History relating the lives of 'they' to the 'Ancient-Men' and 'Young-Men' of the dialogues demonstrates how, in certain profound ways, Bradford's relationship to his material changed in his later years. When he began to write Book Two, he expected to show, as he had in Book One, how magnificently the Holy Spirit had manifested himself in the actions of the Plymouth saints in the preceding fifteen years. Once more he would lay bare the incarnations, the moments of light standing out against the darkness. In his desire to let the truth shine as dispassionately as possible, to have nothing interfere between the reader and the text, Bradford tells *Of Plymouth Plantation* as the story of 'they'; not once does he refer to the people at Plymouth as 'we', although he himself was one of them. As historian, Bradford often explains what he is doing and why, but Bradford the historian never permits Bradford the governor to say 'I'. Always he describes his own acts as those of 'the governor of Plymouth'.

The effect is to create in the reader a strange, almost weird, sense that the Pilgrims were somehow more than ordinary men. Indeed, there was a world of difference between seeing themselves as merely a small group of men and women living somewhere in New England, and, on the other hand, as God's living synecdoches appointed to move through the wilderness toward the heavenly Jerusalem. By referring to his brothers and sisters in Christ as 'they', Bradford removes them from the life of other men; they are children of some unearthly father, citizens inhabiting a new and different world. As 'they', the Pilgrims were made impersonal actors, moving through history as expressions of a will and majesty far greater and other than their own. That Bradford's use of 'they' is deliberate is evident when we compare *Of Plymouth Plantation* with *Mourt's Relation*, the journal published in 1622. Throughout *Mourt's Relation*, Bradford and Winslow write of themselves as 'we', thereby involving the reader in a very different way from the way Bradford does in the History. *Mourt's Relation* tells what happens to men when they face natural hardships: harsh weather, little food, and hostile enemies. In *Of Plymouth Plantation*, the same circumstances are put in a very different context and infused with other meanings.

In the later writings, this belief in the union of actor and act, form and essence, seems to disintegrate. In the dialogues, the dramatist—narrator does not describe 'their' pilgrimage. Instead 'Ancient-Men' speak directly of 'we', 'us', and 'you'. To gain the face-to-face meeting of the generations, Bradford, the writer of the dialogues, breaks into that other world where for decades he had observed the Pilgrims — including his own other and newborn self — moving toward the New Jerusalem, and removes them from their sacred and secret journey. In *Of Plymouth Plantation*, the characters are energetic actors in a dynamic drama; in the dialogues, they stand like immovable statues, only their disembodied voices alive. The actors are outside, no longer one with the act.

In the poems, 'A Word to Plymouth', 'A Word to Boston', 'A word to New England', and 'Some observations of God's merciful dealing with us in this wilderness, and his gracious protection over us these many years. Blessed be his name', the disintegration goes much further. Bradford's mask of 'Ancient-Men' in the dialogues was an attempt to preserve the sense of two worlds; 'Young-Men', he hoped, would see 'Ancient-Men' as inhabitants of the world of faith. But in the poems, Bradford speaks without mask. As 'I', he addresses his 'dear friends, (and children whom I love)', and expresses the hope that his 'few lines' will 'move' them to 'cleave to God' so that the fate which befell Israel 'when the elders and Joshua were dead'[81] would not be New England's. Fearful that a great and terrible 'change'[82] is in store for the land that has lost 'its former glory', he calls on the people to 'repent, amend, and turn to God| That we may prevent his sharp rod,|Time yet thou hast improve it well,|That God's presence may with you dwell'.[83]

Sometime during his last years, Bradford returned to Book One of *Of Plymouth Plantation* and, on a reverse page, wrote a passage that more even than the poems discloses his sense of loss and failure. In 1630, he had quoted a letter of Robinson's and Brewster's in which the two ancients confidently assured Sir Edwin Sandys that their Leyden saints were 'knite togeather as a body in a most stricte and sacred bond and covenante of the Lord, of the violation wherof we make great conscience and by vertue wherof we doe hould our selves straitly tied to all care of each others good, and of the whole by every one and so mutually'.[84] In his note of twenty-five years later, Bradford spoke his pain directly:

O sacred bond, whilst inviollably preserved! how sweete and precious were the fruits that flowed from the same! but when this fidelity decayed, then their ruine approached. O that these anciente members had not dyed, or been dissipated, (if it had been the will of God) or els that this holy care, and constant faithfullnes had still lived, and remained with those that survived, and were in times afterwards added unto them. But (alass) that subtill serpente hath slylie wound in him selfe under faire pretences of necessitie and the like, to untwiste these sacred bonds and tyes, and as it were insensibly by degrees to dissolve, or in a great measure to weaken, the same. I have been happy, in my first times, to see, and with much comforte to injoye, the blessed fruits of this sweete communion, but it is now a parte of my miserie in old age, to find and feele the decay and wante thereof (in a great measure) and with greefe and sorrow of hart to lamente and bewaile the same. And for others warning and admonnition, and my owne humiliation doe I hear note the same.[85]

Mercy no longer seemed to grow out of afflictions. In retrospect, 'the blessed fruits' of Bradford's 'sweete communion' had been greatest in his 'first times'. Disappointed in his expectations for his community as a whole, Bradford, in his 'longing desire', withdrew into a private conversation with the past. Too strong to be relinquished, his dream led him to learn Hebrew in anticipation of the day when resurrected to new and literal life, he would converse with first planters and walk once more before his Lord.

7
The Puritan poetry of Anne Bradstreet
ROBERT D. RICHARDSON, JR

Anne Bradstreet's poetry has been steadily reprinted, anthologized and commented upon since the seventeenth century. Yet she has been praised more often as a phenomenon than as a poet, and her poetry, when it is discussed at all, is sometimes treated in the context of Puritanism and sometimes not. John Berryman's brilliant and moving poem on Mrs Bradstreet is, in one way, an example of the fact that it is now more common to render homage to her than it is to offer critical analysis. The present essay is an attempt to find a suitable focus for the study of her poetry as poetry. In view of the continuing and perhaps even increasing interest in Anne Bradstreet, it seems worth trying to show, in appropriate detail, that she wrote from what might be called the Puritan sensibility, that her best poetry gains rather than loses by being considered as the product of that sensibility, and that her finest work, 'Contemplations', is a splendid and coherent expression of what was best in New England Puritanism.[1]

Puritanism in Massachusetts in the middle of the seventeenth century was a way of life, and its ideal is perhaps best expressed in its injunction that one must somehow live in the world without being of it. This outlook rests firmly on what Perry Miller has called 'the dual contention of the Puritan synthesis', which Miller described as the assertion of 'the fallibility of material existence and the infallibility of the spiritual, the necessity for living in a world of time and space according to the laws of that time and that place, with never once forgetting that the world will pass, be resolved back into nothingness'.[2] In practice, this meant that the Puritan was always trying to achieve a balance between this world and the next. Monastic withdrawal was out of the question; one could not safely turn one's back on this world, for the simple reason that God had made it and had found it good; yet one could not rely upon, or repose in the security of, an earthly life which was, at last, insubstantial. At their most extreme, these apparently conflicting claims on the individual produced what Edmund Morgan calls the Puritan dilemma.

Puritanism required that a man devote his life to seeking salvation, but told him he was helpless to do anything but evil. Puritanism required that he rest his whole hope in Christ but taught him that Christ would utterly reject him unless before he was born God had foreordained his salvation. Puritanism required that man refrain from sin but told him he would sin anyhow.[3]

Thus the Puritan way of life was, at worst, a series of impossible conflicts, and at best a difficult balance. Edward Taylor's extreme and constrasting moods of exaltation and despair are a rather obvious illustration of the effect of the uneasy synthesis upon one sensitive and gifted person. Samuel Sewall's well known apostrophe to Plum Island is a momentary perception of the possible balance between this world and the next.

Anne Bradstreet also wrestled with the problem, at times rebelling, at times submitting. That she had severe doubts about her faith does not make her any the less a Puritan. In fact, according to the carefully safeguarded morphology of conversion developed by New England Puritanism, a firm and doubt-free conviction of salvation was a probable sign of damnation. As Morgan has pointed out, doubt and struggle were built into the fabric of Puritanism.

Delusion continually threatened, because the assurance wrought by grace was easily confused with the false assurance or 'security' of the unregenerate. Arthur Hildersham explained how to distinguish true from false assurance. True assurance came only after attendance on the preaching of the word, and only after a period of doubt and despair.[4]

Thus it becomes possible, I think, to regard Anne Bradstreet's struggles between love of this world and reliance on the next, and the poetic expression of those struggles, not as the rebelliousness of an anti-Puritan temperament but as an attempt to achieve the Puritan ideal of living in the world without being of it.

Her early poetry tends to run to extremes; it is unable to accommodate both worlds. The earliest poem to which a date can be given is the one in ballad measure called 'Upon a fit of Sickness, Anno 1632', written when she was nineteen. Simple and without force, the poem expresses a reliance upon God and a routine dismissal of this world. Her point is not that tribulation or suffering compels her to turn to Christianity; it is rather an expression of contempt for this life in the medieval tradition.

> For what's this life, but care and strife?
> since first we came from womb.
> Our strength doth waste, our time doth hast
> and then we go to th' Tomb.[5]

She turns her back on the world; it means nothing. And as her rejection of the present world is complete, her reliance upon the next reveals an almost mechanical security. The outcome is not in doubt; there is no need to hope or pray. She is simply sure of heaven.

> The race is run, the field is won
> the victory's mine I see.
>
> For ever know, thou envious foe
> the foyle belongs to thee.

In sharp contrast to this easy otherworldliness, the long poems in *The Tenth Muse* show a nearly unqualified worldliness. She writes of the four elements, humours, ages of man, seasons, and monarchies in a surprisingly secular way. There is no emphasis on Adam's fall, no attempt to make her subject subserve Calvinism, very little Christianity of any sort. She seems interested in contemporary knowledge about man, and she appears to have been especially attracted by the old exotic empires glittering with famous men and deeds. 'The Four Monarchies' is, in many respects, conventional and derivative, yet it is not always predictable. In addition to the remarkable absence of Calvinism, there is the unlooked-for approbation of such figures as Nebuchadnezzar and Darius Hyspaspes. There is a quality of spectacle as well; the poem dwells on the sumptuous and the stupendous. It is climaxed by the section on Alexander the Great, by far the longest section in the poem. That Anne Bradstreet was fascinated by Alexander and not just indulging in colorless cribbing from Raleigh and Ussher is attested by the repeated references to the Macedonian conqueror in her elegy on Sir Philip Sidney. The greatest compliment she can pay Sidney is to call him another Alexander. 'The Four Monarchies' is reminiscent of the Fall of Princes literature and it shows a concern with the great Elizabethan theme of mutability. It is a theme that was to occupy Anne Bradstreet for years; here it is given a simple secular expression. As the poem reaches the end of the third monarchy (The Grecian) it rises to a summary:

Here ends at last the Grecian Monarchy
Which by the Romans had its destiny;
Thus Kings and Kingdoms, have their times, and dates,
Their standings, over-turnings, bounds, and fates:
Now up, now down now chief, and then brought under,
The Heavn's thus rule, to fil the earth with wonder. (p. 320)

But however much she muses upon time's inconstant stay, the spectacle of the fallen ancient world does not move the poet to religious reflection. 'The Four Monarchies' is as thoroughly caught up in this world as her earliest poem is in the other world.

Most of the other poems in the first edition of *The Tenth Muse* are similarly secular. Her poems on Sidney, DuBartas, and Elizabeth are applications of the memorializing method of 'The Four Monarchies' to recent figures. Even 'A Dialogue between Old England and New', though informed by Puritan political zeal, is distinctly concerned with such things as terrestrial justice. But the final poem of the early volume 'The Vanity of all worldly things' swings back again to the other extreme. It is a sorrowful lament, a turning to the other world. It is on the theme and in the manner of Ecclesiastes; it is not, however, a simple rejection of the world. In rhymed couplets which are both calmer and more expressive than the early ballad meter, she painfully catalogues the vanities of life.

If not in honour, beauty, age, nor treasure,
Nor yet in learning, wisdome, youth nor pleasure
Where shall I climb, sound, seek search or find
That *summum bonum* which may stay my mind? (p. 387)

The poem turns to God and to hopes of heaven, but only after this world has been ransacked for possibilities. The final effect is weak, however, since the earth is represented only in abstractions. But while the world is still spurned with relative ease, we do not find in this poem any simple assurance of salvation for the poet. Salvation exists — 'who is possessed of [it] shall reign a king' — but she no longer finds it so easy to claim it for herself.

The poems dealt with so far suggest the extreme positions of acceptance and rejection of this world of which Anne Bradstreet was capable. The extremes are, of course, relative. They occur more often in her early work but are by no means confined to it, and they are significant mainly in the light of her better poetry. The early poems

emphasize one side or the other of the problem, but in such well
known poems as 'The Flesh and the Spirit' and 'Upon the Burning of
our House', we see clearly the conflicting claims of earth and heaven.
The form of each poem suggests a foregone conclusion, but the
language and general tone of each show that there is a genuine conflict
which is resolved, if at all, only with difficulty.

'The Flesh and the Spirit', though cast in the traditional debate
form, is more than a routine exercise. Flesh, who speaks first, is not
gross, detestable, sensual or mindless. Flesh begins with a series of
carefully phrased questions which strikes at the heart of the matter.

> Sister, quoth Flesh, what liv'st thou on
> Nothing but Meditation?
> Doth Contemplation feed thee so
> Regardlessly to let earth goe?
> Can Speculation satisfy
> Notion without Reality? (pp. 381–2)

The questions are designed to suggest that Spirit's beliefs are based on
unprovable grounds. Meditation and contemplation are linked to
mere speculation. Flesh exposes the continual doubt of the sceptical
mind, the nagging fear that belief is only 'notion without reality'.
Spirit replies, of course, but the answer is disappointing. Spirit will
not condescend to argue, she simply asserts that she is right and
denounces Flesh rather than answering Flesh's arguments; 'Thy sin-
full pleasures I doe hate | Thy riches are to me no bait.' Spirit asserts
that she has nourishment Flesh knows not of ('The word of life it is
my meat') and by such weak rejoinders tends to validate Flesh's
suspicion that it is indeed all notion without reality. The crowning
irony, however, comes as Spirit describes heaven in the very material
terms she has just scorned.

> My Crown not Diamonds, Pearls, and Gold
> But such as Angels heads infold.
> The City where I hope to dwell
> There's none on Earth to Parallel
> The stately Walls both high and strong
> Are made of pretious Jasper stone;
> The Gates of Pearl . . .

Spirit does not reject jewels; she merely rejects terrestrial jewels in the
hope of finer ones elsewhere. The poem ends conventionally: Spirit

wins. Yet the poem raises more questions than it settles, and we may fairly wonder whether Spirit deserves to win the debate.

The poem 'Upon the Burning of our House' is, from a formal point of view, a conventional Puritan exercise in finding the hand of God behind every apparent disaster. Yet the poem moves back and forth from the human levels to the divine, and it is not impossible to argue that the human level — the fear of fire, the sense of loss — is what genuinely moves the poet, while her submission to the will of God is a somewhat forced acknowledgment of an arrangement that is not really satisfactory.

> And when I could no longer look,
> I blest his Name that gave and took,
> That layd my goods now in the dust:
> Yea so it was, and so 'twas just.
> It was his own: It was not mine;
> Far be it that I should repine. (p. 40)

These lines of submission are clipped and measured, grimly sing-song: they sound forced when placed alongside the following lines which emphasize personal loss.

> Here stood that Trunk, and there that chest
> There lay that store I counted best:
> My pleasant things in ashes lye.

She makes the proper application, interpreting the event as a warning, and as an injunction to look toward the 'house on high erect'. But the vacillation in the poem suggests that the sense of loss outweighs, at least at times, the potential comfort promised by Puritan theology.

Whether or not these two poems are regarded as coming to a resolution, each is alive with conflict, keenly aware of the good things of this world (not just its vanities and vexations) as well as of the folly of a total or ultimate reliance on this world.

In at least one of the short poems to her husband and in the remarkable 'Contemplations', Anne Bradstreet reaches a state of mind which can apprehend both this world and the other, can resolve their apparently conflicting claims, and can find satisfaction in the accommodation or resolution. The poems are orthodox enough, yet they are in no sense forced or mechanical, and the poetic achievement they represent is the best indication of the depth of the poet's acceptance.

The poem to her husband beginning 'If ever two were one, then surely we' is a love poem of twelve lines which, in a Shakespearian manner, considers the love from several points of view and then subsumes the whole argument in a couplet (p. 394). Their love is the best of all the things of this world, more to be prized than 'whole mines of gold' or 'all the riches that the East doth hold'. Her love, she suggests, is such that only his love can equal it, and his love for her is so great that she feels inadequate to 'recompence' it fully. She therefore asks the heavens to reward him. The development of the poem is clear and logical. His love is so great that she is obliged to turn to the only thing greater than her own love in her search for something to equal his, and the concluding couplet simply expands the idea. 'Then while we live, in love lets so persever, | That when we live no more, we may live ever.' The union of the lovers in eternity is the outcome of their earthly love. Earthly love, the best of this world, is thus an emblem of what awaits the saved.

In this poem, this world and the next validate one another. Love is the way to heaven, and the best image of heaven is a realm of eternal love. As the poem expresses it, the transition from this world to the next involves not renunciation, not a change even, but an expansion. The poem stands in contrast to such poems as Sidney's 'Leave me O Love', in which one sort of love must be rejected before another can be accepted. Anne Bradstreet's poem presents a progressive acceptance, which does not need rejection as a spur. Theology rests lightly on this poem, to be sure. It seems less than orthodox in tone, yet it is not really Arminian. The hope of heaven is only a hope. The poem is dominated by a calm sense that the best of this life must indeed be the link between it and the next. In Puritan terms, their love is a possible evidence of justification. In personal terms, heaven holds the only hope that love will have no date.

'Contemplations', the long poem made up of thirty-three seven-line stanzas, is generally, and I think rightly, considered Anne Bradstreet's best poem.[6] Thematically, it is permeated by a concern with time and mutability; stylistically, it is reminiscent sometimes of Shakespeare, and sometimes it anticipates Romantic poetry.[7] 'Contemplations' is marked by an intensity, which, unlike that of most Puritan poems, can still be felt by a reader. It is a complex poem which presents a series of reflections which are sustained and ordered, partly by the continuity of the thought, partly by an almost Romantic use of talismans or symbols. Unlike so much of Puritan poetry which records statements of faith, 'Contemplations' records a reflective search for faith. The idea of the search is the central theme of the poem and it provides the basic structure as well. The poem may be described as a series of imaginative excursions, each of which begins in the natural world with some specific aspect of nature such as a tree or a river, which then leads the poet's mind outward into imaginative speculation or contemplation and ends eventually with a return to the poet and her present condition.

Thus it is the Puritan problem of the balance between this world and the next that actually dominates the poem and supplies its method. In section after section, the sensuous apprehension of the green world of nature leads the mind by easy and logical stages to a consideration of God and the world above the natural one. In turn, speculation about the next world leads not to statements of dogma and belief, but back to man and the natural world. In 'Contemplations', as in few other writings of this period, the interplay between the two worlds is so closely and carefully developed that it may be regarded as Mrs Bradstreet's most successful expression of the Puritan ideal of living fully in the world without being of it.

The opening two stanzas start the poem off firmly in the natural world, and they set the reflective tone that characterizes the whole work. The poet begins with the recollection of a 'time now past in the Autumnal Tide', a time when she was outdoors as evening was coming on. She speaks of the sun as Phoebus, and from this conventional bit of artifice goes on to emphasize the artificiality of her first impression of the scene. The trees were 'richly clad', 'gilded' by the sun, and 'their leaves and fruits seemed painted'. But this splendor, as of art, is of course the real and natural world, a 'true' nature, 'of green, of red, of yellow mixed hew'. This vivid apprehension of the lovely natural world so moves her that, for a moment, she knows 'not what to wish', but she quickly recovers and makes the observation 'If so much excellence abide below; | How excellent is he that dwells on high?' This is the standard Puritan reflex. The natural world, being God's, suggests God. This connection is made several times in the poem. It would be strange if it were otherwise, of course, but the poem is remarkable, not for its unorthodox observations, but for the way it deepens and expands what is normally considered a reflex into a reasonable and persuasive conclusion. Significantly the second stanza does not stop complacently at the thought of God and his perfection, but moves back to his creation, earth.

Sure he is goodness, wisdom, glory, light
That hath this under world so richly dight
More Heaven then Earth was here no winter and no night.

The final line is the culmination of the first two stanzas; it is a perception of the earth and a place approaching Eden, a realm of eternal
day and spring. Thus, in the opening two stanzas we are shown first
the world, beautiful in terms of art, then the world lovely in its own
right, then God, the maker of that world, then the world again, more
beautiful now than art, resembling Eden. The rest of the poem repeats
this movement, swinging back and forth, redoubling on itself, gathering force and conviction as it widens and takes more and more into
account.

Each time the poet takes a fresh look at the world around her, its
excellences — not its vexations — move her to think of the other world,
and each time she reflects on the next world or on God, she returns to
this world since it is the connection between the two that fascinates
her and that gives direction to the poem. The third stanza returns to
the poet and to a 'stately oak', whose age and height move her to
reflect on time (a theme one might claim is announced in the opening
line of the poem). Even if the oak is a thousand years old, it is nothing
to eternity. Again we are given the expected observation, but in an
unexpected manner. Her sense of actuality, her sensuous apprehension
of the world is at least as strong as her abstract sense. She does not
dismiss the oak to dwell upon eternity. The oak remains, and it
remains impressive. That eternity is greater merely occurs to her but
does not lead her off. The oak, indeed, moves her to consider another
even greater part of nature, the sun, to which stanzas four through
seven are addressed.

Looking at the sun 'whose beams was shaded by the leavie Tree',
the poet asks 'What glory's like to thee?' But in place of the ritual
answer, God, she goes on, 'Soul of this world, this Universes Eye. |No
wonder some made thee a Deity.' The lines draw attention now to
the impulse to invest the world with deity, to the process by which
man finds gods in nature. Far from resting on received theological
truths she is speculating on the fact that nature itself, regarded for
itself inevitably leads men's thoughts in certain directions. In the
fifth and sixth stanzas she describes the sun and its beneficent effects,
rising to an apostrophe that sounds, for a moment, almost pagan.
'Hail Creature, full of sweetness beauty and delight.' But at the same

time that she has captured the mood of primitive sun worship, she is careful to call the sun a creature. Though addressed as a god it is not God. For there remains the question, put now in a pointed and forceful phrase, 'Who gave this bright light luster unto thee?' and the acknowledgment that 'admir'd ador'd for ever, be that Majesty'.

Three times now, the natural world has impelled her mind, in seeking for origins and causes, to God. Yet, with a restlessness that continually brings the poem back to this world — the world in which she must live and which she cannot ignore — the eighth stanza doubles back to the poet 'Silent alone, where none or saw, or heard, | In pathless paths I lead my wandering feet.' Moved, lost, bewildered, she does not know how to bear witness to what she perceives. 'To sing some song, my mazed Muse thought meet . . . But ah, and ah, again, my imbecility.' But as nature shows the way to God, so nature prompts the poet. 'I heard the merry grasshopper then sing, | The black clad cricket bear a second part.' Sound breaks the silence, and if the grasshopper and the cricket can seem 'to glory in their little art', why should not she?

The thought-process here is close to the heart of the poem. If the poem achieves the delicate balance between the two worlds of Puritan experience, it is because Anne Bradstreet regards the natural world not as a howling wilderness but as the excellent handiwork of God, as a kind of focal point or point of intersection between this world and the other. Each time she returns to the green world she seeks not to impose something on it, but to emulate it. So in the tenth stanza, she takes a lesson from the black clad cricket and begins to apply her own art in earnest now, broadening the theme in familiar renaissance terms to include time and imagination.

> When present times look back to ages past,
> And men in being fancy those are dead
> It makes things gone perpetually to last,
> And calls back months and years that long since fled.

It is through the imagination or fancy of the living that the past exists. Partly as a way of defeating time and partly as an expression of a sense of history (as opposed to a mere knowledge of it), the poet now proceeds to do what she has just said is possible. Stanzas eleven through fifteen relive, in imaginative form, the old and basic stories of Adam and Eve, and Cain and Abel. It is important to bear in mind that the scenes which follow are not merely recounted. The poet lives in the present and the biblical stories exist also in the present, alive in her imagination. They are all written in the present tense; 'Sometimes in Eden fair, he [one who thus imagines] seems to be, | Sees glorious Adam there made Lord of all.' Further, as she writes of Cain, she sees him as a baby, in Eve's lap, and describes the scene as though it lay before her.

> Here sits our Grandame in retired place
> And in her lap, her bloody Cain new born,
> The weeping Imp oft looks her in the face.

As these scenes from the past rise to her mind's eye, becoming real and present, she generalizes the experience, assuming that others, like her, think often 'upon the Fathers ages'. And inevitably those who are now alive compare their lives with those of the patriarchs. Not only are the lives of the present generation ten times shorter, but we continually shorten even that which we have by 'living so little while we are alive'. Men now seem small and foolish in comparison with men of the past. The eighteenth stanza continues this contrast as the subject broadens again to set man in the perspective of nature as well as time. The verse rises to a richness and fullness which is as reminiscent of Shakespeare as is the theme.

> When I behold the heavens as in their prime,
> And then the earth (though old) stil clad in green,
> The stones and trees insensible of time,
> Nor age nor wrinkle on their front are seen;
> If winter come and greenness then do fade
> A Spring returns, and they more youthful made;
> But Man grows old, lies down, remains where once he's laid.

The natural world is at peace with time. In the endless wheeling of the seasons, gain and loss are equalized. But, for all that nature or history can show, man is subject to loss without the consequent gain. Although man is the noblest work of creation — the argument continues in stanza nineteen — man 'seems by nature and by custome curs'd', and destined for oblivion.

The above argument seems to demonstrate why the natural world is so important to this poem as the meeting-place or imaginative focal point between worlds. Just as the Puritans felt that man must live in the world without being of it, so the poet finds herself surveying the natural world without being of it. While nature is in some sense at peace with time, man is not, and the poem now must turn to the only perspective that offers relief from time. To the question 'Shall I then praise the heavens, the trees, the earth | Because their beauty and their strength last longer', she replies in the twentieth stanza with the promise of Christianity.

> Nay, they shall darken, perish, fade and dye.
> And when unmade, so ever shall they lye,
> But man was made for endless immortality.

Only in ideas of God or immortality can one find an acceptable solution to the problem posed by time.

But the poem cannot come to rest yet. As if to test and retest, as if reluctant or unable to leave the natural world, the poem again doubles back on itself, coming again to the poet herself and to her walk in the woods. The promise of eternity is all very well, but the poet cannot allow herself an easy repose in that promise. She must and does live in this world and she clearly prefers the contemplation of nature to abstract theological discussions. She now sits down by a river 'under the cooling shadow of a stately Elm'. She has already considered the trees, the sun and the heavens, she turns now to the river. Her first reaction, a simple one, is to think how pleasant it would be to live there by the river. She muses about the stream, how it holds its course and overcomes obstacles until it arrives at its eventual goal, the ocean. The river has direction and purpose. It runs its established course, gathering strength from its tributaries, until it empties into an ocean which is only a large version of its own element. It is, she finds, an 'emblem true, of what I count the best'. The river is analogous to her concept of life which runs naturally and inevitably into the next life. Typically, though, she does not digress into a consideration of the next life. Rather, in allowing her imagination to play over what she can see in front of her, she is led on to consider the fishes in the river. They go where they wish, and they lead a happy life. 'So nature taught, and yet you know not why | You watry folk that know not your felicity.' For still another stanza, she lingers over the fish, following them in her imagination to 'Neptun's glassie Hall' and through 'the spacious sea-green fields', and ending by remarking on their protection, 'whose armour is their scales, their spreading fins their shield'. There are analogies or comparisons between the fish and men, of course, but she does not stop here to draw them out, it being perhaps obvious that while time is like the river, the carefree lives of the fish stand in sharp contrast to human life, even though men have, or can have far better armor and shields than those their own bodies provide. The comparison between the lower creatures and man is uppermost in her mind here, though it must be said that the unoriginal diction weakens this section of the poem.

In stanza twenty-six the poem redoubles on itself for the last time. Again the poet comes back to the present, to the real world which she refuses to leave however tempting a subject the other world may offer. And again it is something in nature which allows her to exist for a while in that precarious but delicate position between the two worlds of man and God.

> While musing thus with contemplation fed,
> And thousand fancies buzzing in my brain
> The sweet-tongu'd Philomel perch't ore my head,
> And chanted forth a most melodious strain
> Which rapt me so with wonder and delight
> I judged my hearing better than my sight
> And wisht me wings with her a while to take my flight.

Again it is a sound that breaks in upon her musings, to call her back to earth, but now it is no cricket, but a bird she calls a nightingale that teases her out of thought, and for the next few stanzas her train of thought is oddly similar to the one Keats was to follow 140 years later in his 'Ode to a Nightingale'. The use of 'Philomel' here is unfortunate, as is such diction in the preceding stanzas. Happily it is not repeated, nor does one feel that the bird is to her an abstraction.

Her first impulse is to fly away with the bird and share its happy lot. It 'fears no snares', it 'neither toyles nor hoards', and it 'feels no sad thoughts'. Its food, drink, and resting place are everywhere, and, best of all, it 'Reminds not what is past, nor what's to come dost fear'. Not cursed with thought, it is a part of the natural order, and its function is to sing songs before 'the dawning morn'. The bird leads its fellows, and together

> they pass their youth in summer season
> Then follow thee into a better region
> Where winter's never felt by that sweet airy legion.

As Keats imagined the nightingale to live forever, where no hungry generations could tread it down, so Anne Bradstreet (through an image derived perhaps from the idea of migration) sees the bird as perpetually happy. But she cannot fly away to endless summer any more than could Keats, and, like him, she is brought up short and forced to admit that whatever the nightingale's lot, human life is 'subject to sorrows, losses, sickness, pain'. Pressing the point, she concludes;

> Nor all his losses, crosses, and vexation,
> In weight, in frequency and long duration
> Can make him deeply groan for that divine Translation.

Man without grace is worse than the nightingale in respect both to this life and the next. He does not have the bird's happiness here, nor the nightingale's 'better Region'. But considered from another point of view, the nightingale's life is analogous to a Christian life. The point is only implicit, yet one cannot be sure that the poem would be better if the idea were elaborated.

The poem works to a close now, reaching out in the thirty-first and thirty-second stanzas for yet another image of the human condition. This time she must have an image clearly expressive of the life that has to be lived among the perils of this world. No image from the natural world will do now, for man is apart from nature as the nightingale section has clearly shown. So at last she turns to man himself:

> The Mariner that on smooth waves doth glide
> Sings merrily, and steers his barque with ease,
> As if he had command of wind and tide.

His false security is shattered by a storm and by affliction. He is forced in the end to live more warily in this world and to acknowledge that 'Only above is found all with security.'

The mariner is the last major image of the poem, and it is his state that corresponds most closely to that of the poet. Like the mariner, she can live in this world only under the condition that there is a possibility of some other state which can be inferred from the natural world and which is confirmed in the Bible. The poem concludes with these lines:

> O Time the fatal wrack of mortal things
> That draws oblivions curtains over kings,
> Their sumptuous monuments, men know them not,
> Their names without a Record are forgot,
> Their parts, their ports, their pomp's all laid in th' dust

> Nor wit nor gold, nor buildings scape times rust;
> But he whose name is graved in the white stone
> Shall last and shine when all of these are gone.

'Contemplations' reposes at last in the hope or perhaps just in the possibility of heaven. If, in this poem, earth and earthly life were simply shrugged off and rosy hopes of heaven held out as an alternative, we could with justice dismiss the piece as altogether too easy. But what validates this poem is its intensity, its thoughtfulness, its choice of images, its complex circling movement, its weight of thought, and its continued turning back to earth until every possibility has been explored. The last stanza is a full summation. Man is at last subject to time in this world. With her eye steadily on the human theme, she runs through a renaissance catalogue of time's ruins. Not only will earth and sun pass away, as she has considered earlier, but so will all of man's earthly accomplishments. Not history, not imagination, not poetry will at last avail. At last there is nothing but the promise held out in Revelations:

Let him that hath an eare, heare what the Spirit sayeth unto the churches To him that overcommeth, will I give to eate of the Manna that is yhid and will give him a white stone, and in the stone a new name written, which no man knoweth saving he that receiveth it.[8]

In the Geneva Bible that was favored by the Puritans, the white stone is thus glossed:

Such a stone was wont to be given unto them that had gotten any victory or prize, in sign of honour, and therefore it signifieth here a token of God's favor and grace; also it was a sign that one was cleared in judgement.

The final couplet makes its point theologically no doubt, but it makes it in poetic fashion. The oak, the sun, the grasshopper, the stories of Adam and Cain, the heavens, the river, the ocean, the fish, the bird, and the mariner at sea are all talismans, each offering a starting-point for the contemplative imagination. Each of these images eventually leads the mind to God, but all are temporal, and none has the quiet and final authority of the white stone, the genuine token which gives the new name hidden from all but the receiver.

'Contemplations' comes to rest in a gentle and evocative poetic reference to the selective and unknowable ways of the Puritan God. The poem is a demonstration, in the form of a recorded experience, that nature itself generates belief. In seventeenth-century New England this could only mean that the world itself leads the mind of man to acknowledge God. This search, the speculative trying of a faith, provides the fundamental structure of the poem and emphasizes steadily the idea that the much desired balance between this world and the next is best achieved by a life spent in searching rather than one spent in repose. The poetic level to which 'Contemplations' rises in stanzas nine, eighteen, twenty-one, and twenty-eight is one kind of testimony to the fact that in this poem Anne Bradstreet has reached that ideal but rare state of Puritan consciousness, a carefully reasoned and emotionally convincing resolution of the problem of how to live in the world without being of it. 'Contemplations' spans both worlds. It accepts both worlds, perceives their connection, and acquiesces in that connection.

8
The example of Edward Taylor

KARL KELLER

The neglect and the discovery of Edward Taylor's poetry have been made more interesting by the desire to believe the Taylor family's story about his injunction against publication. Having willed himself into obscurity, Taylor's unexpected emergence in the twentieth century has been almost as interesting as the poetry itself and the gap that it fills in American literary history. The phenomenon of finding Taylor at that point in American literary history where we were sure so good a poet could not appear has become integral to the poetry itself. The find romanticizes him for us; the wooden preacher takes on a little color thereby.

Shortly before his death in 1729, so the family story goes, Taylor 'enjoined it upon his heirs never to publish any of his writing'.[1] Though the existence of his poetry was to be reported a number of times,[2] it was lost to us for over two centuries. The unpublished manuscripts fell first into the hands of Taylor's grandson Ezra Stiles through Taylor's son-in-law Isaac Stiles, then into the hands of his great-grandson Henry W. Taylor and others in the Taylor family, and finally to Yale University, the Westfield and Redwood Athenaeums, and other libraries, whence it has been recovered and now published. It has taken over thirty-five years to locate, transcribe, and publish his poetical works — and there are more to come. None of this was intended; we invade his privacy as we read him today.

Yet publication *was* on Taylor's mind. He was an incessant student and an industrious writer, producing in the course of 67 years works totalling about 3100 manuscript pages. As far as his descendants knew, he had 'an abiding passion for writing poetry during his whole life'.[3]

A number of these writings he apparently intended for the public in one form or another. He wrote a 485-page *Commentary on the Four Gospels*, for example, which was so well thought of that Increase

Mather wrote to Dr John Woodward and other wealthy persons in the Royal Society of London trying to induce them to publish it.[4] The *Christographia* sermons were circulated separately and then later gathered and revised for publication; too complex for the ear, they were to have been printed and read. Eight other sermons, now titled *Treatise Concerning the Lord's Supper*, were his contribution to the public debate over the Stoddardean heresy. There is also supposed to have been a quarto volume containing many short occasional poems prepared for publication,[5] and a few of Taylor's funeral elegies, acrostic love verses, and poems for special occasions were read by the bereaved, the beloved, and interested audiences from Westfield to Boston. Even the poems of *Gods Determinations* and his *Metrical History of Christianity* smack of widely-read genre pieces of the period used for soteriological and educational purposes; they show that Taylor did not write in a social vacuum but had a sense of audience, a sense of what was happening in the religious experience of declining New England.

All of this should show that for the archetype of a private poet in our literary history, Taylor had intents and purpose that were noticeably public. Only the *Preparatory Meditations*, a few of the more meditative sections of *Gods Determinations*, and several of his miscellaneous poems seem to have been composed for purely private rather than public ends. Though Taylor copied out a few of them for slight revision,[6] the form in which they have come down to us suggests intermediacy and private satisfaction rather than finality and publication. Where the more public poems are didactic, even dogmatic, the meditative poems are dramatic. The one type is for the most part in drier, more constrictive, decasyllabic couplets, the other in the freer, more dramatic, sestet of Robert Southwell, George Herbert, and Christopher Harvey (a stanza form which Taylor called 'A brisk Tetrastich, with a Distich sweet'). Most of his poems turn outward and are descriptive, narrative, stilted, and technical, but the private poems turn inward, their substance lost in their inward action. Even the full title of Taylor's *Meditations* suggests a privacy about them: 'Preparatory Meditations Before *My* Approach to the Lord's Supper . . .' Whenever he spoke publicly, he wrote privately; it was another world with a language of its own. It would appear that in not making these poems public, Taylor may have been asking, as Emily Dickinson was later to do, how do you publish a piece of your soul?

To account for the privacy of such poetry, it has been a temptation to turn to Taylor's personality and find there a modesty and humility that would have prevented publication.[7] Items from his biography encourage this for a reason: his choice for his ministerial labors of the humbler, remote Westfield over Boston, the publishing center, or Cambridge, the intellectual center; his notoriously rigid piety and reputation for sweetness, personability, and selfless service; his emphasis on the psychological and occult side of Puritanism. Though we know his life poorly, it appears to have been self-sufficient, defensive, insignificant, inward, and thereby one for which a public was not needed. He simply seems to have lacked the vanity of desiring fame, especially at the end of his life when he was no longer interested in his writing.

Yet he was at the same time a thorny, proud, contentious personality, a man of quick passions, a man who kept a lively interest in the public affairs of the area and the colony and who maintained an association and correspondence with the leading public figures of the period. He was a vigorous advocate of unpopular causes, a curious, constant, powerful man, a man abreast of the issues of his time and sure that God had raised him up in hard times to defend the faith. No one who knew him or knew of him thinks to attribute to him the qualities of modesty and humility of the sort that would have prevented him from baring his soul publicly. So it is unconvincing to presume in him an indifference to his writing, a life too lofty to communicate, an exclusiveness with no responsibility to the world. Because of the Puritan suspicion of the incomprehensible and uncommunicative, to find a modesty and humility behind his injunction against publication is to see his spirituality as schizophrenic, even heterodox.[8]

And though Taylor's orthodoxy is unassailable, at least as he revealed it to congregation and community, in his private life, the inward life which his meditative poetry parallels, he may have been something else — non-covenanting Calvinist, vulgarizer of the faith, secret antinomian, arminian enthusiast, aesthetically an Anglican or even Catholic, liberal neo-platonist or humanist, sensualist and mystic, even pagan.[9] For such positions (take your choice), he might have had to hide his private thoughts and passions from soberer eyes, and so withheld his poetry from publication. He allegedly sensed an incompatibility between his style and his belief.

But in a way, the discovery of Taylor's writings did not so much find a skunk in the garden as point up the carelessness of much of the gardening; we were, perhaps, not well prepared for the sensuously meditative, the joyously logical, the humanistically knowledgeable, and the appropriately personable in high Puritanism, and Taylor has in part forced the adjustment. In view of a life devoted to the hard labor of justifying the *status quo*, a mind sharpened in a very narrow theological groove, and aesthetics that could not possibly be distinguished from dogma, it seems clear that if Taylor would not publish his poems, it would have to have been because of his devotion to Calvinist principles, not because he was afraid of them.

That his devotion to dogma overwhelmed and limited his skill with his art — and that he knew it — might be seen as a more convincing reason for his not publishing. A man of wide reading and aesthetic sensitivity, he might have seen how flawed his verse was by comparison and therefore suppressed it. His meiotic sensibility, as well as his sensitivity to criticism, would have discouraged him. His lack of polish may have embarrassed him, his verses' complexity and obscurity may have warned him, his lack of confidence in his own theory and practice may have humbled him. He may have been simply still another example of a writer conscious of having written something inferior and anxious to forget the fact.

But if Taylor could sense all of this about the unacceptability of his poetry, then he would also have had a sense that the American Puritans would have found his poetry exciting and instructive. He would have known that his work was superior to *The Tenth Muse Lately Sprung Up in America* or *The Day of Doom* or *New England Crisis*, collections of verse that the first century of Puritans had taken pride in. If he were simply stoical about his lack of ability to write well, he would not have been the meticulous craftsman that he was — conscious of technique, working hard to achieve different effects, reworking his lines until they were as dramatic as he could make them — only to do little or nothing to prevent their loss.

It is also likely that Taylor knew he was artistically and intellectually always a little out of touch with his times. His fervor, his style of thought, and his form of verse were all fairly dated. He wrote and thought in 1725 the same as he had written and thought in 1682, as if literary history had been suspended; he was, oddly, a contemporary of Dryden and Swift. The baroque mode that he loved was old-fashioned by at least fifty years; his use of it is a relic. By the eighteenth century the meditative tradition had few apologists and few literary uses, even on the Massachusetts frontier. The year 1700 is too late for a morality-play-cum-versified-theological-sermon like *Gods Determinations*. His *Christographia* sermons are imitative of Increase Mather's sermons *The Mystery of Christ Opened and Applied* (1686) and behind them by two decades; his *Metrical History* is imitative of Matthias Flacius' *Magdeburg Centuries* (1562) and John Foxe's *Actes and Monuments* (1563) and behind them by well over a century. And all of the verse and prose that Taylor wrote in the Stoddardean controversy was written for a cause that was unpopular, untenable, and already pretty well lost.

But though almost everything about him fits an earlier world better, there is nothing to convince one that Taylor had any concern whatever for literary fashion or fashionability of thought – or in fact any reason to concern himself. His call was to the defense of the New England Way in both poetry and prose, and he fulfilled that call with whatever verbal skills he had. That his defense was a strong and almost lone one would hardly be reason for not publishing.

It now seems that these are all reasons without much foundation, reasons that look to Taylor's personality and temperament or to an external world that did not touch his, rather than to his aesthetics or to the lasting qualities of his poetry. Self-effacing, alarmingly personal, botched, and archaic as his poetry is, there is yet something about the nature of Taylor's approach to poetry that justifies its privateness.

In its privateness Taylor's poetry was bound to take on some of the personality of a life lived in the New World, and so a related Taylor issue is how his poetry belongs to an *American* tradition of letters rather than simply to a Puritan tradition. Louis L. Martz answers to this in the negative: 'Is there anything in Taylor's poetry that could be called distinctively American?' How to justify Taylor at the head of American poetry, and not merely as a transitional figure, a link with the heritage, a bridge to what evolved, is a question of historical interest.

To be sure, Taylor was a man of two cultures. He was educated at both an English academy and Harvard. He both taught at Bagworth, Leicestershire, and preached at Westfield on the American frontier. The books he read, the hymns he sang, and the sermons he heard were produced in both London and Boston, and the writers he learned from were British and American. Also, in his dogged loyalism he saw English and New English polity as one, and the confessions of faith on the American frontier were to him no different from those in Puritan England. He appears to have transplanted himself without disturbing his roots, to have become a colonial without dislocation.

The very fact of his writing his more meditative poetry out of personal experience — with that personal experience having its referents, its color, its issues and forms from these shores — could superficially show him to be a provincial. And the earnestness with which he sees his person, his personality, his personal experience as the proper subject for his best poetry perhaps sets him squarely in a tradition of American letters with Walt Whitman and Emily Dickinson. From one point of view, his poetry may indeed be seen as a personal diary which has its typology from an involvement in a New Zion (a typology that was to inform a tradition from Edwards to Faulkner); a diary with its extravagances of metaphor bringing heaven down to New England huswifery and husbandry (a realistic, vernacular metaphoric mode that from Emerson to Frost was to become an American way of poetry); a diary of a self-conscious and lonely poet in the wilderness whose poetry is the fruit of isolation (a recurrent motif in American letters from Anne Bradstreet and Philip Freneau through Hawthorne and Emily Dickinson to James and T. S. Eliot).

Yet these are mere surface connections with what was to be an identifiable American culture. From his poems one could not, I think, really reconstruct his personal life in Westfield, nor the daily Puritan life, nor an attitude toward time and place. Was his verse rugged and raw because he moved to Massachusetts? his metaphors hyperbolic and humor exaggerated because he lived on the frontier? his language excited and engaging because he wrote alone? Was it the environment that made him more than one expects from a devout man of the time who used his imagination and biblical lore and ordinary skill in rhyme to concentrate his attention on the aweful ideas suggested by his faith? Simply because he was here does not mean that the spirit of his work was.

His language too has been overrated for its Americanness. It might be thought possible to turn to Taylor's earthly diction, his homely images, his natural speech, his neologisms, and see there the qualities of an American vernacular. Or one might see in his privateness a freedom to invent and play with the provincial words of his native country. But while Taylor's ideolect is highly non-standard, it is in a number of ways fossilized speech. Much of Taylor's usage is of course difficult to the modern reader though common in his time, but a part of Taylor's diction was obsolete at use (words like 'attent', 'flurr', 'pillard', 'pistick', 'dub', 'tittle-tattle'), another part was made up of archaic survivals in America not current in standard British English but entrenched in regional English dialects ('jags', 'lugg', 'frob', 'grudgens', 'nit', 'frim', 'womble-crops', 'fuddling', 'ding', 'clagd', 'bibble'), and still another part was made up of highly special-ized, technical terms derived from Taylor's reading but not in general use ('anakims', 'mictams', 'calamus', 'catholicons', 'catochee', 'surd-ity', 'syncopee', 'barlybreaks', 'noddy', 'ruff-and-trumpt'). Charles W. Mignon has identified in Taylor's usage diction from several English and Welsh dialects which fossilized in the colonies but which has become obsolete, and in all of Taylor's writings he has found only three Americanisms ('Cordilera', 'dozde', 'Netop').[10] All of which, instead of substantiating the local character of his speech, makes Taylor obscure and relatively much more remote than any other colonial writer. He relies as heavily on the unfamiliar as on that which would communicate with others in his own time and place, and what has often passed for fresh, coined, homely, realistic in him is in large part, it would appear, verbal obscurity and intended for his eyes alone. Instead of speaking New Englandly, Taylor wrote in a per-sonal idiom that was in many ways uncommunicative. Taylor's lan-guage was unique but not because he was on these shores.

More than in his personal experiences and his language, it may be that Taylor's real importance as an *American* poet is in his defense of the New England way of theology. Since that way required him to link his piety with community polity, his introspectiveness with citizenship in the New Israel in America, it might follow that the extent to which Taylor was an ardent defender of New England covenant theology is the extent to which he was an American poet. Taylor's life and writings may indeed be seen as having their main motivation in the idea of the self prepared for grace as a test of visible sainthood, for to Taylor the meditative preparationism re-quired by the Half-Way Covenant justified the whole purpose of the emigration to America, safeguarded the purity of gathered churches, and helped to fulfill God's unique covenant with New England. Therefore, in almost everything he wrote — sermons arguing against

Stoddardean liberalism, historical verses tracing the evolution of religion toward New England purity, poetry dramatizing the personal value of preparing oneself for membership in church and community — he was, it would appear, a kind of nationalist. His meditative poetry may be almost completely dominated by the peculiarities of the New England situation. On no other shores would he have had to be so passionately patriotic in his piety.

But like the reasons for his injunction against publication, these reasons for his relevance to American culture seem imposed with hindsight on the poetry and not derived from any sight that Taylor himself had. While demonstrating something of a New England life, a New England tongue, a New England mind, his poetry still remains apart and aloof from any relationship with the external world. So instead of looking to Taylor's personality — his self-consciousness, his naturalness, his pious defensiveness — we need to look to his works. In his works themselves lies a more convincing reason, a reason that at one and the same time establishes Taylor as an important private poet and an important American poet.

When it comes to Taylor issues of both publication and nationality, it is important to emphasize that Taylor was concerned not so much with poems as products as he was with the production of poems; that it, not so much with the product as with the process, not so much with Meditations as with meditating. He was, as Roy Harvey Pearce has noted, a man 'in action' and a Taylor poem is 'the act of a man whose imagination is *now* engaged in *creating* something'.[11]

For the most part, Taylor deprecates his poems *as products*:

> I fain would praise thee, but want words to do't:
>   And searching ore the realm of thoughts finde none
> Significant enough and therefore vote
>   For a new set of Words and thoughts hereon
>   And leap beyond the line such words to gain
>   In other Realms, to praise thee: but in vain. (II. 106)[12]

As finished products his poems seem to him mere 'blottings', 'wordiness', a 'sylabicated jumble', 'ragged Nonsense', 'Language welded with Emphatick reech'.

> What shall I say, my Deare Deare Lord? most Deare
>   Of thee! My choisest words when spoke are then

> Articulated Breath, soon disappeare.
>> If wrote are but the Drivle of my pen
>> Beblackt with my inke, soon torn worn out ... (II. 142)

It appears as if in their 'steaming reechs', Taylor's poems correspond with, and even symbolize to him, the insufficiency of his own self. Like him, they are products of a fallen world cast off by God and existing passively for recognition and acceptance.

>> Whether I speake, or speechless stand, I spy,
>> I faile thy Glory. (I. 22)

>> Mine Eyes, Lord, shed no Tears but inke.
>> My handy Works, are Words, and Wordiness. (I. 24)

Almost everything that he produces, no matter how well intentioned as praise to God, is poor: his faculties are 'ragged', his pen 'jar [s]', he 'lisps', his voice is 'rough' and his tongue 'blunt' or 'tied', his style is 'homely', his rhymes are 'wracked to pieces', his attempts to write are 'laughable', his finished poems are 'poore Eggeshell[s]' all of which, of course, are Taylor's complaints about the sorry features of his own inadequate life.

>> My tatter'd Fancy; and my Ragged Rymes
>>> Teeme leaden Metaphors: which yet might serve
>> To hum a little touching terrene Shines.
>>> But Spirituall Life doth better fare deserve.
>>> This thought on, sets my heart upon the Rack.
>>> I fain would have this Life but han't its knack. (II. 82)

Taylor's view of created things is so dim that when it comes to evaluating the products of his pen — even though his desires have been intent, his hope sincere, his effort devoted, and his devices polished — what he has written seems to him worthless. As products his poems are 'dirty thing[s]'.

>> My Deare Deare Lord what shall I render thee?
>>> Words spoken are but breesing boxed Winde.
>> If written onely inked paper bee. (II. 158)

Yet in spite of the impossibility of producing anything of worth, Taylor sees importance in the process of using language as a means of meditating on meaning. In fact, he is obsessed with the need to write. Though the purposelessness of a poem itself ought to inhibit

the act of composition, it doesn't, for Taylor finds joy in the duty
of going through the process. He seems even to accept from the outset
the futility of his efforts, but he nonetheless longs to express himself:

> I am this Crumb of Dust which is design'd
> To make my Pen unto thy Praise alone,
> And my dull Phancy I would gladly grinde
> Unto an Edge on Zions Pretious Stone.
> And Write in Liquid Gold upon thy Name
> My Letters till thy glory forth doth flame. ('Prologue')

This insistence on the value of the process of singing/writing
makes Taylor's poems very repetitious. Most of the *Preparatory
Meditations* have a recurring tripartite structure, beginning with a
comment about the desire to write ('Fain I would sing thy Praise'),
continuing with a complaint about the inability to write ('I cannot
sing, my tongue is tide'), and concluding with an affirmation of the
process of writing and the hope that God will make it possible
('Accept this Lisp till I am glorified'), though leaving the poem open
at the end to invite God's poetic closure of this on-going process
(I. 43). So intense was his interest in the process of writing that on
most subjects in his poems he is not finished until he has made some
comment about the difficulty of producing a product from the process, often shifting, contorting, mixing his metaphors to get back
to his theme: process *versus* product. The musical imagery throughout these poems betrays his love of singing — even though it is singing,
as Taylor himself knows, which results in only sour songs. As John
Cotton advised in his *Singing of Psalmes a Gospel-Ordinance* (1650),
a private Christian 'who hath a gift to frame a spirituall Song may
both frame it, and sing it privately for his own private comfort'.
Taylor's poems must be seen as constant complaints about the inability to write amid the need/duty to write.

This is not to say that glory eludes Taylor, for he has glory *as*
he sings rather than *in* his song. The opportunity of carrying out
his duty to sing praise to God is for him enough; and the result
of his singing, his poems, is largely irrelevant. If he is moved to
write, he knows that by some divine favor his life has been made
dynamic, and it is that spiritual momentum which is important.
Without such a process, the product (his life, his poem) is worthless.

Thy Praise shall be my Glory sung in state. (II. 53)

Ile tune thy Prayses while this Crown doth come.
Thy Glory bring I tuckt up in my Songe. (I. 44)

Thy Speech the Liquour in thy Vessell stands,
    Well ting'd with Grace a blessed Tincture, Loe,
Thy Words distilld, Grace in thy Lips pourd, and,
    Give Graces Tinctur in them where they go.
    Thy words in graces tincture stilld, Lord, may
    The Tincture of thy Grace in me Convay. (I. 7)

Such an act as writing was to Taylor a quest for signs of an assured salvation, so to him the process was a matter of spiritual life or death.

Taylor's orthodoxy itself demanded a concern with process rather than product. The condition of the Fall is static and man has mobility only as he works to discover his predetermined spiritual status. His life becomes dynamic as he engages in this process of self-discovery. Nature is in flux and by concentrating on *process* the Puritan participates, if only through his imagination, in the nature of things as they lie beyond the condition of the Fall. Through thinking of his writing as a process, Taylor, like many of Reformed persuasion, could re-enact the process of salvation and live in the illusion of a spiritual development of oneself.

Through introspective meditation the Puritan engaged in a process of transferring truth from the memory and intellect to the affections and the heart and will. In Taylor's predestinarian cosmology, this process was the only thing in which a Puritan could willfully engage in the whole act of salvation: he moved through a series of interior stages of contrition and humiliation, affection and repentance, examining himself mercilessly, arousing in himself a longing desire for help, and thereby predisposing himself for the possibility of saving grace. Without this process, he could not experience the transformation determined for him or even anticipate it, nor would his consciousness be involved in it. But because of the process, he could discover the determined direction of his life. In this there is a careful distinction between the movement and the thing moved, between God in action in a man's life and the man himself, between the process and the product.[13]

This intense, personal process of anticipating salvation dominates the aesthetics of Taylor and lies behind his injunction against publication as well as his relevance to American culture. As a poet, language helped Taylor to achieve the condition of 'preparedness' he desired. Meditation was for Taylor; as for many Puritans, a *verbal* art. Concentration on the means (language) of arriving at meaning (salvation), he finds his life becoming meaningful (the purpose of praise that he finds himself created for). To be sure, to concentrate on such devices of language as sound, syntax, and imagery is to end up with a poem, a product, but it is the process of working at one's praise that is important to him, not the result.

Taylor's private poems are themselves for the most part accounts of the process that Taylor went through in preparing himself to be disposed for saving grace. They are not poems *about* the process, but poems showing Taylor *in the process* of preparation. They are miniature dramas in which Taylor is re-enacting over and over again that which was to him the most meaningful process of man's life. In fact, the form of a number of the Meditations is so close to the experience dramatized that it can legitimately be called imitative. The form of his poems is fully organic to the ideas in them.

And because he was concerned mainly about the process of writing his poetry, Taylor would have considered as largely irrelevant the modern charges against him of bungling ingenuity, lapses of taste, and awkward performance. It was a perfect preparation that he was after, not a perfect poem. The writing of poems no doubt helped Taylor get to that point of self-realization desired, and after that objective had been achieved, they were no longer needed. There would have been no reason whatever to publish them. They were useful as devices, as part of the process, of preparing to preach upon, and partake the sacrament of, the Lord's Supper.

For that reason, a dominant subject in Taylor's poems is Taylor's poems. He is obsessed with writing about writing. He is the Puritan poet's poet, for the poet's worth becomes to him an important metaphor for talking about the business of salvation. Just as he must deprecate himself as a fallen creature of a fallen world, so he depreciates his poems as products. But in addition, just as he accepts the necessity of his existence, so he values the process of writing poetry. Most of the Meditations show Taylor involved dutifully in this process, cursing the results and yet relishing his spiritual activity and hoping for acceptance of his disposition.

A proper preparationist fixes his mind on an object in his meditation, and language was the most natural object for Taylor to use:

My tongue Wants Words to tell my thoughts, my Minde
Wants thoughts to Comprehend thy Worth, alas! (I. 34)

The work of adjusting sound to sense (for example, the agony of the despairing soul in the cramped rhythm of 'My Sin! my Sin, My God, these Cursed Dregs,|Green, Yellow, Blew streakt Poyson hellish, ranck' (I. 39)), the dramatizing with syntax ('And pick mee|headlong hells dread Whirle Poole in' [I. 39]), the structuring of one's illusory movement from despair to hope, and the concentrated involvement of intellect in the Ramist leaps from image to image (in 'The Reflexion', the smells of the food at a banquet become the smell of a rose, the rose suggests a garden of mud, the mud suggests the fallen condition of man, the rose blooms in the mud when there is sunlight, and the light of the Son comes through the church windows and falls on the sacrament, which is the banquet that shows how the Lord rose) — the work with such formal devices of verse-making helped to make Taylor aware of both his human dilemma and the shape of his own personality within that dilemma. The projection of himself into the many minute formal devices of a poem is ultimately a process of self-discovery. Sound, syntax, image, and structure are features of himself in action, and a poem is therefore his body, his mind, his life in all the static worthlessness of his fallen state and in all the active intensity of his spiritual desire.

The process appears to have given Taylor the opportunity to make intense these spiritual desires, so intense in fact that with sensuous language he was able to come as close as a Puritan dared come to the point of mystical union without crossing the line over into sensuality, pride, antinomianism. In the process of writing, Taylor discovers something of the divine; he discovers the divine *in* the process. I do not want to suggest by this that language was for Taylor therapeutic or theoleptic, but that it was a means of making meaning. In fact, language served both to exalt Taylor (dramatizing his desires) and to keep him properly earthbound (the limitations of human speech as a reminder of his human impediments, his fallen condition). Thus, making his hope articulate was both a reaching upward for meaning and a confession of meaninglessness.

Ultimately Taylor's poems do not *mean* very much. They instead show a man watching himself in his worthlessness desiring worth. The meaning of his life therefore lies not in his self nor in his desires (nor even in the object of his desires, God and salvation), *but in the act of desiring.* If he can continually convince himself of the ability to act out his desires, then he can continually reassure himself that God, in His activating love of man, is drawing him to Him. The meditation on one's worthlessness thereby becomes in Taylor's poems the meditation on the process of God's love. In this way the masochistic process of Hookeresque meditation becomes a positive program of conviction of divine love — a moving through the dark self to the realization of light, of worth. This is a re-enactment in miniature of the human condition, giving a spatial condition (the Fall) a time-dimension (eternal salvation). In being self-destructive, the process of Puritan meditation, at least as Taylor performs it in his Meditations, is therefore life-giving. It is important to notice that when Taylor's writing stops, his faith also lags, and when his faith is weak, his writing stops. The process of one is the process of the other.

It comes down to this: because he was interested in the process of writing rather than in his writings themselves, Taylor's private poetry makes one more example of what John A. Kouwenhoven calls 'the national preoccupation with process'.[14] Kouwenhoven finds this fascination to be a central quality common to those artifacts that are peculiar to American culture. The American skyscraper, with its effect of transactive upward motion, arbitrary cut-off, and repeatable upward thrust; the American gridiron town plan, with its unfinished completeness, its infinitely repeatable units; jazz, with its freedom of innovation within a rhythmic pattern, its bounds-ignoring momentum, its unresolved harmony; the Constitution, as an infinitely extendable framework; Mark Twain's fiction, with its irreverence for proportion and symmetry, its river-like momentum, and its characters who are, as was Huck Finn, ready to 'light out' again; Whitman's *Leaves of Grass*, with its restless, sweeping movement on long lines, its imagery of the open road, its openness at the end; comic strips and soap operas, with their lack of ultimate climax, their emphasis on the continued facing of problems without resolution; assembly-line production, with its timed operations, repetitive work, intermediacy, unfinishedness; chewing gum, with its non-consumability, its value for action but valuelessness as commodity — all such things unique to American culture have, when judged aesthetically, the central quality of *process*. To Kouwenhoven, 'America is process'. This quality involves mobility, ever-changing unity, mutability, development, and other facets which militate against the idea of man's (and society's) permanence and perfection and pitches him instead into a condition where change, progress, impermanence, and unfulfilled desire have almost moral value.

Indigenous too to Taylor's aesthetics is this uniquely 'American' principle of process. He has a rigid pattern, a cage or skeleton, within which he works (for the most part, the decasyllabic line, the six-line stanza, the fear-hope-desire pattern or the certainty-despair pattern for a structure, and these repeated over and over again as a process of consecutive occurrences without climax, without conclusion, without concern for time, without finish, without resolution), but he finds a way of moving, of being, within the frame. Through imaginative use of language, he has freedom within fate, freedom of movement within the determined framework of covenant theology. This re-dramatizing of his search for signs of salvation suggests vitality within unity, movement in conflict with stasis, desire *versus* the human condition. And to do this in preparation of oneself for finding an acceptable place in the pattern of the sacrament of the Lord's Supper suggests how poetry served Taylor as illusion: as he wrote he was imagining himself undergoing change in a predetermined universe.

It may be a temptation to think that Taylor's purpose was to try to produce poems that would be so finely wrought, so carefully formed, so fully representative of his mind and spirit that they might serve as signs to Taylor of his election, proving over and over again to himself, like a Puritan merchant realizing proof of his election through his business success, how success with poetic devices is a sign of his justification. But this view must be modified by Taylor's rejection of the products of his pen and the joy he takes in the process alone.

To think of Taylor as conceiving of his poems as great poetry (an assumption that debunkers of Taylor begin with) is the same as saying he lacked critical ability or aesthetic sensitivity or knowledge of poetry. He knew how bad his poems were, just as he knew how insufficient he himself was. But to think of Taylor as thinking primarily of the value of the process he was going through each time he wrote a Meditation is to admit significance in him (to be sure, a different kind of significance) as a poet.

In this light, one begins to see purpose even in the 'flaws' of his poetry—purpose in his choice of old-fashioned baroque for his metaphors; purpose in his annoying insistence on anaphora, anacoluthon, ploce, polyptoton, and other disruptive medieval rhetorical devices;

purpose in his corny borrowings from Ramist logic, biblical typology and the poetry of Herbert and Quarles; purpose in the erratic mechanics of his punctuation, rhymes, syntax; even purpose in his boring repetitiveness, his awkward unevenness, his outmoded fervor, his banality and bathos. They all must have appeared to Taylor effective devices for moving himself to that depth of soul that he desired, and therefore artistically justified, even aesthetically functional.[15] Because he was writing for himself alone and not for others, Taylor was free to write of his soul and his God in the language he wanted. How these devices look and sound to us is not as important as how they moved Taylor

In these ways, Taylor is the examplary private poet. That he should so greatly enjoy the process of meditating by means of the language of poetry is evidence of its centrality to his aesthetics. And being central, it works to include him centrally in American culture as, I feel, no other feature of his thought or style does. Ironically though, his humble love of the poetic process as he knew it almost lost his writings for us. How many other poets were there in early New England who, in being American in the same way, are, as Taylor once was, lost, neglected, undiscovered?

Whether Taylor intended his poetry to provide an example for others to follow we may never know. But by seeing how the process of writing was important to Taylor where the products of his pen were not, I think it is possible to justify his injunction against publication and at the same time make him relevant to the American tradition in literature.

9
Essays to do good for the glory of God: Cotton Mather's *Bonifacius*

DAVID LEVIN

Bonifacius – usually known by its running title, *Essays to Do Good* – has always had a better reputation than the author who published it anonymously in 1710. It is Cotton Mather's historical fate to be considered largely as a transitional figure whose prodigious but narrow mind stretched inadequately between the zealous founding of the Bible Commonwealth and the enlightened struggle for the Republic. His efforts to retain the old Puritan values along with the old Puritan power have tended to diminish him in contrast to the giants who had first established that power in Boston. His advanced ideas on medicine, botany, education, philanthropy, and family discipline look like minor departures from reactionary principles when they are set beside the beliefs of eighteenth-century secular thinkers.

The habit of viewing Mather in the shadow of his potent ancestors began with his parents, who named him for his maternal grandfather, John Cotton, and it continued to affect his life until, in his sixtieth year, he wrote the life of his distinguished father, Increase Mather. When Cotton Mather was an eleven-year-old freshman at Harvard in 1674, his father became embroiled with other members of the Board of Overseers in a public battle that nearly destroyed the college. When the boy became at fifteen the youngest Harvard graduate, the president reminded him publicly of his duty to emulate not only his father but Richard Mather and John Cotton, his two famous grandfathers. Cotton Mather eventually devoted his entire life as a pastor to the very congregation that his father served as teacher. For forty years he worked closely with his father in various political controversies and social crises, from the loss of the colony's original charter, the rebellion against Sir Edmund Andros, the acceptance of a new charter, and the witchcraft trials, through debates about church government and membership and control of Harvard and Yale early in the new century. As a prolific historian, moreover, he wrote the lives of the first governors, the first ministers, the first Harvard presidents — the monumental church-history of New England, *Magnalia Christi Americana*.

Thus Mather unhappily observed the dissolution of the old theocracy even while he cheerfully did his best to extend pious influence in the community through his retrospective writings and his schemes for social action. At the same time, he labored enthusiastically in behalf of the new science. He sent reports of American phenomena to the Royal Society in London, which elected him a Fellow. He collected and published in New England the discoveries of European scientists. He persuaded a medical doctor to try inoculation during a smallpox epidemic in Boston. By the time he died in 1728, it was clear that the millennium he had so confidently predicted thirty years earlier was not yet to be expected. New England would have to settle instead for the imperfect Enlightenment.

For three centuries both Cotton Mather and his works have been discussed almost exclusively in this context of change. The church-history, we say, looks backward to Mather's grandfathers; *The Christian Philosopher* and *Bonifacius* look forward to Benjamin Franklin. Indeed, it was Franklin himself who first stressed the value of *Essays to Do Good* as a transitional document. In his very first published work Franklin paid Mather the tribute of parody by adopting the pseudonym of Mrs Silence Dogood (counting on his Bostonian readers to know that the author of *Essays to Do Good* was rarely silent). Half a century later[1] Franklin told Samuel Mather that *Bonifacius* had turned his own youthful thoughts to methods of doing good, and again in his autobiography he acknowledged *Bonifacius* along with the works of Daniel Defoe and John Bunyan as one of the most valuable influences on his early thought. The relationship would be evident even if Franklin had not written so explicitly. Commentators have repeatedly cited it ever since George Burder quoted Franklin's letter to Samuel Mather in an English edition of *Essays to Do Good* (London, 1807).

Insistence on such historical relationships has taught us much about the changes from pious Puritanism to moralism, from striving in the world for the glory of God to striving for enlightened self-interest. But this perspective has also done considerable harm. Students of historical change have often blurred our understanding of Franklin's and Mather's individual minds and books. The intense light focused on one set of eighteenth-century statements has left others in the darkness. Mather, especially, has been projected so rigidly against what he looked back to, or what he anticipated, that it is unusually difficult to discover what he was.

The modern reader of *Bonifacius* must be prepared to recognize two influential versions of this distortion. The first concerns Puritan piety; the second, Puritan commercial ethics and benevolence.

Perry Miller's magnificent volumes on *The New England Mind* argue that the earliest New England Puritans temporarily united pious faith and reasoned, vigorous action under a grand modification of Abraham's Covenant. The second volume dramatizes the inevitable separation of faith from thought and the inevitable subordination of faith as the Covenant dissolves under the pressure of seventeenth-century events in Europe and America. Cotton Mather is the pivotal figure in Miller's narrative of historical change. At first he preaches jeremiads, long sermons condemning the sins of the land. But as he and other clergymen lose political power in the early decades of the eighteenth century, Mather resorts to new devices, both social and psychological. Now he abandons the jeremiad. Renouncing hope of political power, he tries instead to influence events by publishing 'pietist' instructions for communal life, including proposals for voluntary associations to reform morals. Privately, moreover, he takes emotional refuge from the religious decline of New England by retreating often to his study; there, according to Miller, Mather tries to 'stimulate' his overwrought nervous system to a factitious piety that seeks explicit, divine assurances and demands prostrate, methodical prayer and fasting. In this analysis his correspondence with such foreign reformers as Auguste Francke of Halle is an accidental consequence of Mather's compulsive scribbling and of his response to New England's needs and his own. It has nothing to do with international pietist movements of the time. Mather, indeed, is astonished to find himself in the vanguard, an agent of the new pietism.

Miller presents *Bonifacius* as a milestone on the downward road from John Winthrop to Dickens' caricature of nineteenth-century utilitarianism, Thomas Gradgrind, and he contends that Cotton Mather was further from Winthrop than from Gradgrind. *Bonifacius*, he concedes, is 'not quite a surrender of piety to business', but he declares that Mather found in *Bonifacius* 'a new form of marketing religion'. He describes Mather's appeal to the inherent reward of doing good as a sentimental invitation to luxuriate in the 'delicious swooning joy of the thing itself'. He sees Mather's voluntary associations not as part of an effort to liberate New Englanders but as an attempt to reassert clerical control, and he associates Mather with those service clubs (from the Y.M.C.A. to the Rotary) that work for conformity of various kinds in modern America.[2]

The chief trouble with this interpretation is that it is almost completely subservient to a generalization about the decline in piety. It cannot admit the possibility that Cotton Mather was as pious as his ancestors; it insists on explaining his piety as a neurotic, belated reaction to historical events that occurred when he was past thirty.

The consequent distortion of *Bonifacius* begins at the beginning, with Mather's title. Because of our modern interest in placing Mather on the line from Puritanism to utilitarianism, scholars have customarily shortened the original title of *Bonifacius* in a way that changes its significance. *Bonifacius*, they have called it; *an Essay upon the Good that is to be Devised and Designed by Those who Desire . . . to Do Good While they Live.* This seems in any case a strangely illogical title – as if there were others, *besides* those who desire to do good, who should devise and design good! The important distortion, however, is the change in Mather's purpose. He did not really write for those who desire to do good but for those who desire 'to Answer the Great End of Life', and who *therefore* desire to do good while they live.

The great end of life, for Cotton Mather as for John Winthrop before him and Jonathan Edwards after, was not to do good but to glorify God. Mather had made this plain from the beginning of his career as a preacher, and at the height of his political power. Just after he had served as one of the chief conspirators to overthrow the tyrant Sir Edmund Andros in 1689, he published a volume of sermons at the request of his wealthy father-in-law, John Phillips, who on recovering from a serious illness had offered to subsidize the publication of four sermons on 'Practical Godliness'. None of these sermons is a jeremiad. All relate devotional piety to doing good: ✗

The chief end of man is to *glorify* God . . . To praise God is to *render* and *procure* a due acknowledgment of His excellence . . . This, this *praise* of the LORD is the *end* of our *life* in the world.

This is the *end* of our *being*. We are told that *we have our* being *in God*. Of all things whatever this is then most reasonable, *that we should have our* being *for* God; and our being *for* Him, is not expressed without our praising of Him . . . Every man should say: 'I *live* that God who is worthy to be *praised*, may have the *praises* of my obedience to Him.'

The saints in Heaven, Mather says in the same sermon, have their appropriate way of praising God, by 'shouting Hallelujah, Hallelujah, before the Throne'; but men living on earth have special, additional ways of praising Him here: 'by the discharge of many *relations*, which the dead saints are strangers unto. We may *now* praise God as *parents*, as *masters*, as *officers* in the Church or Common-wealth. All those capacities shall *die* with us.'[3]

In these sermons there is no tension between doing good and praising God. Doing good is one way of praising Him. Of course, we can find sentences that support the emphasis on practical striving in the world: 'To *serve God* was the very errand which we were brought into the wilderness upon'; 'the service of God is His worship'; 'there are two things incumbent upon us, to do good and to get good'. But the good we are to get is the capacity to enjoy God. Lifting such statements out of their pious context is a serious error. Although it may indicate those subtle changes of emphasis that eventually prevailed in American life when the idea of God's sovereignty had been weakened, it can misrepresent not only individual books and the condition of individual minds, but at last the very history that such abstractions were meant to serve.

As early as 1689, then, Cotton Mather had set forth the principle on which he would organize *Bonifacius* twenty years later.[4] He would begin with the reformation of the self and would then move outward into the community, suggesting methods of service in the various 'relations' of life. In the intervening years he often followed this procedure in composing biographies. Thus his life of John Eliot opens outward from personal piety to family government to preaching in the church, and finally to Eliot's evangelism among the Indians.

The organization communicates the central purpose: to praise God in every act of life. By 1688 Mather had adopted the 'delightful and surprising way of thinking' that he attributed to his deceased younger brother Nathanael. His language suggests that he was perhaps as close to Jonathan Edwards and to Emerson, Thoreau, and Whitman as he was to Thomas Gradgrind: Nathanael Mather, Cotton Mather wrote, 'considered that the whole *Creation* was full of God; and that there was not a leaf of *grass* in the field, which might not make an observer to be sensible of the Lord. He apprehended that the *idle minutes* of our lives were many more than a short liver should allow: that the very filings of *gold*, and of time, were exceeding precious; and, that there were little *fragments of hours* intervening between our more stated businesses, wherein our *thoughts* of God might be no less pleasant than frequent with us.'[5] Just as Henry Thoreau would later tell New England's time-passing knitters that it is impossible to kill time without injuring eternity, Mather warned busy Bostonians that God would 'find an *eternity* to *damn* the man that cannot find a *time* to *pray*'.[6]

The terms in which Mather implored Christians to 'redeem time' show that his pietism was in full vigor in 1682, before he was twenty and before the original charter of Massachusetts Bay had been revoked. He was taking John Winthrop's original message to the community but with a new emphasis on method, on the deliberate saturation of one's life in pious action, and especially on ingenuity. 'Thus be *zealous of good works, work for God*', he said in 1689. 'Let even your *eating*, your *trading*, your *visiting*, be done as a *service* for the Lord, and let your *time*, your *strength*, your *estates*, all the *powers* of your spirits and all the *members* of your bodies be ingeniously laid out in that *service*. Often ask your own souls, *What is there that I may do for God?* Even court, and hunt advantages to be serviceable.'[7]

The origins of Mather's interest in such hunting lie deep in seventeenth-century Protestant pastoral work. To understand his career we must remember that Cotton Mather was the *pastor* in the Boston church which his father served as teacher, and that he therefore had a special duty to attend to the people's daily needs. From the beginning of his professional life, he had a remarkable opportunity to apply his great energy over the whole range of Bostonian life. His social action began with secluded meditations in which, with the occasional aid of specific assurances from an angel, he prayed for divine support of afflicted parishioners and of Massachusetts battles against the Devil and the French; it extended to the writing of histories and biographies, to joining the leadership of a revolution, to advising governors, addressing the legislature, offering medical advice, curing the bewitched child of a parishioner, making pastoral visits, catechizing children, administering church discipline to offending members of the congregation, and writing books to teach the most ordinary people methods of becoming Christians and then practicing Christianity in their daily lives.

For some of this work a number of English writers had provided valuable guides. Cotton Mather and his brother Nathanael were especially fond of Joseph Hall's *Occasional Meditations* (3rd edition,

1633), William Waller's *Divine Meditations* (1680), Henry Scudder's *The Christian's Daily Walk* (1628). Cotton Mather also borrowed from Richard Baxter's immense folio *Christian Directory* (1673) and *How to Do Good to Many; or, the Public Good is the Christian's Life* (1682).

All these books have in common with Mather's efforts a determination to bring the common into touch with the divine. Hall's meditations, which both Nathanael and Cotton Mather emulated, drew religious lessons from such conventional earthly experiences as 'the sight of a grave digged up', 'gnats in the sun', 'the sight of a drunken man', 'bees fighting', 'the sight of a piece of money under water', 'a defamation dispersed'. Ready to let every leaf of grass make him sensible of the Lord, Nathanael Mather notes that a kettle of water taken from the fire in a cold New England room is quickly 'seized with lukewarmness'. So, he concludes, are Christians after they have been warmed by some awareness of God's glory. When John Winthrop interprets the killing of a snake during a synod meeting or Nathanael Mather jumps from his 'bed of security', braving the cold to put on 'Christ's garments' and walk to the fire, the lesson in this literary form is always made explicit, and the value of the meditation depends on the aptness of explicit parallels. This is a principle Benjamin Franklin kept in mind when he perfected a quite different kind of anecdote a century later in his autobiography.

In a book like *Bonifacius* the method is reversed. The pastor, accustomed to studying minor events for evidence of God's will, now uses his ingenuity to find explicit ways in which a Christian can express the benevolence with which grace has endowed him. Christians need to be told *how* to do good, especially when they live outside the traditional authority of a hierarchical church and in a swiftly changing society. Yet the movement should not be seen simply as a weakening of old Calvinist reliance on faith and predestination. It seems instead a natural extension of the kind of impulse that led Puritans to establish the New England colonies in the first place. Once the community of saints has established its right to exist, it must set about expanding God's work in the world. 'Though God set up lights so small as will serve but for one room, and though we must begin at home, we must far more esteem and desire the good of multitudes', Baxter said, and we must set 'no bounds to our endeavors, but what God and disability set'. *Bonifacius* echoes: the magistrate is 'the *Minister of God for good*. His *empty name* will produce a *cruel crime*, if he don't set himself to do good, as far as ever he can extend his influences.' Americans in the second half of the twentieth century have seen this kind of rhetoric applied to vast proposals for a Great Society at home and for aid to multitudes in Asia.

For Cotton Mather, moreover, the millennium was not a metaphor for secular achievement. It was literally imminent. He wrote quite seriously, on the one hand, about exactly how the righteous in America might be spared from the fires sweeping the earth before the establishment of the Kingdom here.[8] And he did his best, in the year he wrote *Bonifacius*, to see that Bostonians accepted 'the true doctrine of the Chiliad' so that, by eliminating all 'base dealing' — all 'dirty ways of dishonesty' — from the market place, they might make their street as golden as the one promised in the Book of Revelations from which he had taken his text. He preached this sermon to the General Assembly of the colony, before whom he 'proclaimed unto all the world' that 'ill-dealings are not at all countenanced; no, they are vehemently disallowed, by the religion of NEW-ENGLAND'. The gold he referred to was not profit but precept: 'The street of the city is pure gold' meant to him that 'the business of the CITY, shall be managed by the *Golden* Rule. The things that use to be done in the market-place, shall be done without *corruption*.'[9]

It is in this context that we must consider the second historical distortion of Mather's ideas. Just as emphasis on the decline of piety may overlook his concentration on divine glory, so efforts to trace the Protestant Ethic can ignore not only the divine object of human striving but also his thorough conviction of community. A. Whitney Griswold, in an important essay published more than thirty years ago,[10] cited impressive evidence to show that Mather stressed the Christian's obligations to work diligently in his calling; Mather repeated the biblical promise (so effective with Benjamin Franklin) that the young man who was diligent would stand before kings, and he urged the young man who wished to rise *by* his business to rise *to* his business. But although Griswold scrupulously links this personal calling with the general vocation of a Christian, his interest in linking Mather's advice to the 'rugged individualism' of a later time ignores the perfectly explicit condemnation of all sharp dealing and dishonesty in financial affairs. Mather insisted that New England's professions of extraordinary religion would be worthless if its 'dealing' should be 'defective in honesty ... Let a man be never such a professor and pretender of *religion*, if he be not a *fair-dealer*, THAT MAN'S

RELIGION IS VAIN. A noise about *faith and repentance*, among them that forget MORAL HONESTY, 'tis but an empty noise. The men are utter strangers to *faith* and *repentance* . . . Woe, woe, woe, to you professors, and HYPOCRITES, who can make a show of this and that piety, and *purity*; but can *cheat*, and *cozen*, and *oppress*, and wrong other people in your dealing with them!'[11]

Far from supporting rugged individualism, Mather declared that the golden rule should have its application to business through the scriptural command of Paul (I Corinthians 10: 24): '*Let no man seek his own, but every man another's wealth.*' Lying was to be forbidden, all dealings were to be 'transparent glass', and neither the foolish nor the poor were to be exploited: 'For men to *overreach* others, because they find them *ignorant*, or screw grievously upon them, only because they are poor and low, and in great necessities; to keep up the *necessaries* of human life (I say the necessaries, which I always distinguish from the *superfluities*) at an immoderate price, merely because other people want them, when we can easily spare them; *'tis an abomination!*' For necessities, at least, the law of supply and demand was not supreme.[12]

Thus, although Mather confessed that he knew neither the niceties nor the mysteries of the market place, he did not rest content with prescribing the golden rule. Stating that imperative even in its most positive form[13] would hardly forbid ruthless competition if the individual merchant should be willing to have his neighbor compete just as fiercely as himself. Mather did not supply an ethic fit for the mysteries and niceties, but he did condemn many commercial 'abominations', from the slave trade ('one of the worst kinds of thievery in the world') to the adulteration or misrepresentation of a large number of specified products.[14]

It was a theological principle that gave Mather's sense of community its importance in practical affairs, in his day as well as through the later teachings of Franklin. To consider the principle we must enter that dizzy world of circular argument and begged questions in which Puritans struggled to distinguish faith from works without becoming either antinomians or (to use a word from *Bonifacius*) meritmongers.

In that world a Christian must recognize a central paradox: his assurance of salvation depends on his renouncing all claims to salvation that place any confidence or value in himself. He must become convinced that he does not deserve salvation and that he cannot earn it. If convinced of his inadequacy but unable to attain a conviction of faith, he may fall into the sin of despair, a beginning of hell on earth. If he does find a conviction of Christ's power and willingness to redeem him, he must test the conviction by regularly examining his attitude and his conduct. Good works cannot save him – indeed, no works are truly good unless they proceed from a justifying faith – but the consequence of true faith is a benevolence that impels the converted sinner to praise God through obedient service. *Bonifacius* declares, therefore, that 'a workless faith is a worthless faith'.

Historians gain some value from turning this process around (as some busy, conscientious sinners must have done) to mean not only that worklessness proved worthlessness but also that works proved worth. Often, however, the reversal costs too much, for it blocks appreciation of the great power in one of the chief articles of American faith. The great power comes from the conviction that what is right, works. Both Mather and Franklin worked to propagate this conviction, and both appealed to the reader's self-interest, but neither man ever contended that whatever works is right. Mather and other Puritans actually believed that prosperity could be as threatening a providential judgment as calamity. Merciful dispensations, Mather said, 'are so many trials whether we will hear God speaking in our prosperity; or whether when we wax fat we will kick against the Lord'.

For many people, at least, the drama of guilt, self-doubt, and self-accusation was a terrible reality, and so, too, was the kind of faith that Mather preached. (Even Franklin recognized it during the Great Awakening.) Once that reality stands at the center of our attention, we need not be religious to understand Mather's declaration that good works are a part of, as well as prescribed steps along the way to, 'the great salvation'. The penitent sinner who wanted to join the church might be crushed (in Edward Taylor's phrase) between desire and fear – between a longing to profess his conversion and fear that it is delusory. Having experienced this kind of paralysis, the conscientious sinner might well be grateful for rescue, even in this world, from the psychological self-torture of futility. The ability to act might well be the worldly consequence of such faith.

Not only the motive but the social consequence, too, is a principle or a power rather than a quantitative fact. Just as Mather and Franklin, despite their obvious differences, worked outward from the idea of virtue, gratitude, duty, and wisdom to acts of service, so they conceived of the good done to others as a beginning rather than as charity in the limited sense of alms. *Bonifacius* cites the primitive church's doctrine that the sin of a Christian's neighbor is a sin by the Christian himself. As Richard Baxter ordered Christians to succor poor men's bodies in order to make it possible to save their souls,[15] Mather argues that the American Indians must be 'civilized' so that they can be 'Christianized'. He praises the English philanthropist Thomas Gouge for finding work for the poor, and he commands his own readers to 'find 'em work, set 'em to work, keep 'em to work'. Benjamin Franklin says it is hard for an empty sack to stand upright.

In these years both Old and New England had need of the ingenuity to which Mather appealed. The vigorous new capitalist organizations in 'this projecting age' gave such different authors as Richard Baxter, Daniel Defoe, Jonathan Swift, Cotton Mather, and (by the early 1720s) Benjamin Franklin examples of mutual cooperation that might be used for the public good. Baxter's *Christian Directory* directed Christians 'How to Improve all Helps and Means' toward a Christian life in the world. Defoe's *Essay on Projects* (1697) proposed Friendly Societies for several kinds of life and medical insurance; Swift's ironic *A Project for the Advancement of Religion and the Reformation of Manners* (1709) suggested a scheme for institutionalizing virtue through the Queen's power of preferment and the Court's leadership of fashion.

In England the Societies for the Reformation of Manners had already come under suspicion as petty meddlers by the time Swift published this proposal, but the social need for such organizations seems more interesting than the modern temptation to think of their motives as simply repressive. Systematic welfare programs were of course unknown. Widespread drunkenness seems to have been a relatively new problem, and it existed in a context that may now be difficult to imagine. Wine was often poisonously adulterated; alcoholic and other debtors and petty criminals were locked up indiscriminately in prisons in which conditions were far more abominable than the worst kind of do-gooding. Epidemics in these foul places sometimes made the punishment for civil offenses as lethal as the capital penalty officially attached to so many crimes. There was no effectively organized, properly trained, or trustworthy police force to prevent the growing number of violent crimes on city streets, which were generally unlighted. Private citizens armed to defend themselves. Two years after *Bonifacius* was published, a group of drunken young men who called themselves Mohocks terrorized London with atrocious beatings and mutilations that seemed the more terrible because they were apparently unmotivated.

I do not mean to contend that life in Queen Anne's London was a nightmare. The point is that specific needs in the society, needs unmet by government or other established organizations, encouraged the new techniques for organized benevolence and that in the absence of better preventive methods religious writers naturally encouraged Christians to set an individual example. Nor should we forget, even when considering the restrictive nature of some actions, the disastrous consequences of indiscretions that may seem minor today. Under the prevailing Canon Law, for example, it was easy to find oneself entrapped in a virtually indissoluble marriage, and many Londoners — sailors and young gentlemen alike — suffered from a lucrative conspiracy of clergyman, landlord, prostitute, and lawyer. In such circumstances advice against drinking, which neither Cotton nor Increase Mather ever opposed in its moderate form, and advice against falling into debt need not be officious. Meddlesomely repressive though they might become, societies like Mather's Young Men's Associations, Count Zinzendorf's Slaves of Virtue, and Benjamin Franklin's projected Society of the Free and Easy grew out of a positive desire to free men for the practice of virtue in this world.

What we need to remember, then, is the firmness with which Mather's good-doing is tied to the praise of God, the certainty with which his exhortations to be diligent rely on traditional ethics. *Bonifacius* is addressed to Christians; Mather invites unbelievers to close the book until, by repentance, they begin to live. He is not marketing religion but bringing religion into the market.

Besides a few specific ideas, which deserve separate attention, the key value of *Bonifacius* lies in the resourceful application of methodical ingenuity to pious affairs. Christians, Mather says, should employ their wits for God's service. As Thoreau will later complain that farmers speculate in herds of cattle in order to acquire shoestrings, Mather charges New Englanders with wasting grand capacities on trivial ends. He exhorts them to apply to good works the same ingenuity noted in their business affairs, to equal the degree of contrivance (without the deception) employed by the Devil and the wicked in pursuit of evil ends.

Bonifacius thus appeals simultaneously to one of the most powerful traits in the New England character and to one of the strongest intellectual forces of the eighteenth century. Mather invokes for his divine purpose the desire to invent new means, to contrive, devise, experiment. Nor does he content himself with precepts. He repeatedly sets the example, for the impulse has come from one of the most powerful sources of his own conduct.

Scholarship has rarely found a less appropriate figure than the cliché that says Cotton Mather's knowledge was undigested. Ever since the early 1680s Mather had been scribbling in private as well as for publication, and he worked hard to reduce his experience and his knowledge to usable form. In his *Quotidiana*, copybooks in which he recorded scraps of quotations, scientific curiosities, and historical anecdotes, he laboriously compiled indexes so that he would be able to call on the information in his sermons and other works. In his conversation, moreover, he was remarkably quick to apply his diverse knowledge with an ingenuity that was sometimes startling. His diary, 'Paterna',[16] and *Bonifacius* demonstrate that this quality was more than a natural aptitude. He hunted advantages for pious service in conversation, in idle moments of dinner parties, in the observance of various people as he walked the streets. And of course he wrote down the suggestions, which ranged from prayers to be said on seeing a beautiful woman, and resolutions to drop the name of a poor parishioner when visiting a rich one, to planning the conversation at his family's meals so that the children would be instructed.

It is easy to treat this carefully nurtured habit as comically tasteless by selecting one detail, such as Mather's resolution to meditate while urinating. Even when we supply the context for this example and notice that Mather feared the excruciating pain of kidney stones, which had tortured his grandfather, many of us will find it difficult to accept his resolution to offer up thanks, while urinating, for the grace that has spared him from his grandfather's affliction. Such a meditation can be defended, too, but the criticism misses the point. What matters is the total concentration on developing the discipline of pious resourcefulness. For every ludicrous example there is a passage that seems successful. Benjamin Franklin reports that when he accidentally hit his head on a beam in Mather's house, Mather told him to stoop always as he walked through life, so that he would save himself many a hard thump. Mather resolves in 'Paterna' never to offer his children play as a reward for hard work, lest they come to consider diversion better than diligence. Instead he contrives to punish them by refusing to teach them something, and he resolves to reward them by teaching them 'some curious thing'.

Nor was there any hesitation to work out a much more elaborate meditation relating to recent scientific theories. A long paragraph from 'Paterna' will illustrate the kind of personal resolution that led Mather to write his *Christian Philosopher*. Here he comes very close to using eighteenth-century science in precisely the way that ennobles the works of Jonathan Edwards:

I am continually entertained with *weighty body*, or *matter* tending to the *center of gravity*; or attracted by matter. I feel it in my own. The *cause* of this *tendency*, 'tis the glorious GOD! *Great GOD, Thou givest this matter such a tendency; Thou keepest it in its operation!* There is no other cause for *gravity*, but the *will* and *work* of the glorious GOD. I am now effectually convinced of that ancient confession, and must effectuously make it, 'He is not far from every one of us.' When I see a thing moving or settling that way which its *heavy nature* carries it, I may very justly think, and I would often form the thought, 'It is the glorious GOD who now carries this matter such a way.' When *matter* goes *downward*, my spirit shall therefore mount *upward*, in acknowledgment of the GOD who orders it. I will no longer complain, 'Behold, I go forward, but He is not there; and backward, but I cannot perceive Him: on the left hand, where He does work, but I cannot behold Him: He hideth Himself on the right hand, that I cannot see Him.' No, I am now taught where to meet with Him; even at every turn. *He knows the way that I take*; I cannot stir forward or backward, but I *perceive* Him in the *weight* of every *matter*. *My way* shall be to improve this as a *weighty argument* for the being of a GOD. I will argue from it, 'Behold, there is a GOD, whom I ought forever to love and serve and glorify.' Yea, and if I am tempted unto the doing of any wicked thing, I may reflect, that it cannot be done without some *action*, wherein *the power of matter* operates. But then I may carry on the reflection: 'How near, how near am I to the glorious GOD, whose commands I am going to violate! Matter keeps His laws; but, O my soul, wilt thou break His laws? How shall I do this wickedness and therein deny the GOD, who not only is above, but also is exerting His power in the very matter upon which I make my criminal misapplications!'[17]

The very repetitiousness of Mather's inexhaustible pen demonstrates the persistence of his search for advantages to do good methodically, ingeniously. Besides recording his resolutions, drawing up proposals, preparing indexes, he completely revised his annual diaries so that they might be useful to other readers. Then he copied the relevant portions of these revised versions into 'Paterna', for his son, and he copied relevant incidents, some of them extensive, into *Bonifacius*, making appropriate revisions. At his death he left two grand unpublished books, 'The Angel of Bethesda' and '*Biblia Americana*', which form part of this same resolute plan. 'The Angel of Bethesda' is a collection of medical advice and cures incorporating the kind of spiritual usefulness proposed' in *Bonifacius*, and '*Biblia Americana*' condenses, with Mather's own contributions, centuries of commentary on the Bible.

The energy that performed such prodigies undoubtedly drew some strength from vanity as well as from piety. Although *Bonifacius* was published anonymously, Mather's effort to seem expert in varied professional subjects will seem amusingly pretentious to modern readers, especially when he alludes to legal authors. Yet the conscious purpose of such allusions is to win the respect of those to whom the author offers moral advice useful in their professions, and to exemplify the kind of ingenuity he has been prescribing. The author of *Bonifacius* has taken the trouble to inform himself of at least a few good books and a few specific means for lawyers to do good. In medicine, Mather had no less training and was better read than many practicing physicians.

The pastor's concern with social health leads Mather to express in *Bonifacius* a number of ideas that would be interesting to modern readers even outside the context I have tried to establish. He declares that none but a good man really lives, and that one becomes more alive as one acts for good. Concern for the soul and interest in method led him to encourage rewards rather than punishment in educating children. He opposes beating except for the most serious offenses. He condemns tyrannical schoolmasters as a curse. He advises ministers to preach on subjects of particular use to their congregations and to ask the people to suggest topics for sermons. He favors the practical education of girls. He advises physicians to treat the poor without charge and to attend not only to the patient's soul but also to the 'anxiety' that may be causing his illness. He tells lawyers never to appear in a dirty cause, always to eschew sharp tricks, and to defend the principle of restitution. He condemns that usury which charges interest for money that the debtor never gets to use. He tells the rich to use their money for good while they live, rather than leave large estates.

All these proposals issue from the same pious concern that asks landlords to oblige their tenants to pray, pious societies to look out for their neighbors' sins, schoolmasters to teach Duport's verses on Job instead of Homer. What we must seek if we wish to know Mather is the man who could believe in both these kinds of proposals at once. For him witches, devils, angels, remarkable interventions of Providence, and the certainty of eternal judgment were as real as gravity. For his mind there was no contradiction between working for social justice and spending two or perhaps three days a week in secret fasts; no conflict between hailing Copernicus and Newton and preaching the imminence of the millennium, now that the seven last plagues of the Vial are about to be poured out on the Papal Empire; no conflict between studying the Talmud and preaching the Covenant of Grace.

Evaluation of Mather's literary achievement ought to profit from the same kind of attention to his prose style, which has too often been dismissed as fervid and pedantic. The remarkable quantity of his work, the cleanness of his manuscripts, and the testimony of his son all indicate that he wrote very rapidly, but the charge that his writing is fervid seems superficial. Although a small portion of his work fits the description, its importance has been exaggerated by the typographical devices used in his books and by the dubious belief that he was 'neurotic' and therefore unable to control his rhetoric.

The prevalence of learned allusions and foreign quotations has also been exaggerated, partly because Mather defended these useful ornaments and partly because readers of his history of New England must traverse an unusually thick jungle of classical fact and lore, with a name dropping from every tree, before they can escape from his self-conscious introduction into the history itself. All this may be of little comfort to readers of *Bonifacius*, who will find that Mather studded some pages with what he liked to consider jewels of Latin and Greek. Those who are not completely antagonized may take some comfort in noting how aptly many of these come forth from the index of Mather's *Quotidiana* or the electronic computer of his extraordinary mind. Repeatedly, the quotation is apt, and Mather's comment repeatedly makes it so.

Notice, too, how much of the prose in *Bonifacius* is plain, forceful, precise. Mather's speed makes his paragraphs repetitious, and it is difficult for us to avoid overemphasizing his italics, but I am convinced that much of Mather's writing is plainer than any by Thomas Hooker or John Cotton. Even in *Bonifacius* this passage on brutal schoolmasters seems as representative as the more elaborate classical quotations:

Ajax Flagellifer may be read at the school. He is not fit for to be the master of it. Let it not be said of the scholars, 'They are brought up *in the school of Tyrannus.' Pliny* says that *bears* are the fatter for beating. Fitter to have the conduct of *bears* than of ingenuous *boys*, are the masters, that can't give a *bit* of learning, but they must give a *knock* with it. Send 'em to be tutors of the famous *Lithuanian* school, at *Samourgan.* The harsh, fierce, *Orbilian* way of treating the children, too commonly used in the *school*, is a dreadful *curse* of God upon our miserable offspring, who are *born children of wrath.* It is boasted now and then of a *schoolmaster*, that such and such a *brave man* had his education under him. There is nothing said, how many that might have been *brave men*, have been destroyed by him; how many *brave wits*, have been dispirited, confounded, murdered, by his *barbarous* way of managing them.

Bonifacius is an important historical document because it brings to bear on the world of affairs all the piety and ingenuity that New England Puritanism had been nourishing, despite theological and political troubles, for eighty years. Without wavering from the central conviction of Puritans that man exists to glorify God, Cotton Mather exhorts all Christians to hunt opportunities to do good in the world. It is from this perspective, rather than by focusing on practical rewards, that we can best understand Puritan influences on Benjamin Franklin, later reformers, and American benevolence in the twentieth century. We continue to say, with the author of *Bonifacius*, that the ways of honest men are simple and the ways of the wicked are subtle, but we seek to devise a similar ingenuity for doing good around the world. We may also find it especially interesting that Mather the American, unlike his English predecessor Richard Baxter, says not a word about the danger that our efforts to do good may lead to disaster.

Continuities

The art and instruction of Jonathan Edwards' *Personal Narrative*

DANIEL B. SHEA, Jr

Although the first editor of Jonathan Edwards' *Personal Narrative* described this spiritual autobiography as written for 'private Advantage', he also seems to have felt that Edwards had given him implicit permission to make the document serve a public purpose. The sometimes baffling resemblance between authentic and fraudulent spirituality was, said Samuel Hopkins, 'a point about which, above many other[s], the protestant world is in the dark, and needs instruction, as Mr. Edwards was more and more convinced, the longer he lived; and which he was wont frequently to observe in conversation'.[1] As Hopkins was aware, Edwards' essential act throughout a large body of his published work had been to set nature apart from supernature in the domain of religious experience. The act was no less central to the *Personal Narrative* than it was to other works in which Edwards promoted experimental religion and instructed readers on its glories and pitfalls.

In the controversy between himself and opposers of the Great Awakening, Edwards had put to good use his accounts of the gracious experience of Abigail Hutchinson, Phebe Bartlett, and his own wife, Sarah. But a narrative told in the first person, as Sarah's had been originally,[2] was immensely more valuable to his cause than even the best job of evangelistic reporting. Let the reporter be a 'true saint', said Edwards, still he can only judge 'outward manifestations and appearances', a method 'at best uncertain, and liable to deceit'.[3] No such objection could have been made against his *Account* of the life of David Brainerd, in which Edwards allowed the Indian missionary's diary to speak for itself. A reader's view of 'what passed in [Brainerd's] *own heart*' would thus be cleared of such obstacles as an impercipient narrator; yet the reader would be in the hands of a perfectly reliable guide. As a student, Brainerd may have been rash in remarking that one of his Yale tutors had 'no more grace than this chair', but Edwards could only praise the discretion he revealed when considering 'the various exercises of *his own mind*': 'He most accurately distinguished between real, solid piety, and enthusiasm; between those affections that are rational and scriptural — having their foundation in light and judgment — and those that are founded in whimsical conceits, strong impressions on the imagination, and vehement emotions of the animal spirits.'[4] In the *Personal Narrative* Edwards had performed exactly those functions for which in 1749 he was praising Brainerd. Both men gave their readers, as Edwards said of Brainerd, an 'opportunity to see a confirmation of the truth, efficacy, and amiableness of the religion taught, in the practice of the same persons who have most clearly and forcibly taught it'.[5]

Because Edwards could not have introduced his own autobiography in such glowing terms, Samuel Hopkins admiringly supplied the deficit in 1765. But set next to the cautious distinction-making of the narrative itself, his words were superfluous. Since the manuscript of the *Personal Narrative* is lost, we shall never know just how much care Edwards took in composing it. In fact, the text printed by Hopkins gives the appearance of hurried writing.[6] But if Edwards spent only a day with his spiritual autobiography, he had spent twenty years or more arriving at the criteria by which he judged his experience. It is possible, of course, that we read precision back into the *Personal Narrative* after watching Edwards at work in, say, the *Treatise Concerning Religious Affections*, but the distinction between autobiography and formal argument, especially for an eighteenth-century New England divine, should not be exaggerated. Edwards' narrative is not identical with his spiritual experience but represents a mature articulation of that experience, its form and language determined in varying degrees by the author's reading of sacred and secular writers, interviews with awakened sinners, and his concerns at the time of composition. The Edwards of the *Personal Narrative* bears more resemblance to the author of the *Religious Affections* than to the young student at Yale who entered the perplexing data of daily spiritual upheavals in his diary.[7]

Edwards set down his spiritual autobiography with more than 'private advantage' in mind, then, and he seems in fact to have been governed by the purposes that informed most of his work during the period of the Great Awakening. By narrative example he will teach what is false and what is true in religious experience, giving another form to the argument he carried on elsewhere; and he hopes to affect his readers by both the content and the presentation of his exemplary experience.

I

Something of what Edwards was trying to accomplish in the *Personal Narrative* emerges from a comparison with the *Diary*, which he kept regularly from the last year of his studies at Yale until his settlement in Northampton. The two are profitably read together, but not as if they formed a continuous and coherent piece of writing. A sense of their separate identities is necessary, not only because the *Diary* instructed Edwards alone, while the *Personal Narrative* extends and formalizes its instruction, but also because Edwards was bound to tell his story differently after twenty additional years of introspection and a good deal of pastoral experience. In 1723, for instance, he was greatly troubled by 'not having experienced conversion in those particular steps, wherein the people of New England, and anciently the Dissenters of Old England, used to experience it'.[8] Subsequent events, however, revealed a great variety in the Spirit's operations, so that in 1741 Edwards allowed that a given work might be from the Spirit even though it represented a 'deviation from what has hitherto been usual, let it be never so great'.[9] He may even have reached by this time the more radical conclusion announced in the *Religious Affections*, that although Satan can only counterfeit the Spirit's saving operations, he has power to imitate exactly the order in which they are supposed to appear (pp. 158–9). In any case, the *Personal Narrative* reveals no more brooding on Edwards' part over the absence of 'particular steps'.

The *Diary* exhibits, in general, considerably more doubt, sometimes approaching despair, than could be inferred from an isolated reading of the *Personal Narrative*. Periods of spiritual crisis were marked by such tortured complaints as: 'This week I found myself so far gone, that it seemed to me I should never recover more'; and 'Crosses of the nature of that, which I met with this week, thrust me quite below all comforts in religion.'[10] There are, in addition, all the entries in which, as a kind of running theme, Edwards agonizes over dead, dull, and listless frames of mind. The *Personal Narrative* reflects little of the intensity or number of these entries. Edwards mentions only that at New Haven he 'sunk in Religion' as a result of being diverted by affairs; and in a subsequent paragraph he rounds off a similar recollection with the comment that these 'various Exercises . . . would be tedious to relate' (pp. 32–3).

The difference between the two versions is striking, yet understandable, if we assume that as Edwards grew in his assurance of grace, these drier seasons lost, in recollection, their original impact. But since Edwards seems to have consulted his diary as he wrote ('And my Refuge and Support was in Contemplations on the heavenly State; as I find in my Diary of *May* 1, 1723'), it is more likely that deletions and new emphases were intentional – the choice, for example, to minimize emotions arising from dullness and insensibility in a narrative intended to be affecting. The lingering memory of his uncle Hawley's suicide in 1735 would certainly have enforced Edwards' decision: 'He had been for a Considerable Time Greatly Concern'd about the Condition of his soul; till, by the ordering of a sovereign Providence he was suffered to fall into deep melancholly, a distemper that the Family are very Prone to; he was much overpowered by it; the devil took the advantage & drove him into despairing thoughts.'[11]

Whatever the proximate reason, Edwards felt strongly enough about the dangers of melancholy to edit out any hint of it in the record of his conversion experience, just as in the preface to Brainerd's memoirs he forewarned readers that melancholy was the sole imperfection in an otherwise exemplary man, and just as in his *Thoughts* on the revival of 1740–2 he excepted melancholy as the 'one case, wherein the truth ought to be withheld from sinners in distress of conscience'.[12] It was sufficient for readers to know that a Slough of Despond existed, the foul and miry by-product, as John Bunyan explained, of conviction of sin. Nothing was to be gained, and much would be risked, by bringing on stage the youth who once found himself 'overwhelmed with melancholy'.[13]

Seen from another point of view, the youth of the *Diary* might by the very miserableness of his seeking illustrate an important lesson. The characteristic of the *Diary* which the author of the *Personal Narrative* apparently found most repugnant was its tendency toward spiritual self-reliance. For even as he reminded himself that effort was ineffectual without grace, the young diarist had also been busy drawing up his 'resolutions', seventy of them eventually. In the *Personal Narrative*, Edwards reached back twenty years to untangle these cross-purposes, simplifying his experience somewhat as he fitted it for instruction. Spiritual industry could not be despised; its products were real and of value: 'I was brought wholly to break off all former wicked Ways, and all Ways of known outward Sin.' What had to be emphasized was that the sum of resolutions and bonds and religious duties was not salvation. Edwards spoke beyond the limits of his own case when he concluded, 'But yet it seems to me, I sought after a miserable manner: Which has made me some times since to question, whether ever it issued in that which was saving; being ready to doubt, whether such miserable seeking was ever succeeded.'[14]

2

While the pattern that emerges from Edwards' reshaping of some of the materials of his diary helps suggest the more formal, public nature of the autobiography, the later document represents in most ways a fresh beginning on the analysis of his spiritual experience. The first sentence of the *Personal Narrative* reveals Edwards' anxiety to get at major issues, prefacing the entire narrative with a declaration that nearly sums it up: 'I Had a variety of Concerns and Exercises about my Soul from my Childhood; but had two more remarkable Seasons of Awakening, before I met with that Change, by which I was brought to those new Dispositions, and that new Sense of Things, that I have since had.' A Northampton reader ought not to have missed the distinction being made, or the ascending order of importance in the three clauses. Certainly he would have known that in the 1735 awakening more than 300 persons appeared to have been 'savingly brought home to Christ', but that in the minister's *Faithful Narrative* of the work he had dismissed some as 'wolves in sheep's clothing', while discovering in those for whom he was more hopeful 'a new sense of things, new apprehensions and views of God, of the divine attributes'. For the reader of shorter memory, who might have withdrawn from a battle he thought won at an early age, Edwards was ready at the end of the paragraph to deny that a boy who prayed five times a day in secret, who abounded in 'religious Duties', and whose affections were 'lively and easily moved' had anything of grace in him. He had already explained in 'A Divine and Supernatural Light' (1734) that emotions raised by the story of Christ's sufferings or by a description of heaven might be no different in kind from those elicited by a tragedy or a romance.[15] And it was unnecessary to introduce psychology here, since the course of the narrative itself revealed the nature of these early affections.

In time, Edwards says, they 'wore off', and he 'returned like a Dog to his Vomit'. It was characteristic of Edwards not to hesitate in applying a text (Proverbs 26: 11) to himself, but he may already have conceived an extended application for this simile. In 1746, after his last awakening had ebbed, he used the same expression in charging that persons 'who seemed to be mightily raised and swallowed with joy and zeal, for a while, seem to have returned like the dog to his vomit'.[16]

When Edwards testifies that a sickness so grave it seemed God 'shook me over the Pit of Hell' had only a passing effect on resolution, the implication is undoubtedly both personal and general. The emotion aroused by this image could have no other name but terror, but at almost the same time that he preached 'Sinners in the Hands of an Angry God' (1741), Edwards was disclosing that terror had been irrelevant in his own experience. Whatever moved him in his New Haven years, 'it never seemed to be proper to express my Concern that I had, by the name of Terror' (p. 24). Thus an important distinction was laid down. The experience of terror gave no cause for self-congratulation, since there were persons, like the younger Edwards, 'that have frightful apprehensions of hell ... who at the same time seem to have very little proper enlightenings of conscience, really convincing them of their sinfulness of heart and life'.[17]

Edwards' technique through the initial paragraphs of the *Personal Narrative* is to separate the 'I' of the narrative from his present self and to characterize the younger 'I' as a less reliable judge of spiritual experience than the mature narrator. Thus, Edwards the boy takes much 'self-righteous' pleasure in his performance of religious duties, or Edwards the young man seeks salvation as the 'main Business' of his life, unaware that his manner of seeking is 'miserable'. Soon the reader must adjust his attitude even more carefully, for the mature Edwards will begin to describe genuinely gracious experience, while the 'I' remains largely ignorant of what has happened. Edwards compiles sufficient evidence for a reader to draw his own conclusions from the passage, but subordinates himself to the mind of a youth who was not yet ready to draw conclusions when he says, 'But it never came into my Thought, that there was any thing spiritual, or of a saving Nature in this' (p. 25).

One reason for so oblique an approach may be traced, not to the autobiographer's ignorance of his subject, but to the pastor's close acquaintance with the hypocrite, a brash, colloquial figure who appears often in the *Religious Affections*, drawn no doubt from models near at hand. That part of Edwards' purpose which was public and exemplary dictated that he give a wide margin to the 'bold, familiar and appropriating language' of those who condemned themselves by announcing, '"I know I shall go to heaven, as well as if I were there; I know that God is now manifesting himself to my soul, and is now smiling upon me"' (pp. 170–1). At the same time, Edwards remains faithful to personal experience, accurately reflecting the uncertainty and inconclusiveness he could see in his diary; and by preserving intact the uncertain young man, he provided a character with whom readers similarly perplexed could identify.

The evidence that counters and overwhelms the disclaimers attached to these paragraphs emerges from the history Edwards gives of his assent to the doctrine of God's sovereignty. Even after childhood, his mind, which was 'full of Objections', and his heart, which found the doctrine 'horrible', had struggled against accepting the notion that God in his sovereign pleasure should choose to save some and leave the rest to be 'everlastingly tormented in Hell'. Suddenly and inexplicably the objections had evaporated, but at the time Edwards found it impossible to describe 'how, or by what Means'. Only the effects were clear: 'I saw further, and my Reason apprehended the Justice and Reasonableness of it' (p. 25). Because the next and most significant stage of his conviction deserved separate treatment, Edwards is content for the moment to imply its essential difference: the doctrine that was now reasonable would later appear 'exceedingly pleasant, bright and sweet'. In short, common grace had assisted natural principles by removing prejudices and illuminating the truth of the doctrine; saving grace had infused a new spiritual foundation that underlay a wholly different mode of perception through the 'new sense' or 'sense of the heart' that characterized genuinely spiritual experience.[18]

3

How far Edwards exceeded his Puritan predecessors in the art of uniting instruction with spiritual autobiography, the one reasoned and objective, the other felt and subjective, appears most impressively when he begins to document the experience of the 'new man'. As he relives the first instance of an 'inward, sweet Delight in GOD and divine Things', his prose rises gradually to a high pitch of joyous emotion, sustained by characteristic repetitions and parallelisms and by an aspiring and exultant vocabulary. The paragraph takes its shape so naturally that one nearly overlooks the emergence of relationships that received their fullest elaboration in the *Religious Affections*. Edwards' first ejaculation, 'how excellent a Being that was', is a response to the first objective ground of gracious affections, 'the transcendently excellent and amiable nature of divine things'. When he continues, 'and how happy I should be, if I might enjoy that GOD and be wrapt up to GOD in Heaven, and be as it were swallowed up in Him', Edwards proceeds according to the order of true saints, whose apprehension of the excellency of divine things 'is the foundation of the joy that they have afterwards, in the consideration of their being theirs'. The affections of hypocrites, on the other hand, are aroused in a contrary order; they find themselves 'made so much of by God' that 'he seems in a sort, lovely to them'.[19]

To make clear the order of his own affections became crucial for Edwards as he went on to report his visions, 'or fix'd Ideas and Imaginations'. He ran the risk, after all, of becoming a chief exhibit in the case against enthusiasm should his narrative have fallen into the wrong hands. Nevertheless, when judging experiences similar to his own he was satisfied that lively imaginations could arise from truly gracious affections; and in adding, 'through the infirmity of human nature',[20] he claimed less for his 'visions' than some who read him later. Class distinctions and hierarchies in spiritual experience held little interest for Edwards, because all distinctions resolved finally into the ultimate one between the old and the new man. It was less difficult, however, to point out what was not spiritual experience, even in personal narrative, than it was to render the perceptions of the 'new sense' with an instrument so imperfect as human language and so indiscriminate in itself as to be the common property of both spiritual and natural men. Moreover, narrative prose was only Edwards' second choice to convey what he felt. Insofar as the medium approached anything like satisfactory expression it was by compromise with another that seemed more natural: 'to sing or chant forth my Meditations; to speak my Thoughts in Soliloquies, and speak with a singing Voice'. In admitting that the 'inward ardor' of his soul 'could not freely flame out as it would', Edwards reconciled himself to one kind of defeat, but the attempt, if skillfully managed, might prove affecting to others.

The impossible aim Edwards set for himself in the *Personal Narra-*

tive was to articulate his totally new delight in 'things of religion' for readers who could have 'no more Notion or idea' of it than he had as a boy, no more 'than one born blind has of pleasant and beautiful Colours'. He might have taken solace in the consideration that since all expression was in this case equally imperfect, any expression would do. The prose of the *Personal Narrative* deserves respect to the degree that Edwards refused to avail himself of this consolation or to accept language that by this time flowed easily from his pen. Edwards' continual use of the word 'sweet', for instance, points up some of the difficulty of judging his art and rhetorical effectiveness in the narrative. If the word seems at one moment to derive from a sensationalist vocabulary, we may regard its use as part of his unique project to make Lockean psychology serve the interests of experimental religion. Simply through repetition the word tends to gather to itself all the sensible difference Edwards was trying to express when he said that the easily moved affections of his youth 'did not arise from any Sight of the divine Excellency of the Things of GOD; or any Taste of the Soul-satisfying and Life-giving Good, there is in them'. But Edwards' reading of Locke only added new significance to scriptural passages long familiar to him. In the *Religious Affections* he refers the reader to Psalm 119 for a striking representation of 'the beauty and sweetness of holiness as the grand object of a spiritual taste' (p. 260), and goes on to paraphrase verse 103 ('How sweet are thy words unto my taste! Yea, sweeter than honey to my mouth'). In this light Edwards appears only to be indulging in the kind of reverent plagiarism common to many spiritual autobiographies, among them that of Sarah Edwards.[21]

Occasionally, too, Edwards declines the full potential of personal narrative by taking over, with little change, passages from his 1737 account of Northampton conversions, making them his own by the mechanical act of altering the pronoun. He could not have avoided reporting that in his own experience, as in that of the converts, 'the Appearance of every thing was altered'; but he expands the point by again simply listing natural phenomena over which the 'new sense' played, without vitalizing and re-viewing them through personal expression: 'God's Excellency, his Wisdom, his Purity and Love, seemed to appear in every Thing; in the Sun, Moon and Stars; in the Grass, Flowers, Trees; in the Water, and all Nature; which used greatly to fix my Mind.'[22] However, when Edwards dramatizes a new kind of perception and so involves divine attributes with natural phenomena that abstraction is made vivid and concrete, he begins to communicate something of what it was to confront nature as, in the strictest sense, a new beholder:

I used to be a Person uncommonly terrified with Thunder: and it used to strike me with Terror, when I saw a Thunder-storm rising. But now, on the contrary, it rejoyced me. I felt GOD at the first Appearance of a Thunder-storm. And used to take the Opportunity, at such Times, to fix myself to view the Clouds, and see the Lightnings play, and hear the majestick & awful Voice of God's Thunder: which often times was exceeding entertaining, leading me to sweet Contemplations of my great and glorious GOD. (p. 27)

Taken together, these successive views of nature in its placid and then terrible beauty would adumbrate the symmetry of the divine attributes. Edwards noted as much in another manuscript not published in his lifetime,[23] but the narrative of his conversion imposed special conditions on viewing 'shadows of divine things'. When he scrutinized his own spiritual 'estate', it was absolutely necessary that he be able to acknowledge a view of God's loveliness and majesty in conjunction, for even 'wicked men and devils' were sensible of His 'mighty power and awful majesty'. Against the background of the recent awakening Edwards was moved to observe in the *Religious Affections* that 'too much weight has been laid, by many persons of late, on discoveries of God's greatness, awful majesty, and natural perfection ... without any real view of the holy, lovely majesty of God' (p. 265). To express the ideal vision in the *Personal Narrative*, Edwards chose the language of theological paradox over that of sensationalism, although we do hear symmetry and can observe the proportion Edwards maintains through a dexterous manipulation of his terms. The passage also reveals an infiltration into prose of the 'singing voice', whose rhythms were still alive in the memory, inseparable from the experience that originally provoked them:

And as I was walking there, and looked up on the Sky and Clouds; there came into my Mind, a sweet Sense of the glorious Majesty and Grace of GOD, that I know not how to express. I seemed to see them both in a sweet Conjunction: Majesty and Meekness join'd together: it was a sweet and gentle, and holy Majesty; and also a majestic Meekness; an awful Sweetness; a high, and great, and holy Gentleness. (p. 26)

Through heightened paradox the unawakened reader might be

brought to see dimly and to seek the same sense of God's natural and moral perfections balanced and intermingled with each other. Edwards strove to make the path more clear and more inviting as well when he singled out for relatively extensive treatment that which constituted 'in a peculiar manner the beauty of the divine nature'. At its center the *Personal Narrative* focuses on the experiential realization that holiness is the divine attribute which primarily elicits the love of the true saint. God's underived holiness could not, of course, be encompassed by words; it could only be loved. But the holiness of creatures, deriving from the divine object of their love, yielded to definition in the *Religious Affections* as 'the moral image of God in them, which is their beauty' (p. 258).

In the *Personal Narrative*, Edwards had already embodied the relationship between the holiness of God and the holiness of man in two successive and integrally related 'moral images'. The first describes the soul as 'a Field or Garden of GOD', its multitude of flowers representative of individual moral excellencies. Since holiness comprehends all these excellencies, as its beauty sums up their individual loveliness, Edwards closes in immediately on a single, consummate flower: 'such a little white Flower, as we see in the Spring of the Year; low and humble on the Ground, opening its Bosom, to receive the pleasant Beams of the Sun's Glory; rejoycing as it were, in a calm Rapture; diffusing around a sweet Fragrancy; standing peacefully and lovingly, in the midst of other Flowers round about; all in like Manner opening their Bosoms, to drink in the Light of the Sun' (pp. 29–30). Each felt quality that Edwards noted in his perception of holiness — 'Purity, Brightness, Peacefulness & Ravishment to the Soul' — finds its correspondent physical detail in the image. The life of the flower, as it drinks in light and sustenance from the sun and returns its own fragrance, is the life of grace, continuous in God and the regenerate man; and the second image is finally enlarged to the scope of the first to include a fellowship of saints. Edwards' tendency toward pathetic fallacy, the flower's 'rejoycing as it were, in a calm Rapture', only reminds the reader that this is personal narrative and not an exercise in typology.

4

Not every sight to which the 'new sense' gave access evoked an ecstasy of joy. Acuteness of spiritual perception could also compel

disgust and nausea when eyes seeing for the first time began to search
the depths of one's depravity. So hideous a view as Edwards reported
would have taxed any vocabulary, but his own had so far been richest
and most novel when he expressed the affection of love. For this other
task he might have been forced to depend entirely upon the communal
vocabulary of the Calvinists *vis-à-vis* man's corruption, had his sensitivity to language not intervened. Edwards' awareness of the problems involved in verbal self-chastisement compares with that of his
fictional fellow minister, Arthur Dimmesdale, who found that he
could excoriate himself as the 'vilest of sinners', not only with im-
punity, but with the ironic dividend of being revered the more for
his sanctity. Regardless of their denotative content, formulary expressions, given wide currency, were quickly emptied of meaning —
as Edwards well knew from his experience with hypocrites, men
fluent in 'very bad expressions which they use about themselves . . .
and we must believe that they are thus humble, and see themselves
so vile, upon the credit of their say so'.[24]

When Edwards is most likely to suggest to modern readers an
inverse pride in his corruption rather than the 'evangelical humility'
(the sixth sign of gracious affections) he hoped he had, we discover
that a question of language is at the root of the difficulty. It is not
the rank of 'chief of sinners' that he covets, nor is Edwards vying
with his fellow townsmen for a place in the last ring of hell when he
rejects their expression, 'as bad as the Devil himself', because it
seemed 'exceeding faint and feeble, to represent my Wickedness'.
The full text of this passage, as printed by Hopkins, makes clear that
Edwards is in fact rejecting language he thought inadequately pro-
portioned to its object: 'I thought I should wonder, that they should
content themselves with such Expressions as these, if I had any Reason to imagine, that their Sin bore any Proportion to mine. It seemed
to me, I should wonder at my self, if I should express *my* Wickedness
in such feeble Terms as they did' (p. 37).

The rationale that lies behind Edwards' greater dissatisfaction
with attempts to convey a sense of his wickedness than with parallel
attempts to express his delight in divine things is given fully in the
Religious Affections. There Edwards explained that to the saint the
deformity of the least sin must outweigh the greatest beauty in his
holiness, because sin against an infinite God is infinitely corrupt,
while holiness cannot be infinite in a creature (p. 326). No expression,
then, could take the measure of infinite corruption, and before accept-

ing a simile that only traded on the reputation of Satan, Edwards preferred to draw on the resources of his own rhetoric. He begins by bringing together two images that suggest physical immensity, and then associates them with the key word 'infinite', which is extracted at last from its concrete associations and made to reproduce itself rhythmically:

My Wickedness, as I am in my self, has long appear'd to me perfectly ineffable, and infinitely swallowing up all Thought and Imagination; like an infinite Deluge, or infinite Mountains over my Head. I know not how to express better, what my Sins appear to me to be, than by heaping Infinite upon Infinite, and multiplying Infinite by Infinite. I go about very often, for this many Years, with these Expressions in my Mind, and in my Mouth, 'Infinite upon Infinite. Infinite upon Infinite!' (p. 37)

Even if he had improved on pallid representations of wickedness, Edwards only pushed the question one step further. Did the improvement arise from a greater conviction of sin or from a natural ability in prose expression? Just how rigorously Edwards dealt with himself in answering such questions appears in a subsequent reflection that immediately dissipated any complacency in mere verbal skill: 'And yet, I ben't in the least inclined to think, that I have a greater Conviction of Sin than ordinary. It seems to me, my Conviction of Sin is exceeding small, and faint.' Typically enough, Edwards' ruthlessness here is a double-edged sword that also cuts away from himself. As a public document, the *Personal Narrative* might only provide hypocrites with a new model for their deceptions, a thesaurus of expressions (such as 'infinite upon infinite') that proclaimed conviction or other classic signs of grace. Edwards could not prevent a prostitution of his narrative, but he knew that the hypocrite found it difficult to claim anything in small amounts, and he would explain in the *Religious Affections* how mimicry eventually confounded itself:

But no man that is truly under great convictions, thinks his conviction great in proportion to his sin. For if he does, 'tis a certain sign that he inwardly thinks his sins small. And if that be the case, that is a certain evidence that his conviction is small. And this, by the way, is the main reason, that persons when under a work of humiliation, are not sensible of it, in the time of it.[25]

Simultaneously, then, Edwards convinces the reader that his self-scrutiny has been unremittingly honest, while he offers instruction that is meticulous in its distinctions, and affecting in its language. The *Personal Narrative* is relatively brief, set against Mather's 'Paterna' or Shepard's 'My Birth & Life'; but it is not incomplete. Like all autobiographers, secular or spiritual, Edwards fashioned a coherent narrative by using his total experience selectively; we judge it incomplete only by our curiosity about the interior life of his last harrowing years. He could scarcely have added a word to the felt distillation of all he ever thought on all that finally mattered.

11

Benjamin Franklin and the choice
of a single point of view

JOHN F. LYNEN

Benjamin Franklin's and Jonathan Edwards' modes of vision can be seen as nearly exact inversions of one another. The certainty from which Franklin reasons is experience in time, whereas Edwards' point of departure is the universal scheme revealed by God's word. Yet from their contrasting positions, the two men look at the same world, and this agreement is to be understood not merely in the sense that they both see the world as it appeared to eighteenth-century Americans, nor in the sense that all theories are interpretations of the same reality, but in the stricter sense that Franklin and Edwards both envision a world in which thought must choose between the same set of alternative viewpoints. This common ground is most clearly shown by the tendency of each to make the other's point of view the center of attention. Edwards so organizes dogmatic generalizations as to focus his study of salvation within the momentary personal experience of regeneration, while Franklin interprets experiences as a means of inferring the all-inclusive design. That is why Franklin too often seems a merely typical person and his life full of lessons for everyone. Franklin's paradoxical relation to Edwards can best be understood by recognizing that, since a view — as this term is used in speaking of point of view — is always a view of something other than itself, in the concept of experience the idea of an order transcending experience is implicit. Franklin's great sensitivity to the limits of man's understanding would not be possible without an assumed world having the same orderliness, inclusiveness, and independence of human interests and thoughts as the world which Edwards portrays. The more one insists that an actual experience is always that of someone in particular, the more one becomes aware of the necessity to posit a world which transcends all views except the all-inclusive vision — God's consciousness.

Franklin's fundamental agreement with Edwards serves to explain why his empiricism is often concealed and even seemingly contradicted by his confident rationalism. Considering his moral maxims, his taste for making deistical deductions from the laws of nature, and his fiddling with codes, bylaws, and constitutions, it is hard to imagine that he had any very serious doubts about the scope of human understanding. So assured are his formulas that one can overlook the scepticism they are designed to accommodate. Since the tolerance Franklin recommends is dogma today, one can easily fail to notice that he justifies political and religious liberalism and a morality of rules-of-thumb on the ground that in human thought there is little certainty. Taking his doubts for granted, we doubt much less than he. But Franklin the rationalist is abetted by Franklin the empiricist; indeed the first could not exist without the second. In terms of motive alone, what stronger incitement can there be to the search for broad formulations and general rules than the belief that their usefulness alone is sufficient to justify them? Only, perhaps, Franklin's complementary premise that even the most ambitious generalization can be put to an immediate test. If for no other reason, the empiricist would be a rationalist, because a universe governed by fixed principles is a great convenience.

Franklin will, perhaps, always remain an enigma, for although his rationalism is a function of his empiricism, the two are in continual conflict. But an enigma is a paradox, not an absurdity, and the doubleness of Franklin's thought attests to the unity of his vision. So long as we relate his ideas only to one another, Franklin can be for us no more than a point of collision for contradictory beliefs. We cannot in any convincing way reconcile the gadgetry with the pure science, the faith in Providence with the argument that this belief ought to be maintained merely because the common people need to believe in it, the belief in progress and democratic principles with the sceptical view of human understanding, the financial shrewdness with the voluntary risking of life and fortune. So long as we attend only to relating Franklin's opinions to each other, we are faced with either—or choices and our view of Franklin himself must be arbitrary.

Neither Franklin the hero nor Franklin the humbug seems credible, for each is produced by suppressing a large part of the evidence; either we ignore the scepticism and prudential connivance in favor of the high principles (usually the political ones) or we take the high principles as a mere façade for cynicism and selfish interests. To avoid this false choice, one is tempted to settle for the 'many-sided

Franklin', who is not one person but several, and this typically modern preference has the advantage of flattering our taste for believing that selfhood is a closetful of masks.[1] But one need only ask what a mask may be to recognize the evasion. Franklin's roles are, we say, 'Franklin's'. They must form a system defining some true identity at the center, and that self can be described only as a state or mode of consciousness.

It is, then, only within Franklin's vision that his ideas can be brought into harmony, not in their relations to each other. Each contradiction must be referred to his imaginative view of the human situation; and when this is done, the conflict will then be seen not as an opposition of thought but as a contrast between the senses in which statements are meant. For example, when Franklin asserts the usefulness of belief in Providence as a prop to morality, he is not speaking in the same sense as when he asserts that Providence does in fact govern the affairs of men.[2] The first statement appeals to the limits of man's knowledge as an individual living in time, while the second appeals to the necessity of hypothesizing a universal order. Resting upon the belief that a true generalization can be made — that the real principles of the universe can be expressed in the same form — the second statement intends to assert a truth about the actual order of things, whereas the first asserts a truth only about data lying within the horizon of individual experience.

The paradoxes which make Franklin so difficult to understand have their source in his manner of imagining the thinker's circumstances with reference to two standards — the limits of the thinker's view, on the one hand, and the rational orderliness of the reality of which it is a view, on the other. One must confront this ultimate fiction — this picture of the self — and thus it is Franklin the artist who matters most to those who would understand Franklin the historical personage. Before considering the art of the *Autobiography*, however, I shall briefly survey some particular examples of the mode of thought I have tried to define.

I will cite first that extraordinary work of Franklin's youth, the *Dissertation on Liberty and Necessity, Pleasure and Pain*, an astounding performance in which the nascent exponent of self-help develops a necessitarian thesis and the future moralist concludes that since the individual cannot be free, he is not morally responsible and 'Virtue and Vice are but empty distinctions.'[3] Yet the greatest surprise of the essay is the picture it gives us of a Franklin we do not see again —

Franklin the metaphysician. Franklin, to be sure, soon rejected his shocking little pamphlet, and ever after professed a great distaste for speculations of this kind. The *Dissertation*, then, is the product of a formative phase, yet it is for that very reason of great importance, since it shows us what he believed at an early stage of his development, and, to the extent that it is not typical — that the arguments it contains were rejected — it shows us the reasoning he revolted against — the background of ideas with reference to which his later thoughts were framed.

Franklin's odd criticism of the *Dissertation* in the *Autobiography* — 'I doubted whether some Error had not insinuated itself unperceiv'd into my Argument, so as to infect all that follow'd, as is common in metaphysical Reasonings'[4] — reveals a radical shift of ground: the mere suspicion that his reasoning was faulty is now sufficient to discredit it. Franklin will not even trouble to conjecture what his error might have been, for it is not, indeed, the reasoning of the *Dissertation* that he rejects, but the whole mode of reasoning in terms of which his argument could be judged true or false. Refusing to play the metaphysical game, he dismisses the work not for its questionable arguments but for its practical effects. It is the work of the youthful freethinker, whose arguments misled others, and who was soon to discover that the deists among his friends had turned out to be scoundrels and sybarites.

This change of Franklin's entire perspective, this turning from the question of what in the abstract is true to the problem of what in experience will 'work' is actually foreshadowed in the *Dissertation* itself. Its most crucial argument, that concerning freedom of the will, can only lead to empiricist conclusions. If, the reasoning runs, an individual were entirely free to choose according to his own will, then

Among the many Things which lie before him to be done, he may, as he is at Liberty and his Choice influenc'd by nothing, (for so it must be, or he is not at Liberty) chuse any one and refuse the rest. Now there is every Moment something *best* to be done, which is alone then good, and with respect to which, every Thing else is at that Time *evil*. In order to know which is best to be done, and which is not, it is requisite that we should have at one View all the intricate Consequences of every Action with respect to the general Order and Scheme of the Universe, both present and future; but they are innumerable and incomprehensible by any Thing but Omniscience. As we cannot know these, we have but one Chance to ten Thousand, to hit the right Action; we should then be perpetually blundering about in the Dark, and putting the Scheme in disorder. . . Is it not necessary, then, that our Actions should be governed and over-rul'd by an all-wise Providence?[5]

Franklin could call such a position deism, but it is more properly Puritanism in deistic trappings. The picture of the self's situation is almost exactly that which the Puritan faith assumes: again the individual is seen in his severely isolated present ('there is every Moment something *best* to be done, etc.'); again the problem of knowledge is that of explaining how, from within this moment, the mind can discern how the present facts — its options — fit into the eternal design; and again, to draw the last and most obvious parallel, the eternal design is equated with the consciousness of the omniscient God who foreknows and predestines all things.

For Franklin the 'feel' of experience proves his necessitarian argument. He appeals to our sense that the self is not 'perpetually blundering about in the Dark', but does make the right choices more often than by the laws of chance it could. Even so, the truth as mere feeling and the truth as rationally deduced from fixed principles coincide. Though the self cannot discern the consequences of its sundry options, they are assumed to exist within a pattern as fixed and immutable as the will of the Puritan deity. The whole case for Franklin's radical empiricism is here, and to grant the dissertation's main argument is to recognize, as Franklin quickly did, that in human understanding there is too little certainty to support metaphysical generalizations, since these must be judged, always, within an incomplete vision of reality.

It is of the greatest importance to notice that Franklin's revulsion against speculations of a philosophic kind is not a despairing surrender to ignorance. He does not dismiss the questions philosophy raises as unanswerable — does not, as it were, throw up his hands. Writing to Benjamin Vaughn in 1779, he explains that 'The great uncertainty I found in metaphysical reasonings disgusted me, and I quitted that kind of reading and study for others more satisfactory.'[6] Certainty, then, is the standard, such certainty as metaphysics promises but fails to deliver. As Poor Richard complains, 'Philosophy as well as foppery often changes fashion', a comment which emphasizes the limits of the philosopher's point of view by asserting that his criteria are the

changeable preferences of an epoch rather than the truth itself.[7] And
theology, insofar as it aims at demonstrable truths, is dismissed as
an even more hopeless game: 'Many a long dispute among divines
may be thus abridg'd, It is so: It is not so, It is so; It is not so.'[8]
Such comments reflect a distaste for the methods of the philosopher
and the theologian, not a dismissal of the problems they consider.
Franklin did not simply shuffle aside these problems or satisfy himself with half-hearted answers. Most especially, it is absurd to conclude that Franklin's frequent comments upon religion are only the
gestures of a man trying to get a troublesome subject out of the way.
Those who voice such a lazy answer, will very probably be asking,
in the next breath, why Franklin is so remote from the Puritan world
which nurtured him, and reminding us how, in their one encounter,
Cotton Mather warned him to stoop lest he bump his head.

Franklin's comments on religion, though scattered and often
casual or *ad hoc*, follow an implicit pattern which becomes clear
when they are considered in the light of his idea of Providence. His
faith in providential guidance is supported by so many examples that
only one memorable instance need be cited: his brief speech recom-
mending that prayers be offered at the Constitutional Convention.
Addressing the delegates at a time when their debates had reached
an impasse, he recalled the experience of the revolution.

All of us, who were engag'd in that Struggle must have observ'd frequent
Instances of a superintending Providence in our Favor... I have lived,
Sir, a long time; and the longer I live, the more convincing Proofs I see
of this Truth, *That God governs in the Affairs of Men!* And if a Sparrow
cannot fall to the Ground without his Notice, is it probable that an
Empire can rise without his Aid? — We have been assured, Sir, in the
Sacred Writings, that 'except the Lord build the House, they labor in
vain that build it'.[9]

That this statement and others like it were offered with a practical
end in view does not discredit Franklin's sincerity; the same conviction is often manifest in private jottings and records of conver-
sations in which, were it not that he had it at heart, the subject need
never have come up.

Franklin's trust in Providence will seem cynical or thoughtless
only if we suppose that it requires crediting the notion of a hand
reaching down from the sky — a notion which Edwards also found
absurd. The commonly recognized problem in Puritan thought as to

how providential intervention could be logically reconciled with the natural laws ordained at the creation was quite obvious to Franklin. Sometimes, indeed, he thought the dilemma an apt subject for satire. In the Swiftian hoax perpetrated against a poor astrologer and almanac-maker – Titan Leeds – Franklin, having prophesied Leeds' death, as Swift had Partridge's, explained that if Leeds were still alive, the event foretold had been forestalled by providential intervention.

For the Stars only show to the Skillful, what will happen in the natural and universal Chain of Causes and Effects; but 'tis well known, that the Events which would otherwise certainly happen, at certain Times, in the Course of Nature, are sometimes set aside or postpon'd for wise and good Reasons, by the immediate particular Dispositions of Providence; which particular Dispositions the Stars can by no Means discover or foreshow.[10]

The implications of this pleasantry make it clear that Franklin did not consider Providence as superceding natural law but, like Edwards, as effecting God's will through the medium of nature.

Several bits of evidence which on the surface seem no more than amateurish and fashionably deistical opinions are indications of how Franklin sought to bring nature and Providence into harmony. One example is to be found in the recollections of David Williams, an English thinker who collaborated with Franklin in the project of founding a sect based upon 'a rational Faith in God'. Williams remembered that the liturgy they drew up asserted:

The God of Newton was probably the regulating Principle or Good of the Solar System . . .

What Principles may govern or preserve other Systems we know not, and Therefore know not their Gods. It is probable that all the Systems of Nature are governed and preserved by a relative Principle or Law, and that governing Principle is the Universal God.[11]

Williams' report seems trustworthy, for it makes much sense of that peculiar document, the 'Articles of Belief and Acts of Religion', in which Franklin argues for the existence of a multiplicity of gods: 'There is one Supreme most perfect Being, Author and Father of the Gods themselves'; but since the Supreme Being is infinitely above man and can have no concern for him or satisfaction in his worship, there must be, according to the notion of plenitude, as many degrees of being superior to man as beneath him; therefore, 'The INFINITE has created many Beings or Gods, vastly superior to Man, who can better conceive his Perfections than we, and return him a more rational and glorious Praise.' Franklin concludes that the deity he worships is the 'particular Wise and good God, who is the Author and Owner of our System [i.e. the solar system]'.[12]

We cannot know how long Franklin adhered to polytheism, but two assumptions behind his theory are of great significance. First, polytheism is asserted on the grounds of a post-Lockean idealism. The existence of the Supreme Being depends upon his being known to intelligences able to 'conceive his Perfections'; and, conversely, since men are of too little account for his notice, there must be lesser gods to take thought of them. Clearly, being, as in Edwards, is to be defined as appearing to consciousness. That Franklin ends in what to Edwards would be unspeakable heresy is the result of rather too inconsiderate definitions of great, lesser, and infinite.

Secondly, Franklin's gods are equivalent to 'principles', and the Universal God is 'a relative Principle or Law' which governs all the systems. This equivalence demonstrates well Franklin's way of bridging the gap between the eternal and present points of view. What in reality is principle in experience is process, and men's generalizations from observed phenomena in time — the laws they formulate — bear witness to God's immanence; for while our formulas only approximate the true principles of the universe, the latter are present to experience, though never fully seen. Thus the Puritan contrast between the immanent and transcendent aspects of God is resolved in a manner essentially like that of Edwards.

The system of many gods is not necessary to Franklin's basic design but serves as a means — though a rather awkward means — of accounting for the manifold modes of God's acting. By identifying natural law with God as immanent deity, and explaining the seeming difference between nature and the Eternal Father as a consequence of our inability to view reality in a total conspectus, Franklin at once makes God the cause and ground of all being and yet, quite in Edwards' way, preserves the separateness of the transcendent deity.

That this scheme is patly mechanistic should, I think, be disproved by Franklin's belief that principle is indistinguishable from value. As shown by Williams' phrase, 'the regulating Principle or Good of the Solar System', it is assumed that being is goodness, and the gods are regarded as superior to men in ordering more extensive spheres. Their existence and their excellence are alike functions of their degree of consciousness. In beings, whether men or gods, the degree of value and the scope of awareness are identical.

This belief is, to be sure, susceptible to narrow interpretations and correspondingly ludicrous conclusions. It might easily be put to the service of uncritical materialism and used to show that good is no more than efficiency or orderliness, as if the value of these values did not need to be explained. And at first it may seem that that is just the error of which Franklin himself is guilty. Because he fails to define exactly his habitual value terms — 'benefit', 'success', 'profit', 'felicity', 'convenience' — one might suppose that he thought their meaning self-evident. And, since they are all suggestive of either physical satisfactions or social advantages, one might conclude that such were the values Franklin had most at heart. But comfort or public esteem are not in themselves evil; they may be continuous with virtues, just as the 'little Advantages' of clean streets are continuous with peace of mind and public order. Unless practical and moral value are harshly separated — in which case far the greater part of experience must be considered of no ethical importance — a scale or continuum of values must be assumed; and once the need for such a scale has been granted, the question becomes one of point of view — of where, along the continuum, the approach to an ultimate good begins.

With respect to action, this question concerns the first step, while with respect to thought, it concerns the first perception or most immediate datum. Both, Franklin assumes, are to be found in the area of personal experience, where the good most commonly appears in humble and practical forms. Furthermore, the individual's view is too limited to allow for the definition of absolutes; since he sees processes, not essences, goodness, as it is known to him, is a way of happening, not a timeless object. Franklin's use of value terms is, then, largely dramatic — a means of directing attention to the personal point of view and of defining the situation shared by him and his readers as one in which knowledge is so limited that the only names for values that can be generally agreed upon are those of a practical kind. Beyond this, such words as 'profit' or 'felicity' have only the general meaning 'good'.

Since Franklin is an instrumentalist, it is a vain objection to complain that he neglects ends in his obsession with means: ends, he would reply, are only known to us as means. One may legitimately disagree with this way of thinking, but there is gross illogic in the criticism that Franklin's values are degraded. He has no interest in defining values — does not believe it can be done. His concern, rather, is with the experience of value and the means by which it can be achieved.

This concern is most apparent in the notorious table of virtues which is so frequently decried on the ground that many of the thirteen virtues listed are not virtues at all, but merely traits of prudence. 'Silence' or 'Cleanliness', it is argued, cannot be placed in the same order of value as 'Justice', since the former are but means to the good, whereas justice is a good in itself. Since among the traditional Judeo-Christian virtues, those which are not omitted are given a cynically reductive form — chastity, for example — Franklin seems to have been intent on subverting where he does not deny. But in view of his pragmatic purpose, Franklin's list is not so unorthodox as it appears, for his disconcerting shifts of emphasis are merely the consequence of transposing ends into means, rather than proposing new ends. In subsuming 'Charity' under 'Frugality', for example, he does not intend to exchange the one for the other, but merely to recommend frugality as the means to charity. Franklin's critics commonly imply that he has elevated behavioral modes into intrinsic merits when in fact it is the very purpose of his instrumentalism to preserve this distinction.

In any case, it is well to heed Robert Sayre's warning not to take the table of virtues *au grand sérieux*.[13] It is a part of the autobiographer's highly amused account of a brash enterprise, and the fair-minded reader will find the anecdote of the speckled axe a sufficient proof that in his maturer days Franklin doubted that morality could be learned so easily or so fully. Furthermore, in composing — or, later, editing — the list, Franklin indulged his taste for satiric exaggeration. The rubric on 'Chastity', for example, is an extravagant overstatement of the principle that a virtue is what it does, and surely Franklin's admission that he could only achieve the appearance of humility is meant to imply that human virtues are less merits possessed than modes of behavior which faintly approximate goodness. One hesitates to go quite so far as Prof. Sayre in judging the list a canard; no doubt Franklin believed in it, at least to the extent of thinking that a person who followed its precepts would become a better man. But Prof. Sayre is right in insisting on Franklin's irony; the list is not meant in the sense assumed in most of the earnest attacks upon his ethics.

Franklin's irony is not of a random kind but arises from the essentially comic nature of the self's situation, a situation within which reason and experience never quite match. A man must live by rules, general concepts, formulas, and the like, yet his understanding is so imperfect that he cannot get his principles straight or even understand what they mean. There is always some discrepancy between the universal truth and the human formula for it, and between what we think we mean by a given statement and the meaning our statement would have if we could see all its implications, yet man's rules would not be rules if they did not pretend to universal validity; they mean to be the actual principles of reality, though in fact they are but inferences from a partial view of things. The self is thus placed in the comic position of having to act upon its generalizations as if they were certain truths while, at the same time, remaining aware of their provisional character. To forget that the rules are but rough approximations is to take on their false pretentions, but the man who refuses to accept them as universally valid is hardly less absurd than the credulous believer, since he cannot act at all, except as he is willing to pretend. Sanity is a balancing between belief and doubt in which even the wisest man is forced to some laughable contortions.

Hence Franklin's role-playing is the result of his awareness that a man's self-image is but one more provisional opinion. The wise man must doubt that he is really the person he takes himself to be, and since that personage is, in some degree, an impostor, the self grows accustomed to watching its identity transmigrate through a sequence of roles. But such role-playing should not be regarded as a kind of deception engaged in at will for ulterior motives, whether cynical or playful. Nor are the roles delusions, on the one hand, or, on the other, rhetorical devices, though in writing Franklin does exploit them as such. Franklin's roles emerge from his need to act within particular circumstances, and he assumes new roles as his situation alters. This fact bears witness to the other side of the paradox: though the self's roles are, in one sense, fictions, the self must believe in them, for to act is to assume that the self one has in mind is identical with one's actual self. By this rational necessity, the roles indicate the actor and are far more real than disguises.

That this ambiguous way of viewing his own identity has its source in Franklin's peculiar blend of empiricism and rationalism is illustrated by a well-known letter to his parents.

You both seem concern'd lest I have imbibed some erroneous Opinions. Doubtless I have my Share, and when the natural Weakness and Imperfec-

tion of Human Understanding is considered, with the unavoidable
Influences of Education, Custom, Books, and Company, upon our Ways of
thinking, I imagine a Man must have a good deal of Vanity who believes,
and a good deal of Boldness who affirms, that all the Doctrines he holds,
are true; and all he rejects, are false ...

I think Opinions should be judg'd of by their Influences and Effects;
and if a Man holds none that tend to make him less Virtuous or more
vicious, it may be concluded he holds none that are dangerous; which I
hope is the Case with me.[14]

This is very modest but very self-assured also. The empiricist stands
to the fore, insisting upon the limits which environment places upon
understanding; but the rationalist can easily be detected behind him,
ready with the assurance that Franklin possesses ethical standards so
certain that he can judge the moral effects of his opinions.

In notes listing questions to be asked the Junto, the same paradox
is applied to epistemology:

Q. What is Wisdom?
A. The Knowledge of what will be best for us on all Occasions and of
the best Ways of attaining it...
What is the [*written above:* 'is there any'] Difference between
Knowledge and Prudence?
If there is any, which of the two is most Eligible?[15]

Wisdom is apparently to be defined as the self's knowledge of its
strictly personal interests, but this in turn depends upon knowledge
of universal goodness for this is the only standard by which the self
can judge the actual usefulness of its ideas. One should also notice
that the empiricist bent of Franklin's questions is balanced by his
faith that questions so broad are answerable. If knowing the answer
to Franklin's last question were not an instance of wisdom, Franklin
would not have asked it; but if this answer is an instance of wisdom,
then wisdom involves more than 'knowledge of what will be best for
us on all Occasions'. It would be knowledge of reality itself, as well
as of man's interests. The same doubleness appears in the educational
objective Franklin proposes in his plan for the Pennsylvania Academy.

The Idea of what is *true Merit*, should also be often presented to Youth,
explain'd and impress'd on their Minds, as consisting in an *Inclination*
join'd with an *Ability* to serve Mankind, one's Country, Friends and
Family; which *Ability* is (with the Blessing of God) to be acquir'd or

greatly encreas'd by *true Learning*; and should indeed be the great *Aim* and *End* of all Learning.[16]

'*True Merit*' is not an essence but a process – a way of feeling and of acting – but the latter is dependent upon '*true Learning*', which is 'true' by the standard of reality rather than of usefulness.

Franklin's way of thought is nowhere more clearly summarized than in the Dunker's speech in the *Autobiography*. When Franklin asked this personage why the members of his sect had not drawn up a written creed, he replied:

When we were first drawn together as a Society ... it had pleased God to inlighten our Minds so far, as to see that some Doctrines which we once esteemed Truths were Errors, and that others which we had esteemed Errors were real Truths. From time to time he has been pleased to afford us farther Light, and our Principles have been improving, and our Errors diminishing. Now we are not sure that we are arriv'd at the End of this Progression, and at the Perfection of Spiritual or Theological Knowledge; and we fear that if we should once print our Confession of Faith, we should feel ourselves as if bound and confin'd by it, and perhaps be unwilling to receive farther Improvement; and our Successors still more so, as conceiving what we their Elders and Founders had done, to be something sacred, never to be departed from.[17]

To conceive the human situation in this way is to see it dramatically, because within this scheme ideas appear always as events – as the actual thought of a person in his particular circumstances – and the world itself has the status of an interpretation, being, as it is known, inseparable from the self's act of interpreting. Thus in human thought there is no such thing as a purely objective truth: the truth appears only within a perspective, and man's thinking is right in degree according to the breadth of his vision. The consequent perspectivism explains why it is that of all eighteenth-century Americans Franklin is the most fully rounded historical figure. Modern readers respond to Franklin as a realized character in their myth of the eighteenth century because he so consistently viewed himself in the same way. Though the period did not appear to him as it now does to us, he himself thought of it *as* a period, and his sundry roles – as printer, gentleman of leisure, backwoods' moralist, or sage of the Enlightenment – are the consequence of his world view and of the kind of self-interpretation it called for, rather than of his world as it actually was. Of course, the real conditions of his age caused him to see his situation as he did, and he may have been right in judging that these conditions forced the self to play diverse roles. But granting agreement upon this point, his view of eighteenth-century America is different from ours, and we should not bend his thought to our own conclusions. Since we look back to him from a culture disordered by excessive complexity, it is tempting to see his role-playing as a characteristically modern attempt to rescue identity by seeking a true self among the multiple selves which the conditions of today compel a person to be. But Franklin did not find his own diversity an obstacle, much less a misfortune, and the tone of good-humored confidence which pervades his writings indicates a man who never doubted he had a real identity.

There is an important difference between asking 'What sort of person am I?', as Franklin did, and asking 'Am I a person at all?' Franklin's question assumes that there is a self to be found, and thus his search for identity is a pleasant adventure, while in modern literature, identity itself is often at stake, and seeking it is a desperate struggle to survive. But agreeable as Franklin's quest is, the absence of pain from the record he has left does not lessen its dramatic quality. His drama is of a different kind — comedy, it could be called, since all turns out for the best. It is a drama created by perspectivism, which, instead of juxtaposing distinct characters, as in a play, develops its action through the contrast between the author and his earlier states of mind.

Franklin's reasoning inevitably led to the art of autobiography, for given his view of the self's situation, identity becomes problematical. The self is the center of its own experience, but it is constantly in motion — hovering, as it were, between two different modes of existence, the present event and the accumulated past. It is the person of this moment, but then, too, it is the person of all its moments at once, which is to say, that such a person never existed in any of them. Since both of these selves are equally real, yet each excludes the other, the true self can only be seen in their relation — in the constant interplay between the transcendent and immediate views of identity. The transcendent view is that of the whole lifetime considered at once, and this is such a view as theology would attribute to the Deity, but in looking back upon one's own life, one has to give one's own view the same form. While realizing that he cannot see his entire lifetime perfectly, Franklin must assume that he is omniscient relative to all his earlier states of mind, since his present view of his lifetime is the truest of all those he has to choose from. Thus the author of the *Autobiography* plays God, and the paradox of one God who is both eternal being and immanent spirit is shifted to the self, who is at once a man living in a particular moment and a consciousness which transcends all its lived moments in the act of regarding them from the outside as elements of a single lifetime.

Autobiography is a more demanding form of retrospective literature than either history or biography in the sense that the present from which the past is viewed and judged is more precisely defined. The historian's or biographer's present subsists merely implicitly as a system of tacit assumptions, but when a man writes of his own life, the present is embodied in his personality at the time of writing, and every fact he reports about his past reveals the author by showing what he now thinks of himself. Thus even a dishonest autobiographer would fail far less through the objective falsehood of his facts than through the resultant contrast between what he alleges about his past and the authorial personality his claims imply. More commonly, the failure is unintentional and consists either in making the past self so like the author that there is no development – and hence no story to tell – or in making the past self so different from the author that it is someone else's story rather than his own that is told. An exact balancing of identity and difference is required. The author must show us – and Franklin's theory of experience was ideally suited to express – one self through two persons.

Franklin the author represents the transcendent side of consciousness, the spectator who surveys the whole of his life, and his transcendent view is symbolized by the book's didactic purposes. The lessons and generalizations he offers claim, or at least aim at, universal truth, and they are to be credited on the ground that they hold true for all the author's lifetime.

Whatever Franklin's practical or artistic intentions may have been, it is an essential part of the book's meaning that it was written to instruct. He offers general truths, which are 'proved', as it were, by the success and felicity of his own life. In the opening address to his son, Franklin expresses the hope that 'the conducing Means I made use of, which with the Blessing of God, so well succeeded' may serve his posterity 'as they may find some of them suitable to their own Situations, and therefore fit to be imitated'.[18] The didactic purpose is again emphasized at the beginning of the second part by the insertion of letters from Abel James and Benjamin Vaughn, urging Franklin to complete the work. 'Your Biography', as Vaughn writes, 'will not merely teach self-education, but the education of a *wise man*; and the wisest man will receive lights and improve his progress, by seeing detailed the conduct of another wise man'.[19]

To be sure, the author changes character somewhat in the course of his narrative, and Sayre has suggested that the three main parts correspond to three distinct views of himself, each formed with an eye to Franklin's actual circumstances at the time of writing. But these changes are alterations not so much in the author's role as in that of the actor. It is the young and middle-aged man, not the child or youth, whose projects the elderly narrator criticizes; and Franklin the politician cannot properly emerge until the author reaches that portion of his life. The roles played by past selves must be distinguished from the authorial role, which, throughout, is that of the urbane but venerable sage, offering lessons, whether moral, political, or merely prudential, for the reader's instruction. The fundamental contrast, so far as the book's form is concerned, is not that between the various past selves but that between the man who looks back on the past and the man who lived it. The act of generalizing defines the author as the total consciousness toward which the actor is at every point developing. The author's lessons, though they are not final truths, are the truest opinions he can find, because they are derived from the widest view — the most extensive experience. But since the actor is also engaged in formulating general truths, generalizing unites as well as separates the two. In that the author knows better, he is distinct from the actor; but in that both participate in the same process, they are as one person, the Franklin of the *Autobiography*.

It is significant that Franklin views his childhood as if from the outside. He does so because he supposes that the ability to generalize is not sufficiently developed in the child to permit him to depict the child's state of mind by contrasting its generalizations with the author's. This assumption is quite in line with the typically eighteenth-century view of the mind's development expressed in the *Dissertation*:

All our Ideas are first admitted by the Senses and imprinted on the Brain, increasing in Number by Observation and Experience; there they become the Subjects of the Soul's Action. The Soul is a mere Power or Faculty of *contemplating* on, and comparing those Ideas when it has them; hence springs Reason: But as it can *think* on nothing but Ideas, it must have them before it can *think* at all.[20]

In the first pages, therefore, the child is seen indirectly through his family, and Franklin underlines facts which foreshadow his own maturer traits: his uncle Thomas' 'public-spirited' undertakings, his grandfather Folger's poem in favor of religious toleration, his father's good sense and mechanical ingenuity, the tradition of religious dissent which foreshadows Franklin's rebellion against the Crown.

Franklin's handling of the first experience treated at length, and the only one from childhood – the account of how he and his play-mates stole building stones to construct a wharf – exemplifies his perspectivism very well. The author explains that he was then already 'a Leader among the Boys' who, when the theft had been discovered, 'pleaded the usefulness of the work', and even more obviously turns the episode toward the future by concluding that it illustrates an 'early projecting public Spirit, tho' not then justly conducted'. By such touches the reader is made to feel the identity of the child with the good citizen of Philadelphia who founds a library, improves the streets, and organizes the first fire company. But the difference between child and author is also insisted upon, for Franklin is pictured at that embryonic phase of life when even he did not yet realize that 'nothing was useful which was not honest'.[21]

In the most memorable episode – Franklin's arrival at Phila-delphia – the literary advantages of this perspectivism are apparent. Since the author points it out, every reader recognizes the contrast between the young man's humble beginnings and the venerable auto-biographer's achievements. To be sure, this contrast emphasizes Franklin's success and makes the point that a poor youth can rise to greatness if he follows the precepts of Poor Richard. But these ideas would be far less forcefully expressed were it not for the vividness of the picture of the young man walking up the street with his rolls. It is the image which persuades, and, in the last analysis, the image is created by the contrast of perspectives. Young Franklin has the roundness and movement of a living person, because he is seen within his world – in terms of what he knows – and the youth's knowledge, in turn, is revealed by comparison with what the author knows: 'Thus I went up Market Street as far as fourth Street, passing the Door of Mr. Reed, my future Wife's Father, when she, standing at the Door saw me, and thought I made as I certainly did a most awkward ridiculous Appearance'.[22] That young Franklin did not recognize the girl in the doorway is a nice instance of the way he is placed within his unique moment and circle of consciousness. But since he is shown to have seen himself more accurately than Miss Reed, who would have judged his appearance differently had she known the accidents of his journey or his quite natural mistake about the price of Philadelphia bread, young Franklin and the author become identical in the process of interpretation, for both are engaged in placing the moment within the life already lived.

Because this process is constant, Franklin can exploit it as the means of giving continuity to the events he chronicles. His essential method is to treat each phase of the actor's story as an approximation of the author's consciousness. In almost every episode his opinion at the time contains a truth he will later improve upon in the midst of errors he will come to reject. For example, when he learns the Socratic mode of argument from excerpts in a rhetoric book, young Franklin amuses himself with confounding others by this means, but in time he abandons the method, except for the deferential manner of speaking. Similarly, though his youthful habit of trusting others is soon shaken by the treatment he receives from such men as Governor Keith and James Ralph, later experience tends to confirm the general principle of acting upon good faith.

In the latter part of the *Autobiography* the contrast between actor and author is not so sharp simply because the time gap has narrowed and the two are more nearly of an age. Fortunately, the importance of Franklin's public career keeps the temporal contrasts crucial enough as the gulf between past and present narrows. There is great interest in the differences between Franklin's opinions of 1740–57 and those of 1784–8. The account of his public-spirited projects is written with an eye to their later success, while the more strictly political episodes – those concerning the French and Indian War and the Pennsylvania legislature's struggle with the proprietors – are clearly designed to anticipate the Revolution. Franklin the political leader is always seen to be right in principle though distanced from the author by errors of judgment which, for the most part, only hindsight can correct. During Braddock's disastrous campaign, for example, he is still bemused by the prestige of British power, and yet, even then, he has a shrewd grasp of the difficulties of wilderness fighting which would turn the scales at Saratoga. Similarly, he shows remarkable foresight in recognizing the need for a central government in America and legislative control of taxation, but he has yet to learn that these measures are not possible within the imperial system.

As he sees Franklin approaching, in his opinions, the statesman of 1784, the reader can observe, through beautifully managed gradations, how the coming crisis began to emerge. In a mere joke there is dark prophecy. When a friend of Governor Morris asks Franklin why he has sided with 'these damned Quakers' in the assembly — 'Had not you better sell them? the Proprietor would give you a good price' — Franklin laughingly replies that the Governor 'has not yet black'd them enough'.[23] Whether the colonists were 'slaves' would be discussed in different tones a decade later, but it would be the same question.

The continuity achieved by this use of perspective has the effect of placing all the events within a firm pattern of causation. Though the *Autobiography* is as episodic as Puritan narrative, it moves forward smoothly as a developing action. Like the Puritan historians, Franklin thinks in terms of particular striking events, each of which stands as an epitome of his whole life and is symbolic very much in the Puritan way. As a result, the most memorable moments have the quality of snapshots — Franklin slipping the 'Dogood Papers' under the door of his brother's printing house, Franklin entering Philadelphia, Franklin pushing his wheelbarrow to create the appearance of industriousness, and the like. Yet seen within the autobiographer's double perspective, all the happenings make reference to the beliefs of the author at the end of his life. Thus the gaps between episodes are bridged, and each event is given the status of a phase in the cause-and-effect sequence by which the actor becomes the author. The elaborate web of causation is illustrated by the account of the controversy over the issuance of paper money. The bill enabling the Pennsylvania legislature to do so was opposed by powerful interests, and Franklin wrote a pamphlet in favor of this measure:

It was well receiv'd by the common People in general; but the Rich Men dislik'd it . . . and they happening to have no Writers among them that were able to answer it, their Opposition slackn'd and the Point was carried by a Majority in the House. My Friends there, who conceiv'd I had been of some Service, thought fit to reward me, by employing me in printing the Money, a very profitable Jobb, and a great Help to me.[24]

Franklin had then just bought out his partner in the printing business, and the success of the pamphlet was a crucial step on the road to wealth, but it also served as the cause of future political achievements by enhancing his reputation in the legislature. By writing the pamphlet, Franklin aligned himself with the common people in a progressive cause, and began to move toward the liberal politics of the revolutionary period. Yet if the incident opens upon the future, it also stands as an effect in which earlier events are summarized. Franklin confines himself to saying that the success of the pamphlet was 'another Advantage gain'd by my being able to write',[25] but much more lies behind this episode; Franklin's youthful reading, the founding of the Junto, in which he began to educate himself in public affairs, his previous publications, his experience in printing money for the New Jersey colony, his earlier uses of credit, even the experiments in simplified diet by which he gained time for self-education contribute to this event. Throughout the *Autobiography* each event emerges as an inevitable consequence of earlier ones and, in turn, prepares the way for those which follow.

Yet the effect is never mechanical. The episodes are not fitted together in a diagrammatic pattern but flow and merge naturally. Instead of tracing out the lines of causation, Franklin creates an atmosphere of relevance, so that one feels they *could* be traced. The action develops organically through manifold relations between happenings, relations so subtly reticulated that any given event seems to summarize and anticipate more than the reader can discern. Franklin's narrative is a unified action rather than a maze of potential patterns, because it implies at every point a governing logic whose presence is felt even though it is never made explicit.

In part, this is the consequence of Franklin's fine discretion, his unwillingness, though he is ready enough at proposing general rules of conduct, to explain the cause-and-effect relations in particular cases. On this subject he offers only brief comments here and there, but these suffice to imply much more than he pleases to specify and, indeed, can discern. Such reticence reflects, once again, Franklin's double perspective. As the author of the *Dissertation* argued, only omniscience can see 'all the intricate Consequences of every Action with respect to the general Order and Scheme of the Universe'.[26] But the fact that the author sees more clearly than the actor persuades the reader that there is a real order of which both are approximations. The book is only the author's view, as his tentative manner and sceptical comments constantly remind us. Thus Franklin's episodes stand free — invite other interpretations — exist as events in the real world, having definite meanings but implying also a total meaning which transcends all interpretations.

To see events in this way is to see them with the artist's eye, and it is perhaps the greatest paradox of a paradoxical life that Franklin succeeded so well in his art that he has commonly been judged as if he were no artist at all. His critics, with a few rare and recent exceptions, have proceeded as if they were dealing with the real man, the historical figure. But if it is asked how they know of this personage, the answer is through the imaginative self-image he presents in the *Autobiography*. Much additional evidence is to be found in his other writings, of course, but such is the power of this book that there is no way to avoid interpreting the rest in the light of it, and even its omissions are, by the motives they suggest, almost as influential as the facts it includes. That we cannot avoid taking the Franklin we see in the *Autobiography* as the actual man is the surest proof of his literary achievement. As process is principle seen from within time, the process of Franklin's self-interpretation points toward the principle of his identity. We know Franklin as a way of seeing, but so coherent is the vision and so convincing the drama of its development that we feel we know the man himself. And which of us would say this opinion is false?

It is generally thought that Franklin and Edwards should be placed in the American tradition at a point of transition between the Puritans and the transcendentalists. Edwards' view of symbol does, in an important though limited way, anticipate Emerson. Similarly, Franklin looks forward to Thoreau, who in 'Economy' seems to confirm Franklin's prudential philosophy through the very act of satirizing it. Franklin would surely have agreed with Thoreau's definition of the price of a thing as the amount of life required to procure it, and in Thoreau's humorous lists of expenses and earnings we recognize Franklin's kind of practicality. That Thoreau could not have read the *Autobiography* further strengthens the similarities by making them seem to come from instincts that both inherited rather than from imitation on Thoreau's part. But no one would venture to say that Thoreau is very much like Franklin. They differ most obviously in the relation they assume between the self and society, which for Franklin is nearly identical with the world itself, while for Thoreau it is an antagonist to be circumvented by self-reliance and the formation of a society of one's own choosing. In this Thoreau reflects a common prejudice of his time, which Emerson makes plain in *Nature* when, after defining nature as all that is 'NOT ME', he rather oddly comments that though philosophically speaking nature includes 'art, all

other men and my own body', men's creations amount to no more
than 'a little chipping, baking, patching, and washing'.[27] By this
questionable excuse, institutions, tradition, and the community itself
are excluded from the nature with which the transcendentalist would
bring himself into harmony.

Important as this difference is, it is but an outgrowth of a more
fundamental disagreement concerning the nature of experience itself.
For the transcendentalist, who is closer to the Puritan in this respect,
experience is an event having two distinct aspects. It is the perception of the present moment and it is the revelation of eternal truth.
Though the two are really one and can be recognized as one in
moments of greatest insight, there are no middle grounds between
them, no terms for describing experience which would make it something more than momentary as an event in time or less than eternal
in the meaning it intends and thus epitomizes. But one primary objective of Franklin and Edwards was to provide a middle term. They
undertook to resolve the dualistic tension of the Puritan mind by
discovering the answer which that mind demanded, seeking to unite
the self's experiential moment and the eternal will of God in an image
of perfect harmony. They were able to find their answer within
Puritan thought, with its insistence upon divine foreknowledge and
habitual emphasis on the difference between God's consciousness and
man's. By conceiving of knowledge with respect to where the knower
stands, Edwards and Franklin could explain why experience falls
short of the whole truth and yet is a potential summary of reality.
Thus their answer to the need for a middle term is point-of-view itself.
And the rewards this solution afforded can be seen by comparing
Franklin's kind of experience with that which Thoreau depicts: the
former is harmonious, confident, serene; the latter stressful, excited,
and enigmatic. For Franklin's essential subject is a process of smooth,
progressive development within a temporal continuum which the
juxtaposition of points of view creates, while Thoreau's subject is the
isolated moment which, though all-inclusive in its import, is unique
and autonomous as the only time in which one lives. Therefore, instead of supposing that Edwards and Franklin represent a logical step
toward the development of transcendentalism, it would be wiser to
see in them one response to the Puritan dilemma, a version of experience which is related to that of transcendentalism in that both grew
out of the persistent assumptions of Puritanism.

If Franklin and Edwards foreshadow the transcendentalists, they more directly anticipate Hawthorne, Melville, and James, in whose novels the same double perspective causes the symbol to generate multiple interpretations. Whether the fiery 'A' which Dimmesdale sees from the scaffold means 'Adulterer', as he supposes, or 'Angel', as the good townspeople interpret it, depends upon the observer's personality as the center of the facts he knows. This would not be the case were the symbol merely invented by the perceiving eye. Quite clearly, diverse meanings arise because the symbol exists in a real world which extends beyond those of the interpreters and has a true meaning which is more than what they can discern in it. Here then, already, is the novel of point of view, and we can recognize how natural it was for James to begin as a student of Hawthorne. The rationale of such fiction is summed up by Melville's Pip: 'I look, you look, he looks; we look, ye look, they look'.[28] But the novelists can only make their multiple views add up by adhering also to the other side of the paradox Edwards and Franklin explored. They must assume that there is a true meaning, though we only get views of it. This meaning is 'there', in the symbol, and at one with it, rather than merely a meaning projected upon the symbol by the observer of the moment. The fragment of red cloth radiates its own mysterious heat. To those who deplore Franklin's materialism or Edward's otherworldliness, it is perhaps best to reply that the one loved things for their real meanings, and the other loved God for having created real things.

Christ and Adam as 'figures' in American literature

URSULA BRUMM

Among the important writers of the nineteenth century only Melville and Hawthorne still regard the concepts 'type' and 'emblem' in the light of their religious derivation and substance. In isolated cases later writers in the New England tradition have used them in a way that recalls their religious meaning, without, so far as one can see, a full and precise understanding of it. As early as the time of Hawthorne and Melville the theory of the type coalesced with literary symbolism, contributing to its power to convince from its religious foundation. However, the character components of the type concept exerted an influence on American literature that persisted even longer than this. It is a distinctive trait of American literature far beyond the characterization techniques of Hawthorne and Melville that its characters often are not created as freshly conceived individuals but as based on fixed models, of which the most important are Adam and Christ.[1]

On Adam as the American hero *par excellence*, the ever newly modified archetypal hero of American literature, an important and interesting book has been written by R. W. B. Lewis: *The American Adam: Innocence, Tragedy and Tradition in the 19th Century*.[2] Lewis shows how the young American nation that had recently parted from Europe politically and from Calvinism spiritually chose Adam, the prototype of innocent man, as the symbol and ideal of its destiny. He also shows how the writers of the earlier nineteenth century, from approximately 1820 to 1860, take this ideal as the model for their heroes. In addition to Hawthorne and Melville, Oliver Wendell Holmes, Walt Whitman, and, in another way, Charles Brockden Brown, Cooper, and Montgomery Bird all fashioned their heroes according to the type of Adam. As Lewis shows, even the historians Bancroft and Parkman are under the spell of the innocent Adam.

Thus we may refer to Lewis's account for evidence of Adam

figures and symbolism in these authors, though his point of departure and in some ways his interpretation as well differ from those put forth here. As the guiding idea of his discussion Lewis chooses Emerson's comment on 'The party of the Past and the party of the Future, of Memory and Hope', which he interprets as the party of 'original sin' and that of 'innocence'. But this relativizes his argument in a way that is sometimes confusing. 'Memory' and 'Hope' cannot be exactly co-ordinated with past and future, and the latter pair of concepts can only be fixed relative to some given standpoint.

Lewis views the 'American Adam' only as a myth and archetype, neither recognizing nor mentioning his being anchored in the Calvinist theory of types and antitypes. But this involves a factor important for cultural history. This innocent Adam, who feels free of the burdens of history and faces the future — as anti-Calvinist as he appears in nineteenth-century literature — is as much a product of the Calvinist world drama as his counterpart, the Adam whose fall brought man to sin. With Adam God made the first covenant, the covenant of works; Adam is the 'type' of Christ, the 'second Adam'. This link which comes originally from typology is the reason why the two figures so often appear together and even merge in their literary use, so that some literary Adam figures, for instance Billy Budd, finally turn into Christ figures.[3] Whenever the hero meets a tragic fate, the model of the innocent Adam is linked to that of Christ suffering as, for example, Melville's Steelkilt from the 'Town-Ho's Story' in *Moby Dick*,[4] Pierre, Billy Budd, or Israel Potter.

These works present a double Adam—Christ figure that originates in Calvinism, but is transformed by anti-Calvinist, secular tendencies. The fact is that the Christ of the New Testament was ever characterized by an anti-predestination element, a gentleness and mercy that ill agree with the Old Testament sternness of Puritanism, and this is why Puritanism did not quite grant to Christ the predominant role given him by other Reformation sects. Those who began the rebellion against the severity of Puritanism in the later eighteenth century cast their lot with the merciful Christ.

Harriet Beecher Stowe has given us a fictional account of the beginning of this development in *The Minister's Wooing* (1859). Raised in a family of clergymen that cultivated an intellectual Calvinist tradition even in the middle of the nineteenth century, Harriet Beecher received a formidable education in theology.[5] Two events caused her great inner turmoil. When she was eleven, her

sister's fiancé was drowned in a shipwreck. She was plunged into a
religious crisis over the question whether this dear friend, who according to the Calvinist view was unconfirmed in his faith and thus unregenerate, had been condemned by God to eternal damnation. She
had a similar unfortunate experience in the period when *The Minister's
Wooing* was being written. In 1857 Harriet Beecher Stowe's son
Henry drowned in the Connecticut River. Here too, in addition to
her grief, she was deeply troubled by the question about the eternal
fate of the lad snatched away before his religious awakening.

The Minister's Wooing is a novel about Dr Hopkins, a well known
eighteenth-century New England clergyman. The problem about the
early death of an unregenerate is inserted in the narrative.[6] This
provides Harriet Beecher Stowe an opportunity to discuss the problems of predestination, divine grace, and election. She turns out to be
mainly a follower of Calvinism on essential points, yet at the same
time expresses unorthodox ideas. In the novel the heroine's fiancé is
missed at sea, and his mother is driven to the verge of madness at the
thought that her son, not at all a strict believer, might be condemned
to eternal damnation. In her distress she is comforted by her Negro
servant, Candace, a simple and uneducated woman (uneducated
always means theologically uneducated for the Puritans) who is an
ardent believer. This articulate lay priestess of religious feeling
becomes the antagonist of Dr Hopkins by invoking Christ's help
against the sternly interpreted dogma of predestination. She comforts
her desperate mistress with the following words:

'I knows our Doctor's a mighty good man, an' larned, – an' in fair weather
I hain't no 'bjection to yer hearin' all about dese yer great an' mighty tings
he's got to say. But, honey, dey won't do for you now; sick folks mus'n't
hab strong meat; an' times like dese, dar jest ain't but one ting to come to,
an' dat ar's Jesus ... Why, Jesus did n't die for nothin', – all dat love ain't
gwine to be wasted. De'lect is more'n you or I knows, honey! Dar's de
Spirit, – He'll give it to 'em; and ef Mass'r James is called an' took, depend
upon it de Lord has got him ready – course He has; so don't ye go to layin'
on your poor heart what no mortal creetur can live under, 'cause, as we's
got to live in dis yer world, it's quite clar de Lord must ha' fixed it so we
can, and ef tings was as some folks suppose, why, we could n't live, and dar
would n't be no sense in anyting dat goes on'.[7]

Although Christ's love is called upon here to mitigate the harsh-
ness of the dogma of predestination, his role as the divine redeemer

is not generally affirmed in liberal theology. On the contrary, Christ undergoes a transformation that brings him nearer to man. This is not only because religion grows more emotional, it also results from debates on points of dogma.

When William Ellery Channing defined the position of Unitarianism in 1819 in his ordination speech for Jared Sparks, he staked out his position solidly on the ground of the New Testament, in opposition to orthodox Calvinism: 'Jesus Christ is the only master of Christians'.[8] But when he proceeds to destroy the dogma of the Trinity, he has to place Christ on a lower level than God if he is to avoid a polytheistic conception: 'Jesus Christ is a being distinct from and inferior to God'.[9] There is a new interpretation of Christ as mediator whereby rational explanation is substituted for dogmatic conception. He did not sacrifice himself to redeem mankind from sin by his vicarious suffering. Nor was he acting as God, who assumed human shape because only God Himself could atone for the punishment exacted by divine justice for man's disobedience:

We regard him as a Saviour, chiefly as he is the light, physician, and guide of the dark, diseased, and wandering mind. No influence in the universe seems to us so glorious as that over the character; and no redemption so worthy of thankfulness as the restoration of the soul to purity . . . With these impressions, we are accustomed to value the gospel chiefly as it abounds in effectual aids, motives, excitements to a generous and divine virtue. In this virtue, as in a common centre, we see all its doctrines, precepts, promises meet; and we believe that faith in this religion is of no worth, and contributes nothing to salvation, any farther than as it uses these doctrines, precepts, promises, and the whole life, character, sufferings, and triumphs of Jesus, as the means of purifying the mind, of changing it into the likeness of his celestial excellence.[10]

Here Jesus is regarded primarily as the moral redeemer, by example and by doctrine. The transcendentalist goes beyond the Unitarian theologian to make the Son of God a figure of supreme humanity, whose brotherhood with man attests to man's divine nature. Ralph Waldo Emerson broke with the Unitarian Church in 1832. The immediate cause was his scepticism about the rite of the Lord's Supper, but his criticism of the church was much more far-reaching. In his 1838 address to the young theologians of Harvard Divinity School, he accuses it of overemphasizing the personal, the positive, and the ritual, and of worshipping Christ much as the Orientals and

Greeks worshipped their demigods: 'The stationariness of religion; the assumption that the age of inspiration is past, that the Bible is closed; the fear of degrading the character of Jesus by representing him as a man; — indicate with sufficient clearness the falsehood of our theology.'[11] And he rises to almost hymnic rapture when he proclaims (p. 127f.):

Jesus Christ belonged to the true race of prophets. He saw with open eye the mystery of the soul. Drawn by its severe harmony, ravished with its beauty, he lived in it, and had his being there. Alone in all history he estimated the greatness of man. One man was true to what is in you and me. He saw that God incarnates himself in man, and evermore goes forth anew to take possession of his World. He said, in this jubilee of sublime emotion, 'I am divine. Through me, God acts; through me, speaks. Would you see God, see me; or see thee, when thou also thinkest as I now think.'

The postulated divine nature of man logically requires the human nature of Christ. Three years after Emerson's 'Address', Theodore Parker held his famous sermon on 'The Transient and Permanent in Christianity', severing himself too from the Unitarian Church. Parker views the Bible and Christianity with a sense of history and the scepticism taught by history. What is variable and transient in Christianity are its dogmas: 'Men are burned for professing, what men are burned for denying.' He counts the typological interpretation of the Old Testament among the obsolete dogmas: 'Every fact in the early Jewish history has been taken as a type of some analogous fact in Christian history. The most distant events, even such as are still in the arms of time, were supposed to be clearly foreseen and foretold by pious Hebrews several centuries before Christ.'[12] Parker's conception of Jesus is as revolutionary as his Bible criticism. Jesus is said to combine divine and human features: 'But still was he not our brother; the son of man, as we are; the son of God, like ourselves? His excellence — was it not human excellence? His wisdom, love, piety — sweet and celestial as they were — are they not what we also may attain?'[13] Then Parker completes the transformation of the Son of God into a divine human:

But if, as some early Christians began to do, you take a heathen view, and make him a God, the Son of God in a peculiar and exclusive sense, much of the significance of his character is gone. His virtue has no merit, his love no feeling, his cross no burthen, his agony no pain. His death is an illusion, his resurrection but a show. For if he were not a man, but a god, what are all these things? what his words, his life, his excellence of achievements? It is all nothing, weighed against the illimitable greatness of Him who created the worlds and fills up all time and space! Then his resignation is no lesson, his life no model, his death no triumph to you or me, who are not gods, but mortal men, that know not what a day shall bring forth, and walk by faith 'dim sounding on our perilous way'. Alas! we have despaired of man, and so cut off his brightest hope.[14]

This is a logical development that had its parallels in Europe in the eighteenth and nineteenth centuries. The secularization of early American culture, a pre-eminently theological and rational culture, finds its expression in the humanization of Christ. Parker's words reveal a revolutionary transformation of values. Secular human life now has a significance all its own, and Christ is related to it in a naive and egoistical manner so that this alone lends his suffering significance. He must be human because, in Parker's opinion, this is the only way his suffering and his sacrifice can mean anything to us. Parker is the first to state clearly the necessity of making Christ the paragon of humanity. Christ is 'our brother; the son of man as we are, the son of God, like ourselves'.

'There was never an age, when men did not crucify the Son of God afresh', Parker says elsewhere in this sermon,[15] thereby making the tragic heroes of all ages Christ's brothers in suffering. We discern this same conviction in literary disguise in the fates of Pierre and Billy Budd, of Faulkner's Joe Christmas and his corporal. When Emerson and Parker linked the idealist conviction of man's divinity with Christ's humanity, they sensed that they were establishing a symbolic relation between the two. Christ must bear witness to man's divinity, and Christ's sacrifice is in vain unless man in his suffering regards it as a sign that consoles and exalts him. This means that Christ in his new role was suited for use in literature. Indeed, his metamorphosis even required this use as proof of his new, secularized service to mankind. In a secular age Christ becomes the literary symbol of the innocent man suffering for his brothers.

Even in a novel as deliberately realistic as William Dean Howells' *A Hazard of New Fortunes* (1889), there are unmistakable Christ features in the idealism and self-sacrifice of Conrad Dryfoos, who is shot during a strike. Allusions to Christ are also found in some twentieth-century writers: in Thomas Wolfe, the death of old Grant in *Of Time and the River*;[16] in Ralph Ellison, the shooting and burial of young Tod Clifton in *Invisible Man*;[17] and in Ernest Hemingway's *The Old Man and the Sea*,[18] the old man's endurance and suffering are crowned with the symbols of the Passion. As the luckless fisherman returns home from his battle with the sharks, he drags the mast of his boat to his hut as Christ did the cross, falling down several times with this burden on his shoulders. In his shack he lies face down on the bed with his arms extended out to the sides and the lacerated palms of his hands turned up. This is how he is found by his friend, the fisher boy, who then runs crying to the villagers to report what he has seen. Christ symbolism is used in another way by Nathanael West, namely, as social criticism: his novel *Miss Lonelyhearts* (1932) is the bitter portrait of a modern *ersatz* Christ. Miss Lonelyhearts, the 'comforter of lonely hearts', is the fictitious person of a newspaper who dispenses smooth, tailored consolation in answer to letters from lovelorn readers. This is a cruel travesty of the role of Christ in our time. The hero of the book, the journalist who answers letters from distressed and lovelorn readers, breaks down under the burden of his imitation. He entangles himself in the affairs of those in need of consolation until one of his disappointed letter writers finally shoots him.

No author has invoked the shadow of Christ more often, covertly or openly, than William Faulkner. In *The Sound and the Fury* (1929) it is covertly. Only the Easter services of the Negroes, which Dilsey attends with the thirty-three-year-old child Benjy, tell us that the three days revealing the decline of the Compsons, April 6, 7, and 8, 1928 (given in this order as chapter headings), are the Good Friday, Holy Saturday, and Easter Sunday of that year. *Light in August* (1932) is rife with signs that are more overt. No doubt Faulkner regards the unfortunate hero of this novel as Christ's brother. Joe Christmas, the man with the invisible 'cross' of Negro blood in his veins, was born during the Christmas season and baptized Joseph. 'It is so in the Book', his fanatical grandfather says, 'Christmas, the son of Joe. Joe, the son of Joe. Joe Christmas.'[19] His name is 'an augur of what he will do', and his life follows the example of Christ's suffering in a cruelly twisted way. Every step of this way he is rebuffed, wounded, baited and beaten by fanatics of various sects. Finally, in a horrible reversal of Christ's deed, he is driven to murder the Calvinist Joanna Burden, who tries to hold him with a love distorted by nymphomania. Christmas' life ends in shocking analogy to that of the Redeemer, nor does Faulkner neglect to remind us that at his death he is the same age as Jesus on the cross. On a Friday he is seized, tormented, and murdered, and in death he achieves an entirely unearthly transfiguration and something like a spiritual resurrection:

He just lay there, with his eyes open and empty of everything save consciousness, and with something, a shadow, about his mouth. For a long moment he looked up at them with peaceful and unfathomable and unbearable eyes. Then his face, body, all, seemed to collapse, to fall in upon itself, and from out the slashed garments about his hips and loins the pent black blood seemed to rush like a released breath. It seemed to rush out of his pale body like the rush of sparks from a rising rocket; upon that black blast the man seemed to rise soaring into their memories forever and ever. They are not to lose it, in whatever peaceful valleys, beside whatever placid and reassuring streams of old age, in the mirroring faces of whatever children they will contemplate old disasters and newer hopes. It will be there, musing, quiet, steadfast, not fading and not particularly threatful, but of itself alone serene, of itself alone triumphant. Again from the town, deadened a little by the walls, the scream of the siren mounted toward its unbelievable crescendo, passing out of the realm of hearing.[20]

The drama of the crucifixion is for Faulkner the archetypal human tragedy. Isaac McCaslin, one of his most likeable characters, decides to follow Christ's example. He gives up his life as a landowner and hunter, relinquishing the estate acquired by his ancestors with greed and guilt, and buys himself carpenter tools

not in mere static and hopeful emulation of the Nazarene as the young gambler buys a spotted shirt because the old gambler won in one yesterday, but (without the arrogance of false humility and without the false humbleness of pride, who intended to earn his bread, didn't especially want to earn it but had to earn it and for more than just bread) because if the Nazarene had found carpentering good for the life and ends He had assumed and elected to serve, it would be all right too for Isaac McCaslin.[21]

In scene, plot, and style, *A Fable* (1954) falls so little within the compass of Faulkner's other work that it was an unpleasant surprise and disappointment for most American critics.[22] Yet the theme of the book is very much in the American tradition: the rebellion of an ordinary man against authority, the military, and the war. Some

critics hold that in *A Fable* Faulkner's thought is naive and confused.[23]

From a European writer of Faulkner's stature we would expect in the
treatment of such a theme, even if no answer, at least a sharper and richer
debate in contemporary theological and philosophical terms than Faulkner
gives us: there is a considerable amount of debate in the book, but it tapers
off into nebulous language . . . Faulkner's explicit handling of ideas, outside
as well as within the domain of theology, is usually amateurish. When, for
example, as happens repeatedly in the novel, a cause is assigned to the
war, it is the familiar simplification current in the 1920's: that it was an
international conspiracy of the munitions makers and the generals.

By stating this,[24] Philip Blair Rice shows only that he entirely fails
to understand the monstrous, heretical conception that Faulkner
presents us with here. It is absolutely false that by means of over-
simplification 'an international conspiracy of munitions makers and
generals' is made responsible for the war. Faulkner's accusation is infinitely broader in its sweep: it is aimed at all civilization, at all who
are ambitious, who thirst for fame, who perform great feats, cultural
feats included, at all states, nations, armies, heroes, and at Christianity
as well. His accusation is aimed at *rapacity* as the mother of all culture
and civilization:

Rapacity does not fail, else man must deny he breathes. Not rapacity:
its whole vast glorious history repudiates that. It does not, cannot, must
not fail. Not just one family in one nation privileged to soar cometlike into
splendid zenith through and because of it, not just one nation among all the
nations selected as heir to that vast splendid heritage; not just France, but
all governments and nations which ever rose and endured long enough to
leave their mark as such, had sprung from it and in and upon and by means
of it became forever fixed in the amazement of man's present and the glory
of his past; civilization itself is its password and Christianity its masterpiece, Chartres and the Sistine Chapel, the pyramids and the rock-wombed
powder-magazines under the Gates of Hercules its altars and monuments,
Michelangelo and Phidias and Newton and Ericsson and Archimedes and
Krupp its priests and popes and bishops; the long deathless roster of its
glory — Caesar and the Barcas and the two Macedonians, our own Bona-
parte and the great Russian and the giants who strode nimbused in red
hair like fire across the Aurora Borealis, and all the lesser nameless who
were not heroes but, glorious in anonymity, at least served the destiny of
heroes — the generals and admirals, the corporals and ratings of glory, the

bat-men and orderlies of renown, and the chairmen of boards and the presidents of federations, the doctors and lawyers and educators and churchmen who after nineteen centuries have rescued the son of heaven from oblivion and translated him from mere meek heir to earth to chairman of its board of trade.[25]

Christianity as 'rapacity's masterpiece' — this is unmistakable evidence that Faulkner's interpretation of history and Christianity is intended to jar its audience. As an institution that exercises power, Christianity belongs among nations, generals, and heroes on the side of those who crave fame, wealth, and glory — 'glory' as a motive of historical deeds extends through the book like a *leitmotif* — and whose actions begin wars. But Christ, the 'Son of Man', stands on the other side, the side of ordinary people who want but to live in peace from the work of their own hands. He is the noble hero of the unheroic, the unassuming, the suffering. By setting the two parties in opposition, one acting and one suffering from the action, Faulkner provides his novel with a universal conception above and beyond its treatment of the world war. The world war is then only one of the historical catastrophes wherein the ordinary man is 'crucified'.

'There was never an age, when man did not crucify the Son of God afresh' — Faulkner has undertaken to prove this statement by Theodore Parker several times. Joe Christmas, the man between white and colored, is one such crucified figure; the mutinous corporal of the *Fable* is another. The 'unknown soldier' of the world war is Christ crucified: this comparison is the basic idea of *A Fable*. This is not only expressed by the many analogies in the life of the corporal. It also appears at the end of the novel in a parable, a truely gruesome and grotesque Faulknerian tale of a drunken detachment sent to Verdun to get a corpse from the casemates for the monument to the unknown soldier. Underway this corpse is exchanged for that of the executed Christ-corporal, which in turn is placed in the Paris monument.

The comparison of the hero with Christ is more direct and detailed in *A Fable* than in *Light in August*. Faulkner makes the analogy so exact in regard to Oriental descent, birth, family, and disciples that one would call it an allegory if one forgot that a true allegory has an abstract, conceptual core illustrated in personifications and figurative actions. Here we have a parallelism established between a contemporary character and a historico-religious one, Christ. This parallelism corresponds largely to the old typological comparison while it differs in decisive ways from modern techniques of symbolism and allegory.

Faulkner's reference to Christ does not fit in the category of symbolic structures that today's critics so readily investigate. It is related to the symbol but not identical with it. Where the usual symbol points from the limited to the boundless — it can be defined as a concrete, pictorial form with a nearly unlimited variety of interpretation — the Christ figure is summoned in literature to give a solid and consoling interpretation to the muddled abundance and ambiguity of life which might otherwise seem meaningless or miserable. This is a symbolism in the reverse direction, which points from the unsifted abundance of life to the *one* definite message. The use of exact historical facts represent another departure from usual symbolism and the mythical symbol. The date, day of the week, details of the Passion of Christ, his age, his disciples — all of these facts about unique events are employed symbolically to create the analogy of man with the son of God.[26] Unlike mythical symbols, Christ symbols cannot be freely manipulated and transformed. They stand immutable amidst the infinite variety of human suffering, from where they point toward the ideal, the redemption.

Faulkner's Christ-parallelism is a modern continuation and modification of a typological thought that seeks reincarnations of eternal models in every age. But the age of Calvinism had to pass before Christ, to whom all types were originally connected, could himself become a type who is 'fulfilled' by a man who merges with him. The corporal with the twelve followers, who is betrayed by one of them, and who wants to end the slaughter in the trenches of World War I, fulfills Christ's role in our own time, and he is accordingly a character lacking individual traits and specific features.

Even though the basic idea of the Christ analogy was Calvinistic, its literary execution depended on the anti-Calvinist currents mentioned above. The corporal is a modern and even more radically humanized version of the Christ figure sketched by Emerson and Parker when they made the son of God into the divine brother of man. Faulkner's Christ is the man who suffers symbolically and actually for a mankind entangled in the tragic conditions of this world. The Christ of his conception is more tragic and earthly than Emerson's or Parker's. Both Christ and the corporal die without having provided more than a noble example for mankind. They are destroyed physically by the powers that have organized the world according to their own rules.

As we saw above, the transformation of the image of Christ by the transcendentalists was the result of a rebellion against the absolute authority of a God conceived with Old Testament severity. Faulkner also continues this tendency in his own way, by putting the generalissimo in the place of God. The old general is the supreme military authority, to whom the three allied armies are subordinate — the threefold symbolism of three flags, three armies, is stressed — and in addition he is the natural father of the corporal. The military hierarchy he commands is described in religious terms:

First and topmost were the three flags and the three supreme generals who served them: a triumvirate consecrated and anointed, a constellation remote as planets in their immutability, powerful as archbishops in their trinity, splendid as cardinals in their retinues and myriad as Brahmins in their blind followers; next were the three thousand lesser generals who were their deacons and priests and the hierarchate of their households, their acolytes and bearers of monstrance and host and censer.[27]

Like Melville, Faulkner cannot see how an omnipotent God can avoid direct responsibility for the power exercised on earth. He makes the general represent this power, and this means above all the power that created and that perpetuates the conditions of this world. He is general, Caesar, God the father, and the devil, all in one person. He wants to induce the corporal to flight and to betrayal of himself, his rebellion and disciples, and his meeting and conversation with the corporal correspond to the temptation of Jesus by the devil. Just as the devil takes Jesus to a mountain and then to the pinnacle of the temple overlooking Jerusalem, so the old general takes his son to the Roman citadel overlooking the city and offers him the world:

'Then take the world', the old general said. 'I will acknowledge you as my son; together we will close the window on this aberration and lock it forever. Then I will open another for you on a world such as caesar nor sultan nor khan ever saw, Tiberius nor Kubla nor all the emperors of the East ever dreamed of.'[28]

But the corporal — and herein lies Faulkner's heretical interpretation of Christ — rebels against this father and refuses to submit to him, for which he is executed. Dostoyevsky's *The Great Inquisitor* was mentioned in the discussion of *A Fable*, and Faulkner also coincides with Dostoyevsky in his argument that rather than Christ it was the opposite party of bloody force that converted the world to Christianity:

It wasn't He with his humility and pity and sacrifice that converted the world; it was pagan and bloody Rome which did it with His martyrdom; furious and intractable dreamers had been bringing that same dream out of Asia Minor for three hundred years until at last one found a caesar foolish enough to crucify him . . . Because only Rome could have done it, accomplished it, and even He . . . knew it, felt and sensed this, furious and intractable dreamer though He was.[29]

But Faulkner goes much further than Dostoyevsky. His Christ—corporal opposes not only the church and its rulers but also the ultimate basis of power, God Himself, by Whom he must necessarily be defeated. He is therefore a tragic character, much as Christ himself is a tragic figure in Faulkner's view. Both go down to defeat because they defend the cause of peace against force. But in each case defeat brings a moral victory. As Christ refuses to win followers by deception, changing stone into bread, so the corporal resists the coaxing of the priest whom the general charged with persuading him to save himself and his followers:

'Remember –' the priest said. 'No, you cant remember, you dont know it, you cant read. So I'll have to be both again: defender and advocate. *Change these stones to bread, and all men will follow Thee.* And He answered, *Man cannot live by bread alone.* Because He knew that too, intractable and furious dreamer though He was: that He was tempted to tempt and lead man not with the *bread*, but with the *miracle* of that bread, the deception, the illusion, the delusion of that bread; tempted to believe that man was not only capable and willing but even eager for that deception, that even when the illusion of that miracle had led him to the point where the bread would revert once more to stone in his very belly and destroy him, his own children would be panting for the opportunity to grasp into their hands in their turn the delusion of that miracle which would destroy them . . .'

'Tell him that', the corporal said.

'Power', the priest said. 'Not just power over the mere earth offered by that temptation of simple miracle, but that more terrible power over the universe itself – that terrible power over the whole universe which that mastery over man's mortal fate and destiny would have given Him had He not cast back into the Tempter's very teeth that third and most terrible temptation of immortality: which if He had faltered or succumbed would have destroyed His Father's kingdom not only on the earth but in heaven too because that would have destroyed heaven, since what value in the

scale of man's hope and aspiration or what tensile hold or claim on man himself could that heaven own which could be gained by that base means — blackmail: man in his turn by no more warrant than one single precedent casting himself from the nearest precipice the moment he wearied of the burden of his free will and decision, the right to the one and the duty of the other, saying to, challenging his Creator: *Let me fall — if You dare?'*
'Tell him that', the corporal said.[30]

This rejection of power involves both an external defeat and an inner victory. The priest who wanted to change the corporal's mind bows to him and asks to be saved. Then he goes out and falls on a bayonet.

A Fable is the fable about the tragic fate of the ordinary, peace-loving man in this world. According to the other possibility of interpreting the title, it is the legend of Christ suffering symbolically in the name of the ordinary man. By making Christ into a 'type' of the non-violent rebel against power, Faulkner colors the latter and his cause with a saintly glow. The corporal is the common man ennobled by brotherhood with Christ, an ordinary man who, as the ideal of the unheroic hero, is the true prototype of American literature.

Hemingway, Wolfe, and Ellison had similar aims of elevation and glorification when they lent their modern heroes suffering features of Christ. Their works share with Faulkner's a world view that is tragic in a certain way, something seldom encountered otherwise in American literature. In American fiction Christ becomes the 'type' of the hero who suffers despite his innocence, or perhaps precisely because of it. He thereby fulfills a special function resulting from the peculiar dilemma of the tragic hero in America.

Actually it seems to be a paradox to speak of a 'tragic American hero'. Can there be such a thing as an openly confessed tragic world view in American literature? Does the American regard tragic experience as the unavoidable and necessary lot of man? In both cases the answer is no, and this is a basic difference between American literature and European. A literature that is acknowledged to be democratic, of a nation with an optimistic belief in life, cannot openly affirm the tragic experience of life. If tragic problems are encountered nonetheless, a situation arises where a redeemer is needed and Christ is summoned in aid. The ideal of the American is basically the innocent man, the new Adam of the new world, who lives in the best of all nations, a nation and a society he has shaped according to his own ideals. In this society he devotes himself to peaceful endeavors and the pursuit of happiness, firmly convinced that he is fairly entitled to a happy life.

Of course defects may appear in the social order; at times it may fall short of its ideal and then expose its heroes to distress. This is what happened for instance toward the end of the nineteenth century, and the conflicts that arose were vigorously exploited by naturalistic and sociocritical writers. Their goal, however, was the removal of defects and the restoration of an originally just order rather than revolutionary transformation. This is one possibility of discovering conflicts for literary use in an ideal society without calling the society itself into question and without becoming aware of an inescapable tragedy in life. Henry James explored another possibility by sending his 'innocent' heroes and heroines to old and sinful Europe to become involved in tragic or near-tragic experiences, as innocent victims if not as collaborators.[31]

But the writers now being considered are concerned with a deeper level of experience. Melville, Hemingway, and Faulkner depict innocent people, ordinary Americans, who encounter inexplicable and invincible adversities given along with life itself. Their optimistic view of life yields no explanation for evils that are of an entirely different nature from social abuses. In this sense Billy Budd is the prototype of the tragic American hero. He is absolved of the Calvinist dogma of original sin, but he encounters an evil that persists and 'for which God alone is made responsible', because in this respect He is still the 'omnipotent God' of Calvinism. As in *Moby Dick* Melville here too places evil in close proximity to God. Faulkner's corporal is a more radical successor to Melville's Billy Budd. He rebels against the omnipotent lord of all powers and wars, God-Satan, for which intentional rebellion he meets the same fate encountered by Billy Budd for his unintentional one: a death compared to the crucifixion by the author to tell us that we view an innocent man suffering vicariously.

For Melville, Billy Budd is wholly innocent. He has not the least share in any human failing which for the Greek hero is a precondition of his tragic consummation. Basically the same can be said of Melville's Pierre, and of Faulkner's corporal as well, a character without human weaknesses and faults. At bottom even the cruel Joe Christmas is a basically innocent person who is prevented from being innocent all his life. His constant violence is really nothing other than his reaction to the inexplicable and incessant adversities in life, the helpless rage of innocence defiled that culminates in the murder of his unwelcome benefactress. The enemies of the innocent include not only evil people but good and well-meaning ones in addition. One gets a glimpse of this insight in *Billy Budd*. But the innocent can neither endure nor vanquish evil; instead, they are crushed by it.

The rage, the white-hot indignation and abysmal despair at the world one so often encounters in American literature is frequently the result of this perplexed, helpless innocence of an optimistic faith in life. When the hero who cherishes his own innocence encounters life's adversities, he cannot avoid the conflict. The dilemma of such heroes is that their very innocence prevents them from accepting life's adversities and thereby transcending their fates. The innocent man is at the same time an incomplete man: he must shun experience, for experience brings guilt. His only escape from such a conflict is madness or death. The bitter outbursts of innocent heroes, who often leave an entire world in ruins behind them, would be meaningless if Christ did not lend them the significance of innocence suffering magnificently. Even evil and embittered 'innocents' are apparently unable to do without Christ. Thus we encounter in American literature the strange phenomenon of negative Christ figures, in whom an outraged and unbending 'innocence' is converted to cruelty. This is the case with Joe Christmas, as with the Quaker 'Nick of the Woods' in the novel of the same name by Montgomery Bird. His family having been murdered by Indians, he conceals beneath the mask of a peace-loving Quaker the murderous avenger who slaughters his Indian victims with an ax and marks them with a chilling bloody cross. It is also the case with Ahab, wounded by the incarnation of a neutral evil, Moby Dick, an Ahab who baptizes his helpers in the pursuit of this evil '*in nomine diaboli*' and who hunts Moby Dick with a suicidal, holy madness.

Tragic consummation, the supreme non-religious blessing attainable by man in his earthly struggles, demands of its conferee, paradoxically enough, that he be initiated into guilt. Only the man who can acknowledge that neither he nor life is blameless can transcend his fall. He must accept responsibility and punishment as the price for his inner victory in defeat. But for the innocent hero there is no escape. He cannot be reconciled with his situation as a tragedy because he is convinced that he does not deserve his misfortune. The American hero freed of the conviction of total depravity is unable to deal with the problem of evil in the world. The radical suppression of the dogma of original sin created a dilemma to escape from which American authors called on Christ, not so much the son of God as the innocent one made to suffer persecution and crucifixion. He suffers for mankind and this sanctifies his suffering: it needs no explanation. The innocent hero is consoled at the thought of a brotherhood of all who suffer represented by Christ. The symbol of the crucified one, impressed on the unfortunate American Adam like a stamp, lends him a consecration and transfiguration he could not have attained alone, and it may also satisfy a secret ambition for distinction from and elevation above an egalitarian society.

Christ, the 'hero of the lowest station', is invoked when the ordinary, innocent, suffering democratic hero is defeated by life. His presence lends the defeat the splendor of victorious transcendence that is the mark of tragedy. Santayana once called it 'glorification of life', the glorification of life in the face of death. In American literature it is not the mortal hero that glorifies life in defeat, it is instead the Christ invoked who brings transfiguration and explanation.

Notes

CHAPTER 1

1 The invitation to revaluation was augmented by Miller's polemic style and by the sense of cultural tensions that pervades his work. Undoubtedly, the disparity between his outlook and the Puritans' imaginative achievement seemed a barrier at first to literary studies, but it proved to be a salutary goad to intellectual preparation. For an assessment of Miller's achievement and influence, see (for example): David A. Hollinger, 'Perry Miller and Philosophical History', *History and Theory*, VII (1968), 189–202; Edmund S. Morgan, 'Historians of Early New England', in *The Reinterpretation of Early American History*, ed. Ray Billington (San Marino, Cal., 1966), pp. 41–63; and Gene Wise, 'Implicit Irony in Recent American Historiography: Perry Miller's New England Mind', *Journal of the History of Ideas*, XXIV (1968), 579–600. All of Miller's major works belong to intellectual history and therefore do not appear in the bibliography in this volume. Because of their influence, however, at least some of them deserve mention here: *Orthodoxy in Massachusetts, 1630–1650* (Cambridge, Mass., 1933), the two volumes of *The New England Mind* (New York, 1939, 1953), and the essays collected in *Errand Into the Wilderness* (Cambridge Mass., 1956) and in *Nature's Nation* (Cambridge, Mass., 1967). Recent work in American Puritan typology has generally been antagonistic to Miller, but here again he deserves mention as a major influence: see his introduction to Jonathan Edwards, *Images or Shadows of Divine Things*, ed. Perry Miller (New Haven, 1948), and 'Roger Williams: an Essay in Interpretation', in *The Complete Writings of Roger Williams*, vol. VII, ed. Perry Miller (New York, 1959). In addition to Miller, several other prominant intellectual historians have exerted a strong influence upon colonial literary studies: among others, William Haller, Geoffrey Nuttall, Samuel Eliot Morison, and Edmund S. Morgan. See Michael McGiffert, 'American Puritan Studies in the 1960's', *William and Mary Quarterly*, XXVII (1970), 36–67; David D. Hall, 'Understanding the Puritans', in *The State of*

American History, ed. Herbert J. Bass (Chicago, 1970), and introduction to the Harper Torchbook reprint of Miller, *Orthodoxy in Massachusetts* (New York, 1970); the bibliographical essay in Peter Gay, *A Loss of Mastery: Puritan Historians in Colonial America* (Berkeley, 1966), and Alden T. Vaughan's introduction to his source-book, *The Puritan Tradition in America, 1620–1730* (New York, 1972). Vaughan's anthology, however, generally neglects the literary aspects of 'Puritan Tradition' as do all other anthologies of its kind, including the most recent (e.g., those edited by George M. Waller, Sidney V. James, David D. Hall, Michael McGiffert, and Richard Reinitz). I do not of course refer here to the recent literary anthologies of Puritan writings – those edited by George F. Horner and Roger Bain; Norman S. Grabo; Harrison T. Meserole, Walter Sutton, and Brom Weber; Larzer Ziff; Richard Poirier and William L. Vance; Kenneth Silverman. All of these, as I noted above, express the growing sense of the importance of early New England writing.

2 For a full listing of recent work on Taylor, see: Carol Ann Hoffman, 'Edward Taylor: a Selected Bibliography', *Bulletin of Bibliography*, XXIII (1961), 85–7; Mary Jane Elkins, 'Edward Taylor: a Checklist', *Early American Literature*, IV (1969), 56–63; Kenneth A. Raqua and Karl Keller, 'Additions to the Edward Taylor Checklist', *Early American Literature*, IV (1969), 117–19; Phillip E. Pierpont, 'Edward Taylor Checklist III: Addenda, Corrections, and Clarifications', *Early American Literature*, V (1970), 91–4; Constance J. Gefvert, *Edward Taylor: an Annotated Bibliography, 1668–1970* (Kent, Ohio, 1971); Norman S. Grabo, 'Edward Taylor', in *Fifteen American Authors Before 1900: Bibliographic Essays on Research and Criticism*, eds. Robert A. Rees and Earl N. Harbert (Madison, 1971), pp. 333–56. See also Norman S. Grabo, '*Gods Determinations*: Touching Taylor's Critics', *Seventeenth-Century News*, XXVIII (1970), 22–4; Douglas Grant, 'Edward Taylor: Poet in a Wilderness', in *Purpose and Place: Essays on American Writers* (London, 1965), pp. 7–13; Kenneth B. Murdock, 'The Colonial Experience in the Literature of the United States', *Publications of the American Philosophical Society*, C (1956), 129–32; Austin Warren, 'Edward Taylor', in *Major Writers of America*, ed. Perry Miller (New York, 1962), vol. I, pp. 51–62; Alfred Weber, 'Edward Taylor: Besprechung einer Taylor-Ausgabe und Notizen zu einem Forschungsbericht', *Jahrbuch für Amerikastudien*, VII (1962), 320–34; and the Goldentree Bibliographies compiled by Richard Beale Davis and Alden T. Vaughan. On the discovery of Taylor's poetry, see Richard D. Altick, *The Scholar Adventurers* (New York, 1950), 306–8, and Thomas H. Johnson, 'The Discovery of Edward Taylor's Poetry', in Frederick

B. Adams, 'The Crow's Nest', *Colophon*, New Graphic Series, I, (1939), 101–4.

3 Some representative recent studies in non-literary areas which are pertinent to the study of the American Puritan imagination: Bernard Bailyn, *The New England Merchants in the Seventeenth Century* (Cambridge, Mass., 1955); Emery Battis, *Saints and Sectaries: Anne Hutchinson and the Antinomian Controversy in the Massachusetts Bay Colony* (Chapel Hill, N.C., 1965); Kai T. Erikson, *Wayward Puritans: a Study in the Sociology of Deviance* (New York, 1966); Howard M. Feinstein, 'The Prepared Heart: a Comparative Study of Puritan Theology and Psychoanalysis', *American Quarterly*, XXII (1970), 166–76; Antonello Gerbi, *La Dispute del Nuovo Mundo* (Milan, 1955); George Lee Haskins, *Law and Authority in Early Massachusetts* (New York, 1960); James Fulton Maclear, '"The Heart of New England Rent": the Mystical Element in Early Puritan History', *Mississippi Valley Historical Review*, XLII (1955–6), 621–52; Robert Middlekauff, *The Mathers: Three Generations of Puritan Intellectuals, 1596–1728* (New York, 1971); Walter Ong, *Ramus: Method, and the Decay of Dialogue from the Art of Discourse to the Art of Reason* (Cambridge, Mass., 1958); Edward K. Trefz, 'The Puritans' View of History', *Boston Public Library Quarterly*, IX (1957), 115–36; Michael Walzer, *The Revolution of the Saints: a Study in the Origins of Radical Politics* (Cambridge, Mass., 1965). Also pertinent are the findings in the emergent field of quantitative history (mentioned below), which are gradually beginning to influence literary studies. See, for example, the books by John Demos, Philip Greven, Jr, Kenneth A. Lockridge, Sumner C. Powell, and Darrett B. Rutman. Finally, I want to stress the great value of recent works dealing with other branches of the American Puritan imagination, such as Cyclone Covey, 'Puritanism and Music in Colonial America', *William and Mary Quarterly*, VIII (1951), 378–88, and Allan I. Ludwig, *Graven Images: New England Stone-Carving and its Symbols, 1650–1815* (Middleton, Conn., 1966).

It may be well to note that the Selected Bibliography in this book excludes essay-reviews, annotated bibliographies, and editions, though of course these are valuable auxiliary guides to the study of the American Puritan imagination. Some representative examples: Sacvan Bercovitch, 'Annotated Bibliography' to *Typology and Early American Literature*, ed. Sacvan Bercovitch (Amherst, 1972), pp. 249–338; Delmer I. Davis, 'Critical Editions of Samuel Sewall's *Phaenomena Quaedam Apocalyptica...*' (Dissertation: Colorado, 1968); Shirley W. Harvey, 'Nathaniel Ward: his Life and Works together with an Edited Text of His *Simple Cobler*' (Dissertation: Boston, 1935); J. A. Leo

LeMay, 'Recent Bibliographies in Early American Literature', *Early American Literature*, VII (1973), 66–77; George E. McCandlish, 'Annotations for a New Edition with a Definitive Text of Cotton Mather's *Magnalia Christi Americana* (1702), Books I and II' (Dissertation: Harvard, 1963); and David E. Smith, 'Millenarian Scholarship in America', *American Quarterly*, XVII (1965), 535–49.

4 Some representative recent non-literary studies in cultural continuity: Daniel Boorstin, *The Genius of American Politics* (Chicago, 1953); Richard L. Bushman, *From Puritan to Yankee: Character and the Social Order in Connecticut, 1690–1765* (Cambridge, Mass., 1967); Sidney E. Mead, *The Lively Experiment* (New York, 1963); Richard H. Niebuhr, *The Kingdom of God in America* (New York, 1957); David W. Noble, *Historians Against History* (Minneapolis, 1965); Stow Persons, *American Minds* (New York, 1958); Richard Schlatter, 'The Puritan Strain', in *The Reconstruction of American History*, ed. John Higham (New York, 1962); G. M. Stevenson, *The Puritan Heritage* (New York, 1952); Warren I. Susman, 'History and the American Intellectual: Uses of a Usable Past', in *The American Experience*, ed. Hennig Cohen (New York, 1968), pp. 84–105; Ola Winslow, *Meetinghouse Hill: 1630–1783* (New York, 1952); and Irvin G. Wyllie, *The Self-Made Man in America* (Brunswick, N.J., 1954). Also of interest in this connection are essays on teaching methods, such as Joseph M. Garrison, Jr, 'Teaching Early American Literature: Some Suggestions', *College English*, XXXI (1970), 487–97.

I have excluded scholarship and criticism on Edwards and Franklin in the Selective Bibliography, and, indeed, on all writers after the seventeenth century, except where the discussion pertains to continuities in a general sense — i.e., to groups of writers rather than to writers individually. On Edwards and Franklin, see, for example, Everett Emerson, 'Jonathan Edwards', and Bruce I. Granger, 'Benjamin Franklin', in Rees and Harbert (eds.), *Fifteen American Authors*, pp. 169–84, 185–206, and J. A. Leo LeMay, 'Franklin and the *Autobiography*: an Essay on Recent Scholarship', *Eighteenth-Century Studies*, I (1967–8), 185–211. Regarding nineteenth- of twentieth-century writers — e.g., Poe, Hawthorne, Melville, Emerson, Dickinson, Faulkner — students should consult the many bibliographical guides now available, as well as such thematic bibliographical guides as Abraham Avni's 'The Influence of the Bible on American Literature: a Review of Research from 1955 to 1965', *Bulletin of Bibliography*, XVII (1970), 101–6, and essay-reviews of pertinent works and subjects, such as Carl F. Strauch's 'Typology and the American Renaissance', *Early American Literature*, VI (1971), 167–78.

CHAPTER 2

1 At least this is the confident assertion on the dust jacket of Thomas H. Johnson (ed.), *The Poetical Works of Edward Taylor* (New York, 1939).

2 Arthur O. Lovejoy, 'The Historiography of Ideas', *Essays in the History of Ideas* (Baltimore, 1948), p. 7.

3 The problem of poetic diction, whether blamed upon Edmund Spenser's intentional archaisms or Milton's Latinisms, is a problem of style which does not seriously qualify this assertion. The incidence of individual words with exclusively 'poetic' meaning is minute; not even the popular eighteenth-century term 'contiguous' ever enjoyed the degree of specialization accompanying the modern 'hexachlorophine'. Popular morphemic constructs like Mather Byles's 'the tuneful Nine' or Philip Freneau's 'the generous flame' – a monosyllabic article or adjective followed by a disyllabic adjective followed by a monosyllabic noun – involve a similar question of style.

4 Without implying that her position is always clear, satisfying, or right, I shall limit my discussion to Langer's *Problems of Art: Ten Philosophical Lectures* (New York, 1957), which is a simple and convenient introduction to the aesthetic philosophy she explicates fully in *Feeling and Form: a Theory of Art developed from Philosophy in a New Key* (New York, 1953).

5 This brief resumé cannot do Langer's theory of primary illusions justice; see *Feeling and Form*, esp. pp. 45–68.

6 Langer, *Problems of Art*, pp. 159–60.

7 'The Reflexion', in Donald E. Stanford (ed.), *The Poems of Edward Taylor* (New Haven, 1960), pp. 14–15; I have modified the spelling.

8 Jonathan Edwards, *A Treatise Concerning Religious Affections*, in John E. Smith (ed.), *The Works of Jonathan Edwards*, vol. II (New Haven, 1959), p. 301; Edwards identifies the 'divine sense' with literary taste. Both Carl Gustav Jung, 'Psychology and Literature', and R. W. Gerard, 'The Biological Basis of Imagination', appear in Brewster Ghiselin (ed.), *The Creative Process: a Symposium* (Berkeley, 1952).

9 Langer, *Problems of Art*, p. 72.

10 *Ibid.*, p. 80; cf. 'Art is the creation of forms symbolic of human feeling', *Feeling and Form*, p. 40.

11 Edwin C. Rozwenc, 'Captain John Smith's Image of America', *William and Mary Quarterly*, third ser. XVI (1959), 28; Rozwenc's main emphasis is still on the credibility of Smith's reportage, the reliability of otherwise verifiable data. William R. Taylor, 'William Wirt and the Legend of the Old South', *William and Mary Quarterly*, third ser. XIV (1957), 477–93; Taylor treats the artistic aspects quite satisfactorily, though he does not generalize his method

into a principle of historical procedure, and is certainly incorrect in suggesting that Wirt in 1817 'initiated a kind of historical writing which was almost wholly new' (p. 487).

12 Langer, *Problems of Art*, p. 124.

13 See Edwards, *Religious Affections*, and Taylor's eight manuscript sermons on the Lord's Supper (1694) in the Prince Collection of the Boston Public Library, Boston, Mass., as well as his fourteen 'Christographia' sermons (1701–3) in the Yale University Library, New Haven, Conn.; Taylor's striking anticipation of Edwards must be attained through inference.

14 E. H. Gombrich, 'Icones Symbolicae: the Visual Image in Neo-Platonic Thought', *Journal of the Warburg and Courtauld Institutes*, XI (1948), 163–92, discusses Catholic concern for this same magnetism in this period, esp. pp. 166–7.

15 Edwards, *Religious Affections*, p. 337, presents the 'character' of a truly humble man.

16 Perry Miller, *The New England Mind: the Seventeenth Century* (New York, 1939), pp. 360–1.

17 Alan Simpson, *Puritanism in Old and New England* (Chicago, 1955), p. 21.

18 When they approached poetry from a general, intellectual point of view – as Ramus does – rhetoricians of the Aristotle–Cicero–Quintillian tradition also relegated poetry to the role of handmaid to oratory, except when publicists like Sir Philip Sidney or George Puttenham made some special plea. The names I cite above have all been associated, with varying significance, with Ramus, whose influence on English logic and imagery has only recently been explored. See Rosemund Tuve, *Elizabethan and Metaphysical Imagery: Renaissance Poetic and Twentieth-Century Critics* (Chicago, 1947), esp. pp. 331–53; Wilbur Samuel Howell, *Logic and Rhetoric in England, 1500–1700* (Princeton, 1956); and Walter J. Ong, *Ramus: Method, and the Decay of Dialogue from the Art of Discourse to the Art of Reason* (Cambridge, Mass., 1958).

19 I have tried to demonstrate and document this at length in *Edward Taylor* (New York, 1961), pp. 87–107.

20 Vernon L. Parrington, *Main Currents in American Thought: an Interpretation of American Literature from the Beginnings to 1920*, vol. 1 (New York, 1927), p. iii.

21 Edward Sculley Bradley *et al.* (eds.), *The American Tradition in Literature*, vol. 1 (New York, 1956), p. 39n.

22 Perry Miller, 'Solomon Stoddard, 1643–1729', *Harvard Theological Review*, XXXIV (1941), 277–320; it is only fair to note that Miller dropped this

aspect of his characterization in transplanting this article into *The New England Mind: from Colony to Province* (Cambridge, Mass., 1953).

23 Thomas J. Wertenbaker, *The Puritan Oligarchy: the Founding of American Civilization* (New York, 1947), p. 89.

24. J. Franklin Jameson, (ed.), *Johnson's Wonder-Working Providence 1628–1651* (New York, 1910), pp. 127, 132–3. I have modernized Jameson's text.

25 Samuel Kettel, *Specimens of American Poetry, with Critical and Biographical Notices*, vol. 1 (Boston, 1829), pp. 30–2.

26 Moses Coit Tyler, *A History of American Literature during the Colonial Period, 1607–1765* (2 vols., New York, 1897), p. 305.

27 *Ibid.*, p. 326.

28 Parrington, *Main Currents*, vol. 1, pp. 107–8.

29 Bradley, *American Tradition*, p. 73.

30 Miller, *From Colony to Province*, p. 403.

31 Perry Miller, 'From Edwards to Emerson', *Errand into the Wilderness* (Cambridge, Mass., 1956), p. 190.

32 'Meditation 12', first ser., ll. 43–8. I have modernized the text; see Stanford (ed.), *Poems*, pp. 5, 25.

33 Louis L. Martz, *The Poetry of Meditation: a Study in English Religious Literature of the Seventeenth Century* (New Haven, 1954), p. 16. Professor Martz relates Taylor to this tradition in his foreword to Stanford's edition of Taylor's *Poems*; Miller, discussing Cotton Mather's piety (*From Colony to Province*, pp. 403ff.) refers to this incorrectly as 'a new type of Puritan literature invented after the Restoration' (p. 404). James Fulton Maclear, in '"The Heart of New England Rent": the Mystical Element in Early Puritan History', *Mississippi Valley Historical Review*, XLII (1955–6), 621–52, traces the social implications of this tradition.

34 Richard Baxter, *The Saints Everlasting Rest: or, a Treatise of the Blessed State of the Saints in their enjoyment of God in Glory. Wherein is showed its Excellency and Certainty; the Misery of those that lose it, the way to Attain it, and the assurance of it; and how to live in the continual delightful Foretastes of it, by the help of Meditation.... (London, 1649), p. 662.

35 Samuel Willard, *Some Brief Sacramental Meditations Preparatory for Communion at the Great Ordinance of the Supper* (Boston, 1711), pp. 169–70.

36 Increase Mather, *Meditations on the Glory of the Lord Jesus Christ: Delivered in several Sermons* (Boston, 1705), pp. ii-iv.

37 This is the little sketch usually and capriciously titled 'Sarah Pierrepont', which epitomizes Edwards's elaborate treatises on the will, religious affections, true virtue, and his own personal narrative. See Clarence H. Faust and Thomas

H. Johnson (eds.), *Jonathan Edwards: Representative Selections* (New York, 1935), pp. 56, 63. The quotations above are from Anne Bradstreet, 'Contemplations', ll. 3 and 7, in John H. Ellis (ed.), *The Works of Anne Bradstreet in Prose and Verse* (New York, 1932), p. 370.

38 Miller, *From Colony to Province*, pp. 284–5.

CHAPTER 3

1 This view of Puritanism, I do not believe to be essentially different from that of A. S. P. Woodhouse: 'Puritanism means a determined and varied effort to erect the holy community and to meet, with different degrees of compromise and adjustment, the problem of its conflict with the world'; introduction, *Puritanism and Liberty* (Chicago, 1951), p. 37.

2 The following account of Wright's life is based on information in the *DNB*; H. B. Wilson, *The History of Merchant-Taylor's School* (London, 1812), vol. II; and W. C. Costin, *The History of St. John's College Oxford, 1598–1860* (Oxford, 1958).

3 Costin, *History of St John's*, p. 20.

4 *Ibid.*, p. 46.

5 Abraham Wright, *Five Sermons, in Five Several Styles; or Waies of Preaching* (London, 1656), sig. A3.

6 F. E. Hutchinson (ed.), *The Works of George Herbert* (Oxford, 1953), p. 235.

7 *Ibid.*, p. 225.

8 G. Thorn-Drury (ed.), *Parnassus Biceps* (London, 1927), sigs. A4-A4v.

9 *Ibid.*, sig. A2v.

10 *Five Sermons*, sig. A7v.

11 *Parnassus Biceps*, sig. A4.

12 J. Franklin Jameson (ed.), *Johnson's Wonder-Working Providence, 1628–1651* (New York, 1910), p. 52.

13 Henry James, 'The Modern Warning', *The Aspern Papers, Louisa Pallant, The Modern Warning* (London, 1888), pp. 209–10.

14 William Dean Howells, 'Puritanism in American Fiction', *Literature and Life* (New York, 1902), pp. 278–83.

15 The challenge to look more closely into the matter was most effectively made by Professor Kenneth Murdock in *Literature and Theology in Colonial New England* (Cambridge, Mass., 1949).

16 R. W. B. Lewis, *The American Adam* (Chicago, 1955).

17 Charles Feidelson, *Symbolism and American Literature* (Chicago, 1953).

18 Roy Harvey Pearce, *The Continuity of American Poetry* (Princeton, 1961).

19 Larzer Ziff, *The Career of John Cotton: Puritanism and the American Experience* (Princeton, 1962), esp. pp. 149–69.

20 Richard Chase, *The American Novel and Its Tradition* (New York, 1957).

CHAPTER 4

1 Cyrus L. Dunham, speech, 6 April 1852, 32nd Congress, 1st Session. *Congressional Globe*, Appendix, p. 410; and William Gilpin, *The Mission of the North American People, Geographical, Social, and Political* (Philadelphia, 1874), p. 130, as quoted in Henry Nash Smith, *Virgin Land: the American West as Symbol and Myth* [1950] (New York, 1957), pp. 198, 40. See James Dana, *Two Discourses* (New Haven, 1801), p. 49: and Timothy Dwight, 'Greenfield Hill: a Poem' [1794], especially these lines: 'All hail, thou western world! by heaven design'd | Th' example bright, to renovate mankind.' See, too, the fine discussion of America's language of dedication in Frederick Merk, *Manifest Destiny and Mission in American History* (New York, 1963), p. 261.

2 Patrick Tailfer and others, with comments by the Earl of Egmont, *A True and Historical Narrative of the Colony of Georgia* [1740], ed. Clarence L. Ver Steeg (Athens, 1960), pp. 3, 7, 8. See also Moses Coit Tyler, *History of American Literature*, pp. 504–8.

3 Peter Bulkeley, *The Gospel-Covenant: or The Covenant of Grace Opened* (London, 1646), p. 14.

4 William Stoughton, *New-Englands True Interest: Not to Lie* (Cambridge, Mass., 1670), p. 16.

5 *Ibid.*, pp. 19–20. See John Higginson, *The Cause of God and His People in New England* [1663] in *Elijah's Mantle* (Boston, 1722), pp. 6–9; and Cotton Mather, *Magnalia Christi Americana* (Hartford, 1853, orig. publ. 1702), vol. 1, pp. 25–38.

6 Edward Johnson, *A History of New-England* (London, 1654), p. 26.

7 Stoughton, *New-Englands True Interest*, pp. 16–17. For a characteristic use of the term 'design', see Johnson, *History of New-England*, pp. 24–5; and Increase Mather, *The Day of Trouble Is Near* (Boston, 1674), p. 22.

8 Higginson, *Cause of God*, p. 7.

9 Stoughton, *New-Englands True Interest*, p. 21. Cf. Plutarch in *Morals*: 'It is indeed a desirable thing to be well descended, but the glories belong to our ancestors.'

10 Bulkeley, *The Gospel-Covenant*, p. 15.

11 Cotton Mather, *Magnalia Christi Americana*, vol. 1, p. 25.

12 Stoughton, *New-Englands' True Interest*, p. 21. Cf. William Burnham, *God's Providence in Placing Men* (New London, 1722), p. 33. In 'Democracy and Its Issues', *Lectures and Miscellanies* (New York, 1852), p. 2, Henry James, Sr, states that democracy 'is born of denial'. New England's denial of Old England began early, but it was to a considerable degree a response to being rejected as a model.

13 See Urian Oakes, *The Soveraign Efficacy of Divine Providence* (Boston, 1682), p. 5 and *passim*.

14 Stoughton, *New-Englands True Interest*, p. 17.

15 Oakes, *Soveraign Efficacy*, pp. 15, 13. I have omitted italics in the phrases taken from Oakes. See Thomas Shepard, *A Treatise of Liturgies* (London, 1653), p. 3; and Cotton Mather, *Magnalia Christi Americana*, vol. I, pp. 27–8.

16 The essence of Puritan lamentation is nicely set forth in [Increase Mather] *Necessity of Reformation* (Boston, 1679). Cf. Bulkeley, *The Gospel-Covenant*, pp. 382–3. See also W. D. Love, *The Fast and Thanksgiving Days of New England* (Boston, 1895), and Perry Miller, *The New England Mind: from Colony to Province* (Cambridge, Mass., 1953). Miller's brilliant work on the jeremiad is the point of departure for all subsequent study of the form, in particular my own.

17 See Miller, *From Colony to Province*, p. 30. Michael Wigglesworth's poem 'God's Controversy with New-England', written in 1662, was first published in *Proceedings of the Massachusetts Historical Society*, XII (1871–3), 83–93; and has been reprinted in Perry Miller and Thomas H. Johnson (eds.), *The Puritans: a Sourcebook of Their Writings* (rev. ed., 2 vols., New York, 1963), vol. II, pp. 611–16.

18 John Winthrop, *Journal: History of New England, 1630–1649*, ed. James K. Hosmer (2 vols., New York, 1908), vol. II, pp. 286, 326. Thomas Shepard, *Autobiography*, ed. Allyn B. Forbes, *Publications of the Colonial Society of Massachusetts*, XXVII, (1927–30), 387.

19 Shepard, *A Treatise of Liturgies*, p. 8.

20 Winthrop, *Journal* vol. II, p. 277.

21 Shepard, *A Treatise of Liturgies*, p. 8.

22 Shepard, *Autobiography*, p. 387. See Miller, *From Colony to Province*, pp. 19–39.

23 Cotton Mather, *Magnalia Christi Americana*, vol. I, pp. 27, 26. See Thomas Buckingham, *Moses and Aaron* (New London, 1729), p. 4.

24 Bulkeley, *The Gospel-Covenant*, p. 14.

25 Stoughton, *New-Englands True Interest*, p. 29.

26 Increase Mather, *A Discourse concerning the Uncertainty of the Times of Men* (Boston, 1697), pp. 9–11, 20–1. Italics omitted.

27 Oakes, *Soveraign Efficacy* pp. 15, 37. Italics omitted. Cf. John Webb, *The Government of Christ Considered and Applied* (Boston, 1738), pp. 7, 11–12.

28 *Ibid.*, p. 37.

29 See Miller, *From Colony to Province*, pp. 19–39 and *passim*.

30 Thomas Prince, *The People of New-England* (Boston, 1730), p. 36. See F. O. Matthiessen, *American Renaissance: Art and Expression in the Age of Emerson and Whitman* (New York, 1941), p. 629. Matthiessen quotes Thomas Mann, 'Freud and the Future', wherein Mann states that life in myth is 'life, so to speak, in quotation', that myth 'is a kind of celebration, in that it is a making present of the past', and that in myth – in 'the performance by a celebrant of a prescribed procedure' — the celebration of life 'becomes a religious act'.

31 Shepard. *A Treatise of Liturgies*, p. 3. See John Davenport, *A Sermon Preach'd at the Election of the Governor, at Boston in New-England, May 19, 1669*, (Boston, 1670), p. 15.

32 Cotton Mather, *Magnalia Christi Americana*, vol. I, p. 25.

33 Prince, *People of New-England*, p. 22.

34 Jonathan Mitchel, *Nehemiah on the Wall in Troublesom Times* (Cambridge, Mass., 1671), p. 27.

35 Cotton Mather, *Magnalia Christi Americana*, vol. I, p. 25.

36 *Ibid.*, p. 26.

37 Prince, *People of New-England*, p. 26. See Cotton Mather, *Magnalia Christi Americana*, vol. I, pp. 25–8.

38 Cotton Mather, *Ibid.*, p. 26.

39 Oakes, *Soveraign Efficacy*, p. 13.

40 Cotton Mather, *Magnalia Christi Americana*, vol. I, p. 27.

41 Prince, *People of New-England*, pp. 24, 28. Italics omitted. In this passage Prince is echoing mainly the prophet Isaiah.

42 Prince, *ibid.*, p. 36.

43 Cotton Mather, *Magnalia Christi Americana*, vol. I, p. 27.

44 Wallace Stevens, 'The Poem That Took the Place of a Mountain', *Collected Poems* (New York, 1964), p. 512. Cf. what Stevens calls, in 'The Well Dressed Man with a Beard' (p. 247), the yes that follows the final no.

45 Auden, 'In Memory of W. B. Yeats', pp. 141–3. Cf. Yeats, *The King's Threshold* [1904], *The Collected Plays of W. B. Yeats* (London, 1952), p. 114, where Seanchan, a poet, says: 'And I would have all know that when all falls | In ruin, poetry calls out in joy, | Being the scattering hand, the bursting pod, | The victim's joy among the holy flame, | God's laughter at the shattering of the world.'

CHAPTER 5

1 The term, found in Urian Oakes, *New-England Pleaded With* (Cambridge, Mass., 1673), p. 23, referred to a wider group of Puritan historians than will be considered in this discussion, where it designates only writers of large-scale New England histories. Admittedly for the sake of focusing discussion I take some liberties by conglomerating distinctive works. The purpose of this essay is to reveal a special thematic and generic kinship among these historians, and for that reason their variations will be minimally treated.

2 For examination of historiographical standards current during the Renaissance and into the seventeenth century, see James Westfall Thompson, *A History of Historical Writing* (New York, 1942), vol. I. Also helpful are F. Smith Fussner, *The Historical Revolution: English Historical Writing and Thought, 1580–1640* (New York, 1962), who discusses the emergence of local and regional histories increasingly written by laymen, and Kenneth B. Murdock, *Literature and Theology in Colonial New England* (Cambridge, Mass., 1949), who examines the impact of the Reformation on the Puritan conception of history. Peter Gay, *A Loss of Mastery* (Berkeley and Los Angeles, 1966), succinctly traces the course of Christian historiography as it comes to influence New England Puritan historians.

3 See Norman S. Grabo, 'The Veiled Vision'. In raising the important question of the disparity between Puritan literary theory and Puritan literary practice, Grabo opens the way toward a more fruitful exploration of the nature of Puritan literature than has generally been attempted.

4 See William H. Whitmore, 'Life and Labors of Thomas Prince', *North American Review*, XVI (1860), 354–75.

5 Thomas Prince, *A Chronological History of New-England in the Form of Annals* (Boston, 1736), vol. I, p. ii.

6 *Ibid.*, p. i.

7 *Ibid.*, dedication.

8 Perry Miller, *Errand into the Wilderness* (Cambridge Mass., 1956), p. 143.

9 John Winthrop, *A Modell of Christian Charity* (1630), in Perry Miller and Thomas H. Johnson (eds.), *The Puritans: a Sourcebook of their Writings* (rev. edn., 2 vols., New York, 1963), vol. I, p. 195.

10 William Hubbard, *The Happiness of a People* (1676), in Miller and Johnson (eds.), *Puritans*, vol. I, p. 247.

11 Miller, *Errand into the Wilderness*, p. 143.

12 Daniel J. Boorstin, *The Americans: the Colonial Experience* (New York, 1958), p. 19.

13 Winthrop, *Christian Charity*, in Miller and Johnson (eds.), *Puritans*, vol. I, p. 199.

14 Perry Miller, *The New England Mind: the Seventeenth Century* (New York, 1939), p. 416.

15 Edmund S. Morgan, *Visible Saints: the History of a Puritan Idea* (Ithaca, 1965, orig. publ. 1963), p. 88, writes that 'within ten years the procedures for founding a church and admitting new members to it did include a test. During this decade some twenty thousand settlers landed in New England, and eighteen churches were set up in Massachusetts alone. By 1640 the New Englanders had evolved practices so uniform that both critics and advocates could agree in describing them, and evidence is so abundant that we need not resort to speculation.'

16 Boorstin, *The Americans*, p. 17.

17 Larzer Ziff, 'The Social Bond of Church Covenant', *American Quarterly*, x (1958), 462.

18 Ziff, 'Social Bond', pp. 454, 460, argues that the Puritans developed 'an abundance of external expressions of holiness whereby they deliberately widened the gulf between themselves and others'. He demonstrates tribal strength by citing cases where the church covenant was kept under the most unlikely circumstances.

19 Edmund S. Morgan, *The Puritan Family* (New York, 1966, orig. publ. 1944), p. 168.

20 Sumner Chilton Powell, *Puritan Village* (Middletown, Conn., 1963), pp. 143–4.

21 An examination of selected New England spiritual biographies may be found in Daniel B. Shea, Jr, *Spiritual Biography in Early America* (Princeton, 1968). Murdock, *Literature and Theology*, pp. 117–18, examines the formal progression from the diary, to autobiography, to biography intended for publication as a work of religious edification.

22 Thompson, *Historical Writing*, vol. I, pp. 605–6, discusses the exemplary influence of Plutarch's *Lives*, as does Douglas Bush, *English Literature in the Earlier Seventeenth Century, 1600–1660*, 2nd ed. (Oxford, 1962), p. 229.

23 Roy Pascal, *Design and Truth in Autobiography* (Cambridge, Mass., 1960), pp. 22–3.

24 *Ibid.*, p. 23.

25 See Wayne Shumaker, *English Autobiography: its Emergence, Materials, and Form* (Berkeley and Los Angeles, 1954), p. 52.

26 William Haller, *The Rise of Puritanism* (New York, 1957, orig. publ. 1938), pp. 101–2.

27 George A. Starr, *Defoe and Spiritual Biography* (Princeton, 1965), p. 5.

28 John Bunyan, *Grace Abounding to the Chief of Sinners*, ed. Roger Sharrock (Oxford, 1962), p. xxvii.

29 Murdock, *Literature and Theology*, pp. 110–11. Starr, *Defoe*, p. 18, remarks similarly that 'a man could tell which way he was headed, and how far he had come, by consulting the signposts and milestones set up for his guidance in spiritual autobiographies.' In my discussion spiritual biography and autobiography are treated as one.

30 Starr, *Defoe*, p. 17.

31 *Ibid.*, pp. 17–18.

32 *Ibid.*, p. 17.

33 *Ibid.*

34 *Ibid.*

35 *Ibid.*, p. 22.

36 *Ibid.*

37 *Ibid.*, pp. 22–3.

38 *Ibid.*, p. 23.

39 Francis Higginson, *New-England's Plantation* (1630), in Alexander Young (ed.), *Chronicles of the First Planters of Massachusetts Bay Colony, from 1623 to 1636* (Boston, 1846), pp. 243, 246, 248, 251.

40 William Wood, *New-Englands Prospect* (1635), in Young (ed.), *Chronicles*, pp. 390–4.

41 Nathaniel Morton, 'Epistle Dedicatory', in Howard J. Hall, (ed.), *New Englands Memoriall* (New York, 1937). Hereafter cited as Morton, *New Englands Memoriall*.

42 *Ibid.*

43 Morton, 'To the Christian Reader', *ibid.*

44 Richard S. Dunn, 'Seventeenth-Century English Historians of America', in James Morton Smith (ed.), *Seventeenth-Century America: Essays in Colonial History* (Chapel Hill, 1959), p. 196.

45 Striving in vain to delineate specific referents for the 'wilderness' abounding in Puritan writings, Gay, *Loss of Mastery*, p. 29n, concludes that ' "Wilderness" became an all-purpose, and hence almost meaningless, metaphor.' Gay fails to recognize the emotional synthesis operating in a metaphor spiritually all encompassing. Peter N. Carroll, *Puritanism and the Wilderness: the Intellectual Significance of the New England Frontier, 1629–1700* (New York, 1969), examines the palpable aspects of the word's referent, while George H. Williams, *Wilderness and Paradise in Christian Thought: the Biblical Experience of the Desert in the History of Christianity and the Paradise Themes in the Theological Idea of the University* (New York, 1962), p. 74, explores the psychology of the Puritan wilderness, remarking that 'the word *wilderness* became indeed, in the seventeenth century, an almost incantational term'.

46 Unfavorable criticism of the Puritan historians centers in two indictments, the first of which is plagiarization from Bradford and Winthrop. Most vulnerable to the charge have been Nathaniel Morton and William Hubbard, one or both of whom has been so criticized by Moses Coit Tyler, *A History of American Literature 1607–1765* (New York, 1897), p. 132; Dunn, 'English Historians of America', in Smith (ed.), *Seventeenth-Century America*, pp. 211, 214; Miller and Johnson (eds.), *Puritans*, vol. I, p. 82; Michael Kraus, *The Writing of American History* (Norman, 1953), p. 29. The second failing ascribed to the 'Lords Remembrancers', notably to Edward Johnson and to Cotton Mather, is an undisciplined and super-abundant imagination, which is in Johnson blamed on lack of education and in Mather ascribed to excess of it. The following scholars condemn one or both men for prolixity, verbosity, lack of cogent organization, incoherence, vacillation, and above all lack of control: Gay, *Loss of Mastery*, pp. 53, 61; Miller and Johnson (eds.), *Puritans*, vol. I, p. 90; Tyler, *American Literature*, pp. 143, 334; Dunn, 'English Historians of America', in Smith (ed.), *Seventeenth-Century America*, pp. 204–5, 217; Kraus, *Writing of American History*, pp. 27–8, 37, Murdock, *Literature and Theology*, p. 88; J. Franklin Jameson, *The History of Historical Writing in America* (Boston, 1891), p. 55. Thus, while critics have been quick to cite Puritan historians' stylistic similarities to Bradford and Winthrop as proof of plagiarization and to denounce the Puritans' departures from current desiderata for historical writing (namely, that verbal coloration be subservient to a carefully controlled logic of argument), still there has been very little effort at discerning shared cultural factors in the works of the 'Lords Remembrancers'.

47 Edward Johnson, *Wonder-Working Providence of Sions Saviour in New England*, ed. J. Franklin Jameson (New York, 1910), p. 151. Hereafter cited as Johnson, *Wonder-Working Providence*.

48 John Winthrop, *Winthrop's Journal*, ed. James Kendall Hosmer, vol. II (New York, 1946, orig. publ. 1908), p. 71. Hereafter cited as Winthrop, *Journal*.

49 Johnson, *Wonder-Working Providence*, p. 56.

50 *Ibid.*, p. 62.

51 *Ibid.*, pp. 62–3.

52 William Bradford, *Of Plymouth Plantation, 1620–1647*, ed. Samuel Eliot Morison (New York, 1952), p. 61. Hereafter cited as Bradford, *Plymouth Plantation*.

53 Morton, *New Englands Memoriall*, p. 22.

54 Johnson, *Wonder-Working Providence*, p. 82.

55 *Ibid.*, p. 104.

56 Bradford, *Plymouth Plantation*, p. 329.

57 Johnson, *Wonder-Working Providence*, p. 52.

58 Cotton Mather, *Magnalia Christi Americana*, vol. 1 (Hartford, 1853, orig. publ. 1702), p. 109.

59 William Hubbard, *A General History of New England from the Discovery to 1680* (Boston, 1815), pp. 57–8.

60 Mather, *Magnalia Christi Americana*, vol. 1, p. 54.

61 Hubbard, *General History*, p. 643.

62 *Ibid.*, p. 197.

63 *Ibid.*, p. 52.

64 Mather, *Magnalia Christi Americana*, vol. 1, p. 68.

65 *Ibid.*, p. 275.

66 Morton, *New Englands Memoriall*, pp. 150, 151.

67 *Ibid.*, p. 63.

68 Hubbard, *General History*, p. 556.

69 Mather, *Magnalia Christi Americana*, vol. 1, p. 154.

70 *Ibid.*, p. 575.

71 Hubbard, *General History*, p. 661.

72 *Ibid.*, p. 552. I have been unable to attribute these lines, which are not listed in the most comprehensive bibliography of New England verse, that of Harold S. Jantz, *The First Century of New England Verse* (New York, 1962).

73 Hubbard, *General History*, p. 499.

74 Mather, *Magnalia Christi Americana*, vol. 1, p. 128.

75 *Ibid.*, p. 25.

76 *Ibid.*, p. 107.

77 *Ibid.*

78 *Ibid.*, p. 355.

79 Mather writes, 'It must be confessed, that the Palm is given unto Church History; wherein the dignity, the suavity, and the utility of the subject is transcendent'. *Ibid.*, p. 28.

80 *Ibid.*, p. 25.

81 *Ibid.*, pp. 253, 459.

82 See Kenneth B. Murdock, 'Clio in the Wilderness: History and Biography in Puritan New England', *Church History*, XXIV (1955), 221–38. Murdock makes clear his understanding that biblical and cultural allusions in Puritan writings emphasize Christian unity and not New England singularity, and are not a vaunting of erudition, notably on Mather's part. Discussion of Mather's spiritualizing is found in Austin Warren, *The New England Conscience* (Ann Arbor, 1966), p. 84, and observed in Mason I. Lowance, Jr., 'Typology and the New England Way: Cotton Mather and the Exegesis of Biblical Types', *Early American Literature*, IV (1969), pp. 15–37.

83 Bradford, *Plymouth Plantation*, pp. 165–6.

84 Winthrop, *Journal*, pp. 12–13.

85 *Ibid.*, p. 13.

86 Johnson, *Wonder-Working Providence*, p. 136.

87 Prince, *Chronological History*, p. xxi.

88 Thomas Prince's election sermon of 1730 has been reprinted in A. W. Plum-
     stead (ed.), *The Wall and the Garden: Selected Massachusetts Election Sermons
     1670–1775* (Minneapolis, 1968), pp. 184–220.

89 *Ibid.*, p. 180.

CHAPTER 6

1 The Hebrew exercises preceding the History have been published in Isidore
    S. Meyer, 'The Hebrew Preface to Bradord's History of the Plymouth Planta-
    tion', *Publications of the American Jewish Society*, XXXVIII (June 1949), 289–
    305.

2 Meyer, 'Preface', p. 296. The 'hourglass' was first published in *Proceedings
    of the Massachusetts Historical Society*, XI (Boston, 1870), p. 402.

3 Peter Gay, *A Loss of Mastery* (Berkeley and Los Angeles, 1966), pp. 3–52.

4 Henry Ainsworth, *Annotations* (2 vols., Edinburgh, 1843).

5 *Ibid.*, vol. II, pp. 404–5.

6 *Ibid.*, p. 200.

7 *Ibid.*, p. 404.

8 *Ibid.*, p. 405.

9 See Richard Reinitz, 'The Separatist Background of Roger William's Argu-
    ment for Religious Toleration', in Sacvan Bercovitch (ed.), *Typology and Early
    American Literature* (Amherst, 1972), pp. 107–37.

10 See Alan Heimert, 'Puritanism, the Wilderness, and the Frontier', *New Eng-
     land Quarterly*, XXVI (1953), p. 370.

11 John Robinson, *A Justification of Separation from the Church of England . . .*,
     in *Works* (3 vols., London, 1851), vol., II, p. 304. Hereafter cited as *Works*.

12 William Bradford, *History of Plymouth Plantation, 1620–47*, ed. Worthing-
     ton C. Ford (2 vols., Boston, 1912), vol. I, p. 156. Hereafter cited as *Ply-
     mouth Plantation*.

13 II Cor. 6; I Pet. 2: 5.

14 *Plymouth Plantation*, vol. I, pp. 131–4.

15 'Governor Bradford's Letter Book', *Collections of the Massachusetts Historical
     Society*, 1st ser., III, (Boston, 1794), p. 45.

16 *Plymouth Plantation*, vol. I, p. 76.

17 *Ibid.*, vol. II, p. 153.

18 (London, 1622). The following quotation is on pp. 5–8.

19 *Sermon at Plimmoth*, p. 15.

20 *Ibid.*, p. 20.

21 *Ibid.*, 'The Epistle Dedicatorie'.

22 In Robert C. Winthrop, *Life and Letters of John Winthrop* (2, vols., Boston, 1869). The quotation is from vol. I, p. 309.

23 Cushman, *Sermon at Plimmoth* 'The Epistle Dedicatorie'.

24 Edward Winslow, *Hypocrisie Unmasked* (London, 1646), quoted in *Chronicles of the Pilgrim Fathers of the Colony of Plymouth from 1602 to 1605*, ed. Alexander Young (Boston, 1844), pp. 397–8.

25 Robinson, *Works*, vol. II, p. 66.

26 *Plymouth Plantation*, vol. I, p. 55.

27 See Sacvan Bercovitch, 'The Historiography of Johnson's *Wonder-Working Providence*', *Essex Institute Historical Collections*, CIV (1968), pp. 138–61.

28 *Plymouth Plantation*, vol. II, p. 63.

29 William Bradford, *A Dialogue of the Sum of A Conference Between some Young Men Born in New England and Sundry Ancient Men That Came out of Holland And Old England Anno Domini 1648*, in Young (ed.), *Pilgrim Fathers*, p. 423.

30 William Bradford, *A Dialogue or 3d Conference*, in *Proceedings of the Massachusetts Historical Society*, XI (Boston, 1870), p. 448.

31 *Plymouth Plantation*, vol. I, pp. 14–16.

32 *Ibid.*, vol. II, p. 128.

33 *Ibid.*, vol. I, pp. 218–19.

34 *Ibid.*, vol. II, pp. 393–4.

35 *Ibid.*, vol. I, p. 20.

36 Zechariah 2: 12.

37 I am indebted to Professor John Demos' discussion of the parent–child relationship in Plymouth. See John Demos, *A Little Commonwealth: Family Life in Plymouth Colony* (New York, 1970); see also Professor William Scheick's perceptive essay, 'Anonymity and Art in *The Life and Death of That Reverend Man of God, Mr. Richard Mather*', *American Literature*, XLII (January 1971), pp. 457–67.

38 *Plymouth Plantation*, vol. I, pp. 155–8.

39 See Samuel Eliot Morison, *The Story of the 'Old Colony' of New Plymouth [1620–1692]* (New York, 1956), pp. 138–40; George D. Langdon, *Pilgrim Colony: a History of New Plymouth, 1620–91* (New Haven, 1966), pp. 38–57; and Darrett B. Rutman, *Husbandmen of Plymouth: Farms and Villages in the Old Colony 1620–1692* (Boston, 1967), pp. 3–27.

40 *Plymouth Plantation*, vol. I, p. 52.

41 *Ibid.*, vol. I, p. 120.

42 *Ibid.*, p. 317.
43 *Ibid.*, p. 106.
44 *Ibid.*, p. 43.
45 *Ibid.*, vol. II, p. 350.
46 *Ibid.*, pp. 350–1.
47 *Ibid.*, pp. 351–3.
48 *Ibid.*, p. 343.
49 *Ibid.*
50 *Ibid.*, p. 353.
51 Robinson, *Works*, vol. I, p. 8.
52 *Ibid.*, p. 140.
53 *Ibid.*, p. 143.
54 *Ibid.*, pp. 140–1.
55 *Ibid.*, p. 142.
56 *Ibid.*, p. 144.
57 *Plymouth Plantation*, vol. I, p. 30.
58 *Ibid.*, p. 33.
59 *Ibid.*, p. 35; David Levin, review of Gay, *Loss of Mastery* in *History and Theory*, VII (1968), p. 389.
60 The events for 1639 and 1640 are combined into one annal.
61 *Plymouth Plantation*, vol. I, p. 117.
62 *Ibid.*, p. 325.
63 *Ibid.*, pp. 446–7.
64 *Ibid.*, p. 258.
65 *Ibid.*, p. 263.
66 *Ibid.*, vol. II, pp. 107–8.
67 Robinson, *Works*, vol. II, p. 183.
68 *Plymouth Plantation*, vol. II, p. 352.
69 Robinson, *Works*, vol. II, p. 207.
70 For a later development of this concept in Puritan thought, see Mason I. Lowance, Jr, 'Cotton Mather's *Magnalia* and the Metaphors of Biblical History', in Bercovitch (ed.), *Typology*, pp. 139ff.
71 Robinson, *Works*, vol. II, p. 43.
72 *Ibid.*, p. 298.
73 *Ibid.*, p. 119.
74 *Ibid.*, p. 424.
75 *Plymouth Plantation*, vol. I, p. 3.
76 Robinson, *Works*, vol. II, p. 134.
77 *Plymouth Plantation*, vol. II, p. 397.
78 *A Dialogue*, in Young (ed.), *Pilgrim Fathers*, p. 456.

79 *Dialogue, or 3d Conference*, pp. 463–4.

80 *Ibid.*, p. 407.

81 William Bradford, 'Some observations of God's merciful dealing with us in this wilderness, and his gracious protection over us these many years. Blessed be his name', *Proceedings of the Massachusetts Historical Society*, XI (Boston, 1870), p. 477.

82 *Ibid.*, p. 473.

83 William Bradford, 'A word to New England', *Collections of the Massachusetts Historical Society*, third ser., VII (Boston, 1838), p. 28.

84 *Plymouth Plantation*, vol. I, p. 76.

85 *Ibid.*

CHAPTER 7

1 There is no complete bibliography of work on Anne Bradstreet, much of which is hard to locate. Significant estimates of her poetry include Moses Coit Tyler, *A History of American Literature During the Colonial Period 1607–1765* (New York, 1897), vol. I, pp. 277–92; L. N. Richardson, 'Anne Bradstreet', *Dictionary of American Biography* (New York, 1929); S. E. Morison, 'Mistress Anne Bradstreet', *Builders of the Bay Colony* (Boston, 1930), pp. 320–36; G. F. Whicher, *Alas, All's Vanity: or A Leaf from the First American Edition of Several Poems by Anne Bradstreet, printed at Boston, anno 1678* (New York, 1942); Elizabeth Wade White, 'The Tenth Muse — A Tercentenary Appraisal of Anne Bradstreet', *William and Mary Quarterly*, VIII, (1951), 355–77; Josephine Piercy, *Anne Bradstreet* (New York, 1965), contains a useful bibliography.

2 Perry Miller and Thomas H. Johnson (eds.) *The Puritans: a Sourcebook of Their Writings* (rev. edn. 2 vols., New York, 1963), p. 287. See also Perry Miller, *The New England Mind: the Seventeenth Century* (New York, 1939), ch. 2.

3 E. S. Morgan, *The Puritan Dilemma* (Boston, 1958), pp. 7–8.

4 E. S. Morgan, *Visible Saints* (New York, 1963), p. 69.

5 J. H. Ellis (ed.), *The Works of Anne Bradstreet in Prose and Verse* (New York, 1932), p. 391. Hereafter, page references to the Ellis edition will be given only for the first quotation from any given poem.

6 Ellis, *Works of Bradstreet*, pp. 370–81. This poem was first anthologized in Samuel Kettell's *Specimens of American Poetry* (Boston, 1829), pp. xxii–xxvii, and has since been praised and excerpted by nearly every commentator on early American poetry. In addition to the work cited in note 1, see, for example,

William B. Otis, *American Verse 1625–1807: a History* (New York, 1909), p. 228; Kenneth B. Murdock, *Literature and Theology in Colonial New England* (Cambridge, Mass., 1949), pp. 150–2; Harold S. Jantz, *The First Century of New England Verse* (New York, 1962), p. 36; Roy Harvey Pearce, *The Continuity of American Poetry* (Princeton, 1961), p. 23.

7 Shakespearian influence on Anne Bradstreet has been discussed by J. Piercy in her *Anne Bradstreet*, esp. pp. 59–64. Similarities between 'Contemplations' and Keats' 'Ode to a Nightingale' have been pointed out by R. Crowder in 'Anne Bradstreet and Keats', *Notes and Queries*, III (1956), 386–8.

8 Revelations 2: 17, Geneva Version.

CHAPTER 8

1 Henry W. Taylor, in William B. Sprague, *Annals of the American Pulpit* (New York, 1857), vol. I, pp. 177–81; and in John L. Sibley, 'Edward Taylor', *Biographical Sketches of Graduates of Harvard University* (Cambridge, Mass., 1881), vol. II, pp. 397–412, 534–6.

2 Cotton Mather, *Right Thoughts in Sad Hours* (London, 1689) includes a portion of one of Taylor's poems 'Upon Wedlock and Death of Children'. Other sources where one might have discovered that Taylor had been a poet are: Sprague, *American Pulpit* and Sibley, 'Edward Taylor'; John H. Lockwood, *A Sermon* (Westfield, 1879) and *Westfield and Its Historic Influences* (Springfield, Mass., 1922); H. W. Taylor, in *The Westfield Jubilee* (Westfield, 1870); and Thomas G. Wright, *Literary Culture in Early New England* (New Haven, 1920).

3 Taylor, *Westfield Jubilee*, p. 180.

4 However, the work was never published. 'An Extract of Several Letters from Cotton Mather, D. D., . . .', *Philosophical Transactions of the Royal Society of London*, XXIX (1714), 62–3.

5 Taylor, *Westfield Jubilee*, p. 179.

6 Donald Junkins, 'Edward Taylor's Revisions', *American Literature*, XXXVII (1965), 135–52. The argument here is about Taylor's craftsmanship, but in spite of the few revisions in diction, the poems for the most part do not seem prepared for publication.

7 Those who argue thus are: Thomas H. Johnson, *The Poetical Works of Edward Taylor* (New York, 1939), pp. 11–15; Emma L. Shepherd, 'Edward Taylor's Injunction Against Publication', *American Literature*, XXXIII (1962), 512–13; and Donald E. Stanford, cited in *Early American Literature*, I (1966), 4.

8 Charles W. Mignon argues this point in his unpublished dissertation, 'The American Puritan and Private Qualities of Edward Taylor the Poet' (Conn., 1963); 'Diction in Edward Taylor's *Preparatory Meditations*', *American Speech*, XLI (1966), 243–53; and 'Edward Taylor's *Preparatory Meditations: A Decorum of Imperfection*', *Publications of the American Language Association*, LXXXIII (1968), 1423–8.

9 The debate over Taylor's orthodoxy between Thomas H. Johnson, Donald E. Stanford, Norman S. Grabo, and Michael J. Colacurcio on the one hand and Perry Miller, Kenneth B. Murdock, Roy Harvey Pearce, Nathalia Wright, Mindele Black, Willie T. Weathers, and Sidney E. Lind on the other hand seems to have been fairly decided in favor of orthodoxy, the argument of the former group.

10 Mignon, 'Taylor's *Preparatory Meditations*'. Professor Mignon shows how there is something about the meiotic and hyperbolic character of Taylor's conceits which makes him substantially different from the English metaphysicals and perhaps peculiarly American.

11 *The Continuity of American Poetry* (Princeton, 1961), pp. 45–54. Pearce gets only a glimpse of the importance of process to the poetry of Taylor, however. He says that Taylor's 'eloquence lay immanent in what he knew, not in the telling of it – in the object of his discovery, not in the act of discovering the object'.

12 All Taylor poems quoted here are from the edition of Donald E. Stanford, *The Poems of Edward Taylor* (New Haven, 1960). Numerals indicate the series of *Preparatory Meditations*, and numbers refer to the particular Meditation in the series.

13 The key study of the subject of Puritan meditation as a process is Norman Pettit, *The Heart Prepared: Grace and Conversion in Puritan Spiritual Life* (New Haven, 1966).

14 John A. Kouwenhoven, 'What is American about America?', in *American Literary Essays*, ed. Lewis Leary (New York, 1960).

15 See Peter Thorpe's discussion of the justification of such 'flaws' – 'Edward Taylor as Poet', *New England Quarterly*, XXXIX (1966), 356–72

CHAPTER 9

1 12 May 1784.

2 Perry Miller, *The New England Mind: from Colony to Province* (Cambridge, Mass., 1953), pp. 402–16.

3 Cotton Mather, *Small Offers toward the Service of the Tabernacle in the Wilder-*

ness. Four Discourses accommodated unto the Designs of Practical Godliness (Boston, 1689), pp. 108–11.

4 Here Mather seems clearly to have been following Richard Baxter's *How to Do Good to Many: or, the Publick Good is the Christian's Life. Directions and Motives to It* (London, 1682), p. 5: 'But as all motion and action is first upon the nearest object, so must ours; and doing good must be in order: First we must begin at home with our own souls and lives, and then to our nearest relations, and friends, and acquaintance, and neighbors, and then to our societies, church, and kingdom, and all the world. But mark that order of execution, and the orders of estimation and intention differ. Though God set up lights so small as will serve but for one room, and though we must begin at home, we must far more esteem the desire and good of the multitude, of city and church and commonwealth; and must set no bounds to our endeavours, but what God and disability set'.

5 Cotton Mather, *Early Piety, Exemplified in the Life and Death of Mr. Nathanael Mather. . .* (London, 1689), p. 39.

6 Mather, *Small Offers*, p. 37.

7 *Ibid.*, pp. 19ff.

8 See *Theopolis Americana. An Essay on the Golden Street of the Holy City: Publishing a TESTIMONY against the CORRUPTIONS of the Market-Place. With some Good HOPES of Better Things to be yet seen in the AMERICAN World* (Boston, 1710), p. 48.

9 *Ibid.*, p. 5. The text was Revelations 21: 21. The sermon was preached on 3 November 1709.

10 See A. Whitney Griswold, 'Three Puritans on Prosperity', *New England Quarterly*, VII (1934), 475–93.

11 *Theopolis Americana*, pp. 13–14.

12 *Ibid.*, p. 21.

13 He did not say, 'Do unto others as you would have them do unto you', but rather: '*All things whatsoever* ye would, that men should do to you, do ye even so unto them.' He cited Matthew 7: 12. See *Theopolis Americana*, pp. 14–16.

14 *Ibid.*, pp. 18–22.

15 Baxter, *How to Do Good to Many*, p. 15.

16 A book-length autobiographical manuscript addressed to Mather's son and concentrating on the father's devices for piety. The manuscript is in the Alderman Library, University of Virginia. Many of these passages had been copied in turn from Mather's Reserved and Revised Memorials, which have since been published as *The Diary of Cotton Mather*, two vols., ed. Worthington C. Ford, in *Massachusetts Historical Society, Collections*, seventh ser., VII–VIII (Boston, 1911–12).

17 This passage is quoted, with the permission of the University of Virginia, from the manuscript 'Paterna', pp. 304–5. I have modernized the spelling and capitalization.

CHAPTER 10

1 *The Life and Character of the Late Reverend Mr. Jonathan Edwards* (Boston, 1765), p. iii.

2 *The Works of President Edwards: with a Memoir of his Life*, ed. Sereno E. Dwight (New York, 1829–30), vol. I, pp. 171–86; hereafter cited as *Works*. Sarah's original relation was drawn up, according to Dwight, at the request of her husband. Edwards then retold her experiences as part of his attempt to vindicate experimental religion in *Some Thoughts Concerning the Present Revival of Religion* (*Works*, vol. IV, pp. 110–18).

3 *A Treatise Concerning Religious Affections*, ed. John E. Smith (New Haven, 1959), p. 181.

4 From Edwards' preface to the *Account* of Brainerd's life, 'chiefly taken from his own diary and other Private Writings', *Works*, vol. X, p.29.

5 *Works*, vol. X, p. 27.

6 Although anthologies of American literature continue to reproduce the *Personal Narrative* from the Austin (Worcester, 1808) or Dwight editions, the text printed by Hopkins in his 1765 *Life of Edwards* is clearly preferable. As was their habit, the nineteenth-century editors 'improved' Edwards' style and also omitted several important passages. All my references are to the Hopkins text, but it is beyond the scope of this study to call attention to all the omissions and revisions of later editions. The indications in the Hopkins text of relatively hasty composition are: (1) the number of sentences lacking a pronominal subject ('On one Saturday Night, in particular, had a particular Discovery'), more than appear in later editions; (2) redundancy of a sort that invites improvement and that Edwards himself might have revised had he taken a second look ('my Concern that I had', or the phrase just quoted). If Edwards intended to make the manuscript more fit for posthumous publication, he apparently never found time to do so.

7 It is very doubtful that the *Personal Narrative* was written after the *Religious Affections* appeared in 1746, but it might conceivably have been written as Edwards prepared a series of sermons given in 1742–3, on which the *Religious Affections* is based. The only absolute certainty, of course, is that he did not conclude the narrative before January 1739, the date he mentions in its final paragraph.

8 *Works*, vol. I, p. 93.

9 *Ibid.*, pp. 84, 104. Entries for 7 Apr. 1723 and 12 Sept. 1724.

10 *Works*, vol. III, p. 561.

11 *Jonathan Edwards: Representative Selections*, ed. Clarence Faust and Thomas Johnson (rev. cdn., New York, 1962), p. 83.

12 *Works*, vol. IV, p.163.

13 Entry for 17 January 1723, *Works*, vol. I, p. 81.

14 Hopkins, *Life of Edwards*, p. 24. By deleting 'was' from the final phrase of this sentence, editors after Hopkins also silenced the passive voice that reminded readers, however awkwardly, whence grace originates.

15 *Works*, vol. VI, pp. 175–6.

16 *Religious Affections*, p. 119.

17 *Religious Affections*, p. 156.

18 The full context for these distinctions may be found in the 'Miscellanies' published in *The Philosophy of Jonathan Edwards From His Private Notebooks*, ed. Harvey G. Townsend (Eugene, 1955), pp. 249–51. See especially numbers 397, 408, 628.

19 *Religious Affections*, pp. 240–50.

20 *Ibid.*, p. 291.

21 The word 'sweet' is used frequently in Sarah's first person narrative.

22 The comparable passage in the *Faithful Narrative* reads: 'The light and comfort which some of them enjoy ... cause all things about them to appear as it were beautiful, sweet, and pleasant. All things abroad, the sun, moon, and stars; the clouds and sky, the heavens and earth, appear as it were with a cast of divine glory and sweetness upon them.' *Works*, vol. IV, p. 50.

23 'As thunder and thunder clouds, as they are vulgarly called, have a shadow of the majesty of God, so the blue skie, the green fields, and trees, and pleasant flowers have a shadow of the mild attributes of God, viz., grace and love of God, as well as the beauteous rainbow.' *Images or Shadows of Divine Things*, ed. Perry Miller (New Haven, 1948), p. 49.

24 *Religious Affections*, pp. 316–17.

25 *Religious Affections*, p. 334. The relationship between Edwards' personal experience and his public pronouncements on experience often presents interesting problems. In the passage quoted above, Edwards almost seems to be settling for himself the question of why he could record no more conviction of sin than we find described in the *Personal Narrative*. But another cross-reference, a sentence from the narrative, printed only by Hopkins, contains the essential logical distinction he employed to discuss conviction in the *Religious Affections* (pp. 323–36): 'That my Sins appear to me so great, don't seem to me to be, because I have so much more Conviction of Sin than other Christians, but because I am so much worse, and have so much more Wickedness to be convinced of' (p. 37).

CHAPTER 11

1 I have borrowed this phrase from the title of *The Many-Sided Franklin*, ed. Paul L. Ford (New York, 1899).
'For, without the belief of a Providence that takes cognisance of, guards, and guides, and may favor particular persons, there is no motive to worship a Deity, to fear his displeasure, or to pray for his protection' (Letter to Thomas Paine, *Ibid.*, p. 166).

3 *The Autobiography of Benjamin Franklin*, ed. Leonard W. Larabee *et al.* (New Haven, 1964), p. 114.

4 *Ibid.*

5 Leonard W. Larabee *et al.* (eds.), *The Papers of Benjamin Franklin*, vol. 1 (11 vols., New Haven, 1959), p. 62.

6 *Benjamin Franklin: Representative Selections*, ed. Frank Luther Mott and Chester E. Jorgenson (New York, 1936), p. 411.

7 *Poor Richard's Almanac: Selections from the Prefaces, Apothegms and Rimes*, ed. Benjamin E. Smith (New York, 1898), p. 142.

8 *Ibid.*, p. 116.

9 Mott and Jorgenson, *Franklin Selections*, p. 490.

10 *Papers of Franklin*, vol. 1, p. 350.

11 David Williams, 'More Light on Franklin's Religious Ideas', *American Historical Review*, XLIII (July 1938), 812.

12 *Papers of Franklin*, vol. 1, pp. 102–3.

13 Robert F. Sayre, *The Examined Self: Benjamin Franklin, Henry Adams, Henry James* (Princeton, 1964), pp. 27–31.

14 *Papers of Franklin*, vol. III, pp. 202–3.

15 *Ibid.*, vol. 1, pp. 262–3.

16 *Ibid.*, vol. III, p. 419.

17 *Autobiography*, p. 190.

18 *Ibid.*, p. 43.

19 *Ibid.*, p. 136.

20 *Papers of Franklin*, vol. 1, p. 69.

21 *Autobiography*, p. 54.

22 *Ibid.*, p. 76.

23 *Ibid.*, p. 214.

24 *Ibid.*, p. 124.

25 *Ibid.*

26 *Papers of Franklin*, vol. 1, p. 62.

27 *Nature*, in *Complete Works of Ralph Waldo Emerson*, ed. Edward Waldo Emerson (12 vols., Boston, 1903–4), vol. 1, p. 5.

28 *Moby-Dick*, ed. Charles Feidelson, Jr (New York, 1964), ch. 99, p. 556.

CHAPTER 12

1 Ursula Brumm, 'The Figure of Christ in American Literature', *Partisan Review*, XXIV (1957). Parts of this article are used in the present chapter.

2 (Chicago, 1955).

3 Lewis notes this too and comments on it thus (p. 130): 'When this conviction [the saving strength of the Adamic personality] became articulate in *Billy Budd*, the American hero as Adam became the hero as Christ and entered, once and for all, into the dimension of myth.'

4 Cf. Don Geiger, 'Melville's Black God. Contrary Evidence in the "Town-Ho's Story"', *American Literature*, XXV (1954), 464–71.

5 This has been shown by Charles H. Foster, *The Rungless Ladder: Harriet Beecher Stowe and New England Puritanism* (Durham, N.C., 1954).

6 Cf. what Edmund Wilson has recently said of this novel in *Patriotic Gore* (London, 1962), pp. 38ff.

7 *The Writings of Harriet Beecher Stowe*, vol. V (Boston, 1896), *The Minister's Wooing*, pp. 253f.

8 *The Works of William E. Channing* (Boston, 1878), p. 367.

9 *Ibid.*, p. 376.

10 *Ibid.*, p. 380.

11 *Complete Works of Ralph Waldo Emerson*, ed. Edward Waldo Emerson (12 vols., Boston, 1903–4), vol. I, p. 142.

12 Theodore Parker, 'A Discourse of the Transient and Permanent in Christianity', in Perry Miller (ed.), *The Transcendentalists: an Anthology* (Cambridge, Mass, 1950), pp. 267f.

13 *Ibid.*, p. 275.

14 *Ibid.*

15 *Ibid.*, p. 274.

16 Thomas Wolfe, *Of Time and the River* (New York, 1935).

17 Ralph Ellison, *Invisible Man* (New York, 1952).

18 Ernest Hemingway, *The Old Man and the Sea* (New York, 1952).

19 *Light in August*, The Modern Library (New York, 1950), p. 337.

20 *Ibid.*, p. 407.

21 'The Bear', *Go Down, Moses* (New York, 1942), p. 309.

22 It is indeed a matter for debate whether this book is successful in conception, form, and style. There are stretches where Faulkner's narration is mushy and lacking in contour, bogged down with unproductive detail, and the tone and technique of Saturday evening village small talk is sometimes out of place.

23 The German reviews were mostly favorable. The one by Wolfgang von Einsiedel in *Merkur*, X (1956), 282ff., is worthy of special note.

24 *Kenyon Review*, XVI (1954), 668f.

25 *A Fable* (New York, 1954), pp. 259f. 'Rapacity does not fail' is a parody on I Cor. 13: 8, 'charity never faileth', and the entire section on rapacity is the ironic counterpart of ch. 13 of I Corinthians, the theme of which is 'charity'.

26 In addition there is a mythical sort of Christ symbolism: cf. Eliot's 'Christ the tiger', *The Complete Poems and Plays* (New York, 1952), p. 21. The animal parallels for Christ are reminiscent of Physiologus.

27 *A Fable*, pp. 239f.

28 *Ibid.*, p. 348.

29 *Ibid.*, pp. 363f.

30 *Ibid.*, pp. 365f.

31 James occasionally uses Christ symbolism with these heroes, for instance Milly Theale, the heroine of *The Wings of the Dove*, but it is not pronounced enough to be studied from our standpoint.

Selected bibliography

The bibliography is divided into three parts, corresponding to the organization of the essays in this anthology. It does not include M.A. theses, reviews, anthologies of primary sources, editions, and bibliographies. For brief bibliographical guides to works in areas pertinent to the study of the American Puritan imagination, see the footnotes to the Introduction.

A. GENERAL

Benton, Robert M. 'The American Puritan Sermon before 1700', Dissertation. Colorado, 1967.

Bercovitch, Sacvan. 'Horologicals to Chronometricals: the Rhetoric of the Jeremiad', *Literary Monographs*, III, ed. Eric Rothstein. Madison, 1970. Pp. 1–124, 187–215.

'Puritan New England Rhetoric and the Jewish Problem', *Early American Literature*, V (1970), 63–71.

(ed.) *Typology and Early American Literature*. Amherst, 1972.

Brumm, Ursula. *American Thought and Religious Typology*. Trans. John Hoaglund. New Brunswick, N.J., 1970. First published in German, Leiden, 1963.

Cantor, Milton. 'The Image of the Negro in Colonial Literature', *New England Quarterly*, XXXVI (1963), 452–77.

Carleton, Philips D. 'The Indian Captivity', *American Literature*, XV (1943), 169–80.

Carroll, Peter N. *Puritanism and the Wilderness: the Intellectual Significance of the New England Frontier, 1629–1700*. New York, 1969.

Carroll, Richard S. 'Studies in the Background and Practice of Prose Style in New England, 1640–1750', Dissertation. Harvard, 1951.

Davis, Thomas M. 'Traditions of Puritan Typology', *Typology and Early American Literature*, ed. Sacvan Bercovitch. Amherst, 1972. Pp. 11–46.

'Typology in New England Puritanism', Dissertation. Missouri, 1969.

Emerson, Everett (ed.). *Major Writers of Early American Literature*. Madison, 1972.

Engdahl, Bonnie T. 'Paradise in the New World: a Study of the Image of the Garden in the Literature of Colonial America', Dissertation. U.C.L.A., 1967.

Faust, Clarence H. 'The Decline of Puritanism', *Transitions in American Literary History*, ed. Harry Hayden Clark. Durham, North Carolina, 1953. Pp. 1–47.

Fritzell, Peter A. 'Landscapes of Anglo-America During Exploration and Early Settlement', Dissertation. Stanford, 1967.

Gilsdorf, Aletha J. 'The Puritan Apocalypse: New England Eschatology in the Seventeenth Century', Dissertation. Yale, 1965.

Gummere, Richard M. *The American Colonial Mind and the Classical Tradition.* Cambridge, Mass., 1963.

Heimert, Alan. 'Puritanism, the Wilderness, and the Frontier', *New England Quarterly*, XXVI (1953), 361–82.

Henson, Robert. 'Sorry After a Godly Manner: a Study of the Puritan Funeral Elegy in New England, 1625–1722', Dissertation. U.C.L.A., 1957.

Hibler, David J. 'Sexual Rhetoric in Seventeenth Century American Literature', Dissertation. Notre Dame, 1971.

Horner, George F. 'A History of American Humor to 1765', Dissertation. North Carolina, 1938.

Howard, Alan B. 'The Web in the Loom: an Introduction to the Puritan Histories of New England', Dissertation. Stanford, 1969.

Howard, Leon. 'The Influence of Milton on Colonial American Poetry', *Huntington Library Bulletin*, VII (1935), 169–79.

Hudson, Robert L. 'American Sermons: a Study in Purpose, Background, and Psychological Approach', Dissertation. Peabody, 1948.

Hudson, Roy F. 'The Theory of Communication of Colonial New England Preachers, 1620–70', Dissertation. Cornell, 1954.

Israel, Calvin. 'American Puritan Literary Theory: 1620–1660', Dissertation. U.C.D., 1970.

Jackson, Frank M. 'An Application of the Principles of Aristotelian Rhetoric to Certain Early New England Prose', Dissertation. Texas, 1967.

Jantz, Harold S. 'The First Century of New England Verse', *Proceedings of the American Antiquarian Society*, LIII (1943), 219–523. Published as a separate book, New York, 1962.

Jones, Howard Mumford. *O Strange New World: American Culture, The Formative Years.* New York, 1964.

Kretzoi, Charlotte. 'The Concept of Poetry in Colonial America', *Hungarian Studies in English*, III (1967), 5–21.

Lesser, Marvin X. 'All for Profit: the Plain Style and the Massachusetts Election

Sermons in the Seventeenth Century', Dissertation. Columbia, 1967.

Levy, Babette M. *Preaching in the First Half Century of New England History.* Hartford, Conn., 1945.

Lowance, Mason I., Jr. 'Images and Shadows of Divine Things: Puritan Typology in New England from 1660 to 1750', Dissertation. Emory, 1967.

Manning, Stephen. 'Scriptural Exegesis and the Literary Critic', *Typology and Early American Literature*, ed. Sacvan Bercovitch. Amherst, 1972. Pp. 47–68.

Martin, Howard H. 'Puritan Preachers on Preaching: Notes on American Colonial Rhetoric', *Quarterly Journal of Speech*, L (1964), 385–92.

Miller, Perry. Introduction to *The Puritans: a Sourcebook of their Writings*, ed. Perry Miller and Thomas H. Johnson. New York, 1938. Rev. edn., 2 vols., New York, 1963.

Murdock, Kenneth B. 'Clio in the Wilderness: History and Biography in Puritan New England', *Church History*, XXIV (1955), 221–38.

'The Colonial and Revolutionary Period', *The Literature of the American People*, ed. Arthur Hobson Quinn. New York, 1951. Pp. 3–171.

Literature and Theology in Colonial New England. Cambridge, Mass., 1949.

Pearce, Roy Harvey. 'The Significance of the Captivity Narrative', *American Literature*, XIX (1947), 1–20.

Perluck, Herbert A. 'Puritan Expression and the Decline of Piety', Dissertation. Brown, 1955.

Pettit, Norman. *The Heart Prepared: Grace and Conversion in Puritan Spiritual Life.* New Haven, 1966.

Piercy, Josephine K. *Studies in Literary Types in Seventeenth Century America (1607–1710).* New Haven, 1939.

Plumstead, A. W. Introduction to *The Wall and The Garden: Selected Massachusetts Election Sermons, 1670–1775*, ed. A. W. Plumstead. Minneapolis, 1968. Pp. 3–37.

Roddey, Gloria J. 'The Metaphor of Counsel: a Shift from Objective Realism to Psychological Subjectivism in the Conceptual Cosmology of Puritanism', Dissertation. Kentucky, 1969.

Rosenmeier, Jesper. 'New England's Perfection: the Image of Adam and the Image of Christ in the Antinomian Crisis, 1634 to 1638', *William and Mary Quarterly*, XXVII (1970), 435–59.

'VERITAS: the Sealing of the Promise', *Harvard Library Bulletin*, XVI (1968), 26–37.

Searl, Stanford J., Jr. 'The Symbolic Imagination of American Puritanism: Metaphors for the Invisible World', Dissertation. Syracuse, 1971.

Shea, Daniel B., Jr. *Spritual Autobiography in Early America*. Princeton, 1968.

Silverman, Kenneth. Introductions in *Colonial American Poetry*, ed. Kenneth Silverman. New York, 1968.

Simpson, Alan. *Puritanism in Old and New England*. Chicago, 1955.

Smith, Wilbur M. 'The Prophetic Literature of Colonial America', *Bibliotheca Sacra*, C (1943), 67–82.

Spencley, Kenneth J. 'The Rhetoric of Decay in New England Writing, 1665–1730', Dissertation. Illinois, 1966.

Stein, Roger B. 'Seascape and the American Imagination: the Puritan Seventeenth Century', *Early American Literature*, VII (1972), 10–32.

[Tichi], Cecelia L. Halbert. 'The Art of the Lords Remembrancers: a Study of New England Puritan Histories', Dissertation. U.C.D., 1969.

'The Puritan Historians and Their New Jerusalem', *Early American Literature*, VI (1971), 143–55.

'Thespis and the "Carnall Hipocrite": a Puritan Motive for Aversion to Drama', *Early American Literature*, IV (1969), 86–103.

Trefz, Edward K. 'Satan as the Prince of Evil: the Preaching of New England Puritans', *Boston Public Library Quarterly*, VII (1955), 3–22.

'Satan in Puritan Preaching', *Boston Public Library Quarterly*, VIII (1956), 148–59.

Twomey, Rosemary. 'From Pure Church to Pure Nation: Massachusetts Bay, 1630–1692', Dissertation. Rochester, 1971.

Tyler, Moses Coit. *A History of American Literature during the Colonial Period, 1607–1765*. 2 vols., New York, 1897. First published, 1878.

Waggoner, Hyatt H. 'Puritan Poetry', *Criticism*, VI (1964), 291–312.

Wright, Thomas G. *Literary Culture in Early New England, 1620–1730*. New Haven, 1920.

B. INDIVIDUAL WRITERS

Bay Psalm Book [*Thomas Weld, John Eliot, and Richard Mather*]

Dorenkamp, John H. 'The *Bay Psalm Book* and the Ainsworth Psalter', *Early American Literature*, VII (1972), 3–16.

'The New England Puritans and the Name of God', *Proceedings of the American Antiquarian Society*, LXXX (1970), 67–70.

Grabo, Norman S. 'How Bad is the Bay Psalm Book?' *Publications of the Michigan Academy of Science, Arts, and Letters*, XLVI (1961), 605–14.

Haraszti, Zoltan. *The Enigma of the Bay Psalm Book*. Chicago, 1956.

Turner, Maxine Thompson. 'A History of the *Bay Psalm Book*', Dissertation. Auburn, 1971.

William Bradford

Akiyama, Ken. 'William Bradford and Cotton Mather: a Stylistic Analysis of the New England Mind', *Studies in English Literature* (Japan), XLI (1964–5), 59–71.

Bradford, E. F. 'Conscious Art in Bradford's *History of Plymouth Plantation*', *New England Quarterly*, I (1928), 133–57.

Daly, Robert, 'William Bradford's Vision of History', *American Literature*, XLIV (1973), 557–69.

Fritscher, John J. 'The Sensibility and Conscious Style of William Bradford', *Bucknell Review*, XVII (1969), 80–90.

Grabo, Norman S. 'William Bradford: *Of Plymouth Plantation*', *Landmarks of American Writing*, ed. Hennig Cohen. New York, 1969. Pp. 3–19.

Howard, Alan B. 'Art and History in Bradford's *Of Plymouth Plantation*', *William and Mary Quarterly*, XXVIII (1971), 237–66.

Levin, David. 'William Bradford: the Value of Puritan Historiography', *Major Writers of Early American Literature*, ed. Everett Emerson. Madison, 1972. Pp. 11–32.

Major, Minor W. 'William Bradford Versus Thomas Morton', *Early American Literature*, V (1970), 1–13.

Runyan, Michael G. 'The Poetry of William Bradford: an Annotated Edition with Essays Introductory to the Poems', Dissertation. U.C.L.A., 1971.

Anne Bradstreet

Contenti, Alessandra. 'Anne Bradstreet, il Petrarchismo e il "Plain Style"', *Studi Americani*, XIV (1968), 7–27.

Galinsky, Hans. 'Anne Bradstreet, Du Bartas und Shakespeare in Zusammenhang Kolonialer Verpfanzung und Umbormung Europäischer Literatur', *Festschrift für Walther Fischer*, ed. Carl Winter. Heidelberg, 1959. Pp. 145–80.

Hambler, Abigail Ann, 'Anne Bradstreet: Portrait of a Puritan Lady', *Cresset*, XXXII (1962), 11–13.

Hensley, Jeannine. 'Anne Bradstreet's Wreath of Thyme', introduction to *The Works of Anne Bradstreet*, ed. Jeannine Hensley. Cambridge, Mass., 1967. Pp. xxi–xxxv.

Hutchinson, Robert. Introduction to *The Poems of Anne Bradstreet*, ed. Robert Hutchinson. New York, 1969. Pp. 1–33.

Johnson, Carol. 'John Berryman and Mistress Bradstreet: a Relation of Reason', *Essays in Criticism* (Oxford), XIV (1964), 388–96.

Johnston, Thomas E., Jr. 'American Puritan Poetic Voices: Essays on Anne Bradstreet, Edward Taylor, Roger Williams and Philip Pain,' Dissertation. Ohio, 1968.

Laughlin, Rosemary M. 'Anne Bradstreet: Poet in Search of Form', *American Literature*, XLIII (1971), 1–17.

McMahon, Helen. 'Anne Bradstreet, Jean Bertault, and Dr. Crooke', *Early American Literature*, III (1968), 118–23.

Piercy, Josephine. *Anne Bradstreet*. New York, 1965.

Rich, Adrienne. 'Ann Bradstreet and Her Poetry', foreward to *The Works of Anne Bradstreet*, ed. Jeannine Hensley. Cambridge, Mass., 1967. Pp. ix–xx.

Rosenfeld, Alvin H. 'Anne Bradstreet's "Contemplations": Patterns of Form and Meaning', *New England Quarterly*, XLIII (1970), 79–96.

Rowlette, Edith J. 'The Works of Anne Bradstreet', Dissertation. Boston, 1964.

Stanford, Ann. 'Anne Bradstreet', *Major Writers of Early American Literature*, ed. Everett Emerson. Madison, 1972. Pp. 33–58.

'Anne Bradstreet: Dogmatist and Rebel', *New England Quarterly*, XXXIX (1966), 373–89.

'Anne Bradstreet as a Meditative Writer', *California English Journal*, II (1966), 24–31.

'The Poetry of Anne Bradstreet', Dissertation. U.C.L.A., 1962.

Tedeschini Lalli, Biancamaria. 'Anne Bradstreet', *Studi Americani*, III (1957), 9–37.

White, Elizabeth Wade. *Anne Bradstreet, 'The Tenth Muse'*. New York, 1971.

'The Tenth Muse – a Tercentenary Appraisal of Anne Bradstreet', *William and Mary Quarterly*, VIII (1951), 355–77.

John Cotton

Bercovitch, Sacvan. 'Typology in Puritan New England: the Williams–Cotton Controversy Reassessed', *American Quarterly*, XIX (1967), 166–91.

Emerson, Everett. *John Cotton*. New York, 1965.

Grabo, Norman S. 'John Cotton's Aesthetic: a Sketch', *Early American Literature*, III (1969), 4–10.

Gummere, Richard M. 'Church, State and the Classics: the Cotton–Williams Debate', *Classical Journal*, LIV (1959), 175–83.

Habegger, Alfred. 'Preparing the Soul for Christ: the Contrasting Sermon Forms of John Cotton and Thomas Hooker', *American Literature*, XLI (1970), 342–54.

Rosenmeier, Jesper. 'The Image of Christ: the Typology of John Cotton', Dissertation. Harvard, 1966.

'The Teacher and Witness: John Cotton and Roger Williams', *William and Mary Quarterly*, XXV (1968), 408–31.

Ziff, Larzer. *The Career of John Cotton: Puritanism and The American Experience.* Princeton, 1962.

Thomas Hooker

Bush, Sargent. 'The Growth of Thomas Hooker's *The Poor Doubting Christian*', *Early American Literature*, VII (1973), 3–20.

Darrow, Diane M. 'Thomas Hooker and the Art of Puritan Preaching', Dissertation. U.C.S.D., 1969.

Emerson, Everett H. 'Thomas Hooker and the Reformed Theology: the Relationship of Thomas Hooker's Conversion Preaching to Its Background', Dissertation. Louisiana, 1955.

Frederick, John T. 'Literary Art in Thomas Hooker's *The Poor Doubting Christian*', *American Literature*, XL (1969), 1–8.

Habegger, Alfred. 'Preparing the Soul for Christ: the Contrasting Sermon Forms of John Cotton and Thomas Hooker', *American Literature*, XLI (1970), 342–54.

Pellman, Hubert R. 'Thomas Hooker: a Study in Puritan Ideals', Dissertation. Pennsylvania, 1958.

Zolla, Elémire. 'Lo Stile di Thomas Hooker', *Studi Americani*, XI (1965), 43–52.

Edward Johnson

Bercovitch, Sacvan. 'The Historiography of Johnson's *Wonder-Working Providence*', *Essex Institute Historical Collections*, CIV (1968), 138–61.

Brumm, Ursula. 'Edward Johnson's *Wonder-Working Providence* and the Puritan Conception of History', *Jahrbuch für Amerikastudien*, XIV (1969), 140–51.

Gallagher, Edward J. 'A Critical Study of Edward Johnson's *Wonder-Working Providence of Sions Savior in New England*', Dissertation. Notre Dame, 1971.

'An Overview of Edward Johnson's *Wonder-Working Providence*', *Early American Literature*, V (1971), 30–49.

Trimpey, John E. 'The Poetry of Four American Puritans: Edward Johnson, Peter Bulkeley II, Nicholas Noyes, and John Danforth', Dissertation. Ohio, 1968.

Vanccura, Zdeněk. 'The Humble Song of Captain Johnson (a Note on Edward Johnson's *Wonder-Working Providence of Sions Saviour in New-England*)', *Philologica*, supplement to *Casopis Pro Moderni Filologii*, VII (1955), 1–11.

Cotton Mather

Akiyama, Ken. 'William Bradford and Cotton Mather: a Stylistic Analysis of the New England Mind', *Studies in English Literature* (Japan), XLI (1964–5), 59–71.

Andrews, William D. 'The Printed Funeral Sermons of Cotton Mather', *Early American Literature*, V (1970), 24–44.

Bercovitch, Sacvan. 'Cotton Mather', *Major Writers of Early American Literature*, ed. Everett Emerson. Madison, 1972. Pp. 93–150.

'"Delightful Examples of Surprising Prosperity": Cotton Mather and the American Success Story', *English Studies* (The Netherlands), LVI (1970), 40–3.

'A Literary Study of Cotton Mather's *Magnalia Christi Americana*', Dissertation. Claremont, 1965.

'New England Epic: Cotton Mather's *Magnalia Christi Americana*' *English Literary History*, XXXIII (1966), 337–51.

Cifelli, Edward, 'More of Cotton Mather's "Verbal Patterns"', *Quarterly Journal of Speech*, LVII (1971), 94–7.

Duffy, John P. 'Cotton Mather Revisited', *Massachusetts Studies in English*, I (1967), 30–8.

Heimert, Alan. Introduction to, Barrett Wendell, *Cotton Mather: the Puritan Priest* (1891). New York, 1963. Pp. vii–xxxix.

Lazenby, Walter. 'Exhortations as Exorcism: Cotton Mather's Sermon to Murderers', *Quarterly Journal of Speech*, LVII (1971), 50–6.

Levin, David. 'The Hazing of Cotton Mather: the Creation of a Biographical Personality', *New England Quarterly*, XXXIV (1963), 147–71.

Lowance, Mason I., Jr. 'Cotton Mather's *Magnalia* and the Metaphors of Biblical History', *Typology and Early American Literature*, ed. Sacvan Bercovitch. Amherst, 1972. Pp. 139–62.

Manierre, William R., II. 'Cotton Mather and the Biographical Parallel', *American Quarterly*, XIII (1961), 153–60.

'Cotton Mather and the Plain Style', Dissertation. Michigan, 1957.

'Some Characteristic Mather Redactions', *New England Quarterly*, XXXI (1958), 496–505.

'Verbal Pattern in Cotton Mather's *Magnalia*', *Quarterly Journal of Speech*, XLVII (1961), 402–13.

Murdock, Kenneth B. Introduction to *Selections from Cotton Mather*. Ed. Kenneth B. Murdock. New York, 1926. Pp. ix–lviii.

Silverman, Kenneth. Commentary on *Selected Letters of Cotton Mather*. Ed. Kenneth Silverman. Baton Rouge, La., 1971.

Warren, Austin. 'Dr. Cotton Mather's *Magnalia*', in Austin Warren, *Connections*. Ann Arbor, 1970. Pp. 24–44. Revised from 'Grandfather Mather and His Wonder Book', *Sewanee Review*, LXXII (1964), 96–116.

Watters, Reginald E. 'Biographical Technique in Cotton Mather's *Magnalia*', *William and Mary Quarterly*, II (1945), 154–64.

White, Eugene E. 'Cotton Mather's *Manuductio ad Ministerium*', *Quarterly Journal of Speech*, XLIX (1963), 308–19.

Woody, Kennerly M. 'Cotton Mather's *Manuductio ad Theologiam*: the "More Quiet and Hopeful Way"', *Early American Literature*, IV (1969), 3–48.

Samuel Sewall

Arner, Robert D. 'Plumb Island Revisited: One Version of the Pastoral', *Seventeenth-Century News*, XXVII (1969), 58–61.

Dykema, Karl W. 'Samuel Sewall Reads John Dryden', *American Literature*, XIV (1942), 157–61.

Highfill, Robert D. 'The Vocabulary of Samuel Sewall from 1673 to 1699', Dissertation. Chicago, 1927.

Isani, Mukhtar Ali. 'The Growth of Sewall's *Phaenomena Quaedam Apocalyptica*', *Early American Literature*, VII (1972), 64–75.

Millar, Albert E., Jr. 'Spiritual Autobiography in Selected Writings of Sewall, Edwards, Byrd, Woolman and Franklin: a Comparison of Technique and Content', Dissertation. Delaware, 1968.

Edward Taylor

Akiyama, Ken 'Edward Taylor's Poetry: an Introduction'. *Studies in Humanities* [Osaka, Japan], LXIV (1963), 27–44.

Alexis, Gerhard T. 'A Keen Nose for Taylor's Syntax', *Early American Literature*, IV (1969), 97–101.

Allen, Judson Boyce. 'Edward Taylor's Catholic Wasp: Exegetical Convention in "Upon A Spider Catching a Fly"', *English Language Notes*, VII (1970), 257–60.

Arner, Robert D. 'Edward Taylor's Gaming Imagery: "Meditation 1.40"', *Early American Literature*, IV (1969), 38–40.

'Folk Metaphors in Edward Taylor's "Meditation 1.40"'. *Seventeenth-Century News*, XXI (1973), 6–8.

Bach, Bert C. 'Self-Depreciation in Edward Taylor's Sacramental Meditations', *Cithara*, VI (1966), 49–59.

Bales, Kent, and William J. Aull. 'Touching Taylor Overly: Note on "Meditation Six"', *Early American Literature*, V (1970), 57–9.

Ball, Kenneth R. 'Rhetoric in Edward Taylor's *Preparatory Meditations*', *Early American Literature*, IV (1969), 78–88.

Benton, Robert M. 'Edward Taylor's Use of His Text', *American Literature*, XXXIX (1967), 31–41.

Berkowitz, Morton. 'Edward Taylor and the Seventeenth Century', Dissertation. Massachusetts, 1968.

Black, Mindele. 'Edward Taylor: Heavens Sugar Cake', *New England Quarterly*, XXIX (1956), 159–81.

Blau, Herbert. 'Heaven's Sugar Cake: Theology and Imagery in the Poetry of Edward Taylor', *New England Quarterly*, XXVI (1953), 337–60.

Boll, Robert N., and Thomas M. Davis. 'Saint Augustine and Edward Taylor's "Meditation 138.2"', *English Language Notes*, VIII (1971), 183–7.

Bottorff, William K. 'Edward Taylor: an Explication: "Another Meditation at the Same Time"', *Early American Literature*, III (1968), 17–21.

Brown, Wallace C. 'Edward Taylor: an American "Metaphysical"', *American Literature*, XVI (1944–5), 186–97.

Brumm, Ursula. 'Der "Baum des Lebens" in den Meditationen Edward Taylor', *Jahrbuch für Amerikastudien*, XII (1967), 109–23. Reprinted in English translation, *Early American Literature*, III (1968), 72–87.

'Edward Taylor and the Poetic Use of Religious Imagery', *Typology and Early American Literature*, ed. Sacvan Bercovitch. Amherst, 1972. Pp. 191–208.

Bush, Sargent, Jr. 'Paradox, Puritanism, and Taylor's *Gods Determinations*', *Early American Literature*, IV (1969), 48–66.

Callow, James T. 'Edward Taylor Obeys Saint Paul', *Early American Literature*, IV (1969), 89–96.

Carlisle, E. F. 'The Puritan Structure of Edward Taylor's Poetry', *American Quarterly*, XX (1968), 147–63.

Clare, Sister M. Theresa. 'Taylor's "Meditation Sixty-Two"', *Explicator*, XIX (1961), no. 16.

Clendenning, John. 'Piety and Imagery in Edward Taylor's "The Reflexion"', *American Quarterly*, XVI (1964), 203–10.

Colacurcio, Michael. '*Gods Determinations* Touching Half-Way Membership: Occasion and Audience in Edward Taylor', *American Literature*, XXXIX (1967), 298–314.

Curtis, Jared. 'Edward Taylor and Emily Dickinson: Voices and Visions', *Susquehanna University Studies*, VII (1964), 159–67.

Davis, Thomas M. 'Edward Taylor and the Traditions of Puritan Typology', *Early American Literature*, IV (1969–70), 27–47.

'Edward Taylor's "Occasional Meditations"', *Early American Literature*, V (1971), 17–29.

Dunn, Hough-Lewis. 'Edward Taylor's Poetic Sequences', Dissertation. Texas, 1966.

Ellzey, Diana S. 'Edward Taylor's *Christographia*: the Poems and the Sermons', Dissertation. Michigan, 1971.

Emerson, Everett (ed.). Special Edward Taylor issue of *Early American Literature*, IV, no. 3 (1969).

Epperson, William Russell. 'The Meditative Structure of Edward Taylor's "Preparatory Meditations"', Dissertation. Kansas, 1966.

Fender, Stephen A. 'Edward Taylor and "The Application of Redemption"', *Modern Language Review*, LIX (1964), 331–4.

'Edward Taylor and the Sowers of American Puritan Wit', Dissertation. Manchester, 1963.

Garrison, Joseph M., Jr. 'The "Worship-Mould": a Note on Edward Taylor's *Preparatory Meditations*', *Early American Literature*, III (1968), 127–31.

Gilman, Harvey. 'From Sin to Song: Image Clusters and Patterns in Edward Taylor's *Preparatory Meditations*', Dissertation. Penn. State, 1967.

Giovannini, G. 'Taylor's *The Glory of and Grace in the Church Set Out*', *Explicator*, VI (1948), no. 26.

Goodman, William B. 'Edward Taylor Writes His Love', *New England Quarterly*, XXVII (1954), 510–15.

Grabo, Norman S. 'Catholic Tradition, Puritan Literature, and Edward Taylor', *Papers of the Michigan Academy of Science, Arts, and Letters*, XLV (1960), 395–402.

Edward Taylor. New York, 1961.

'Edward Taylor on the Lord's Supper', *Boston Public Library Quarterly*, XII (1960), 22–35.

'Edward Taylor's Spiritual Huswifery', *Publications of the Modern Language Association*, LXXIX (1960), 554–60.

Introduction to *Edward Taylor's Christographia*, ed. Norman S. Grabo. New Haven, 1962. Pp. xiv–xlviii. Revised from Dissertation, U.C.L.A., 1958.

Introduction to *Edward Taylor's Treatise Concerning the Lord's Supper*, ed. Norman S. Grabo. Lansing, Mich., 1966. Pp. ix–li.

Griffin, Edward M. 'The Structure and Language of Taylor's Meditation 2.112', *Early American Literature*, III (1968–9), 205–8.

Griffith, Clark. 'Edward Taylor and the Momentum of Metaphor', *English Literary History*, XXXIII (1966), 448–60.

Hedberg, Johannes. 'Meditations Linguistic and Literary on "Meditation Twenty-Nine" by Edward Taylor (c. 1644–1729)', *Moderna Språk* [Stockholm], LIV (1960), 253–70.

Hodges, Robert R. 'Edward Taylor's "Artificiall Man"', *American Literature*, XXXI (1959), 76–7.

Howard, Alan B. 'The World as Emblem: Language and Vision in the Poetry of Edward Taylor', *American Literature*, XLIV (1972), 359–84.

Isani, Mukhtar Ali. 'Edward Taylor and the "Turks"', *Early American Literature*, VII (1972), 120–3.

Israel, Calvin. 'Edward Taylor's *Barleybreaks*', *American Notes and Queries*, IV (1966), 147–8.

Johnson, Thomas H. 'Edward Taylor: a Puritan "Sacred Poet"', *New England Quarterly*, X (1937), 290–322.

Introduction to *The Poetical Works of Edward Taylor*, ed. Thomas H. Johnson. New York, 1939. Pp. 11–28.

Johnston, Thomas E., Jr. 'American Puritan Poetic Voices: Essays on Anne Bradstreet, Edward Taylor, Roger Williams and Philip Pain', Dissertation. Ohio, 1968.

'Edward Taylor: an American Emblematist', *Early American Literature*, III (1968–9), 186–98.

Jordan, Raymond J. 'Taylor's "The Ebb and Flow"', *Explicator*, XX (1962), no. 67.

Junkins, Donald. 'An Analytical Study of Edward Taylor's *Preparatory Meditations*', Dissertation. Boston, 1963.

'Edward Taylor's Creative Process', *Early American Literature*, IV (1969), 67–78.

'Edward Taylor's Revision', *American Literature*, XXXVII (1965), 135–52.

'"Should Stars Wooe Lobster Claws?": a Study of Edward Taylor's Poetic Practice and Theory', *Early American Literature*, III (1968), 88–117.

Keller, Karl. 'The Rev. Mr. Edward Taylor's Bawdry', *New England Quarterly*, XLIII (1970), 382–406.

'"The World Slickt Up in Types": Edward Taylor as a Version of Emerson', *Typology and Early American Literature*, ed. Sacvan Bercovitch. Amherst, 1972. Pp. 175–90.

Krishnamurthi, M. G. 'Edward Taylor: a Note on the American Literary Tradition', *Indian Essays in American Literature: Papers in Honor of Robert E. Spiller*, eds. Sujit Mukherjee and D. V. K. Raghavacharyulu. Bombay, 1969. Pp. 27–39.

Lang, Erdmute. 'Meditation 42 von Edward Taylor', *Jahrbuch für Amerikastudien*, XII (1967), 92–108.

Laurentia, Sister M. 'Taylor's *Meditation 42*', *Explicator*, VIII (1949), no. 19.

Lind, Sidney E. 'Edward Taylor: a Revaluation', *New England Quarterly*, XXI (1948), 518–30.

Link, Franz H. 'Edward Taylors Dichtung als Lobpreis Gottes', *Jahrbuch für Amerikastudien*, XVI (1971), 77–101.

Manierre, William R., II. 'Verbal Patterns in the Poetry of Edward Taylor', *College English*, XXIII (1962), 296–9.

Martz, Louis L. Foreword to *The Poems of Edward Taylor*, ed. Donald E. Stanford. New Haven, 1960. Pp. xiii-xxxvii.

McNamara, Anne Marie. 'Taylor's "Sacramental Meditation Six"', *Explicator*, XVII (1958), no. 3.

Mignon, Charles W. 'The American Puritan and Private Qualities of Edward Taylor, the Poet', Dissertation. Connecticut, 1963.

'Diction in Edward Taylor' *Preparatory Meditations*', *American Speech*, XLI (1966), 243–53.

'Edward Taylor's *Preparatory Meditations*: a Decorum of Imperfection', *Publications of the Modern Language Association*, LXXXIII (1968), 1423–8.

'A Principle of Order in Edward Taylor's *Preparatory Meditations*', *Early American Literature*, IV (1969), 110–16.

Nicolaisen, Peter. *Die Bildlichkeit in der Dichtung Edward Taylors*. Neumünster, 1966.

Pearce, Roy Harvey. 'Edward Taylor: the Poet as Puritan', *New England Quarterly*, XXIII (1950), 31–46. Reprinted in *Critical Approaches to American Literature*, ed. Ray B. Browne and Martin Light. New York, 1965. Vol I, pp. 13–25.

Penner, Allen Richard. 'Edward Taylor's Meditation One', *American Literature*, XXXIX (1967), 193–9.

Pérez Gallego, Cándido. '"Sweet" en Edward Taylor: una clave para valorar al primer poeta metiafisico americano', *Filologia Moderna*, VI (1966), 273–92.

Peterson, Richard. 'The "Art of Meditation" in Edward Taylor's *Preparatory Meditations*', Dissertation. Kent State, 1967.

Prosser, Evan. 'Edward Taylor's Poetry', *New England Quarterly*, XL (1967), 375–98.

Reiter, Robert E. 'Poetry and Doctrine in Edward Taylor's *Preparatory Meditations*, Series II, 1–30', *Typology and Early American Literature*, ed. Sacvan Bercovitch. Amherst, 1972. Pp. 163–74.

Rowe, Karen E. 'A Biblical Illumination of Taylorian Art', *American Literature*, XL (1968), 370–4.

Russell, Gene. 'Dialectal and Phonetic Features of Edward Taylor's Rhymes: a Brief Study Based upon a Computer Concordance of His Poems', *American Literature*, XLIII (1971), 165–80. Taken from Dissertation of the same title, Wisconsin, 1970.

Scheick, William J. 'Nonsense from a Lisping Child: Edward Taylor on the Word as Piety', *Texas Studies in Language and Literature*, XIII (1971), 39–53.

'Tending the Lord in All Admiring Style: Edward Taylor's *Preparatory Meditations*', *Language and Style*, IV (1971), 163–87.

'A Viper's Nest, The Featherbed of Faith: Edward Taylor on the Will', *Early American Literature*, V (1970), 45–56.

'The Will and the Word: the Experience of Conversion in the Poetry of Edward Taylor', Dissertation. Illinois, 1970.

Schulze, Fritz W. 'Strophe, Vers und Reim in Edward Taylor's *Meditations*', *Literatur und Sprache der Vereinigten Staaten: Aufsätze zu Ehren von Hans Galinsky*, eds. Hans Helmcke, Klaus Lubbers, and Renate Schmidt von Bardeleben. Heidelberg, 1969. Pp. 11–33.

Shepherd, Emma L. 'The Metaphysical Conceit in the Poetry of Edward Taylor', Dissertation. North Carolina, 1960.

Siebel, Kathy, and Thomas M. Davis. 'Edward Taylor and the Cleansing of *Aqua Vitae*', *Early American Literature*, IV (1969), 102–9.

Smith, Roy H. 'A Study of the Platonic Heritage of Love in the Poetry of Edward Taylor', Dissertation. Bowling Green, 1969.

Stanford, Donald E. *Edward Taylor*. Minneapolis, 1965.

'Edward Taylor', *Major Writers of Early American Literature*, ed. Everett Emerson. Wisconsin, 1972. Pp. 59–92.

'Edward Taylor and the "Hermophrodite" Poems', *Early American Literature*, VII (1973), 59–61.

'Edward Taylor and the Lord's Supper', *American Literature*, XXVII (1960), 172–8.

'Edward Taylor's Metrical History of Christianity', *American Literature*, XXXIII (1961), 279–97.

Introduction to *The Poems of Edward Taylor*, ed. Donald E. Stanford. New Haven, 1960. Pp. xxxix-lxii.

'The Puritan Poet as Preacher: an Edward Taylor Sermon', *Studies in American Literature*, eds. Waldo McNeir and Leo B. Levy. Baton Rouge, La., 1960. Pp. 1–10.

Tedeschini Lalli, Biancamaria. 'Edward Taylor', *Studi Americani*, II (1956), 9–43.

Thomas, Jean L. 'Drama and Doctrine in *Gods Determinations*', *American Literature*, XXXVI (1965), 452–62.

Thorpe, Peter. 'Edward Taylor as Poet', *New England Quarterly*, XXXIX (1966), 356–72.

[Tichi] Halbert, Cecelia L. 'Tree of Life Imagery in the Poetry of Edward Taylor', *American Literature*, XXXVIII (1966), 22–34.

Wack, Thomas G. 'The Imagery of Edward Taylor's *Preparatory Meditations*', Dissertation. Notre Dame, 1961.

Warren, Austin. 'Edward Taylor's Poetry: Colonial Baroque', *Kenyon Review*, III (1941), 355–71. Revised as 'Edward Taylor', in *Rage for Order: Essays in Criticism*. Chicago, 1948. Pp. 1–18.

Weathers, Willie T. 'Edward Taylor and the Cambridge Platonists', *American Literature*, XXVI (1954), 1–31.

'Edward Taylor, Hellenistic Puritan', *American Literature*, XVIII (1946), 18–26.

Werge, Thomas. 'The Tree of Life in Edward Taylor's Poetry: the Sources of a Puritan Image', *Early American Literature*, III (1968–9), 199–204.

Wiley, Elizabeth. 'Sources of Imagery in the Poetry of Edward Taylor', Dissertation. Pittsburgh, 1962.

Wright, Nathalia. 'The Morality Tradition in the Poetry of Edward Taylor', *American Literature*, XVIII (1946), 1–17.

Michael Wigglesworth

Alexis, Gerhard T. 'Wigglesworth's "Easiest Room"', *New England Quarterly*, XLII (1969), 573–83.

Brack, O. M., Jr. 'Michael Wigglesworth and the Attribution of "I Walk'd and Did a Little Molehill View"', *Seventeenth-Century News*, XVIII (1970), 41–4.

Crowder, Richard. *No Featherbed to Heaven: a Biography of Michael Wigglesworth*. East Lansing, Mich., 1962.

Matthiessen, Francis O. 'Michael Wigglesworth, a Puritan Poet', *New England Quarterly*, I (1928), 491–504.

Roger Williams

Bercovitch, Sacvan. 'Typology in Puritan New England: the Williams – Cotton Controversy Reassessed', *American Quarterly*, XIX (1967), 166–91.

Gummere, Richard M. 'Church, State and the Classics: the Cotton–Williams Debate', *Classical Journal*, LIV (1959), 175–83.

Hunsaker, Orvil Glade. 'Calvinistic Election and Arminian Reparation: a Striking Contrast in the Works of Roger Williams and John Milton', Dissertation. Illinois, 1970.

Johnston, Thomas E., Jr. 'American Puritan Poetic Voices: Essays on Anne Bradstreet, Edward Taylor, Roger Williams and Philip Pain', Dissertation. Ohio, 1968.

Miller, Perry. *Roger Williams: his Contribution to the American Tradition*. Indianapolis, 1953.

Morgan, Edmund S. *Roger Williams: the Church and the State*. New York, 1969.

Reinitz, Richard. 'The Separatist Background of Roger Williams' Argument for Religious Toleration', *Typology and Early American Literature*, ed. Sacvan Bercovitch. Amherst, 1972. Pp. 107–37.

Rosenmeier, Jesper. 'The Teacher and the Witness: John Cotton and Roger Williams', *William and Mary Quarterly*, XXV (1968), 408–31.

Other Writers

I have included a writer in this category if there have been only one or two literary studies of his work; the category itself, however, is by no means intended as a judgment (e.g., 'minor' authors). It seems safe to say that some of these writers, like Increase Mather and Thomas Shepard, will rise in significance as literary artists — as will others who have not yet been individually treated, such as Joshua Scottow.

Arner, Robert D. '*The Simple Cobler of Aggawam*: Nathaniel Ward and the Rhetoric of Satire', *Early American Literature*, V (1971), 3–16.

Fussell, Edwin. 'Benjamin Tompson: Public Poet', *New England Quarterly*, XXVI (1953), 494–511.

Gildrie, Richard P. 'Francis Higginson's New World Vision', *Essex Institute Historical Collections*, CVI (1970), 182–9.

Hahn, T. G. 'Urian Oakes's *Elegie* on Thomas Shepard and Puritan Poetics', *American Literature*, XLV (1973), 163–81.

Johnston, Thomas E., Jr. 'American Puritan Poetic Voices: Essays on Anne Bradstreet, Edward Taylor, Roger Williams and Philip Pain', Dissertation. Ohio, 1968. Note abstracted from Dissertation appears in *Early American Literature*, III (1968), 125–6.

Kaiser, Leo M. 'The Oratorio Quinta of Urian Oakes, Harvard, 1678', *Humanistica Lovaniensia*, XIX (1970), 485–508.

LeMay, J. A. Leo. 'Jonson and Hilton: Two Influences in Oakes's *Elegie*', *New England Quarterly*, XXXVIII (1965), 90–2.

Lowance, Mason I., Jr. Introduction to Samuel Mather, *Figures or Types of the Old Testament* (reprint of 2nd edn., London, 1705). New York, 1969. Pp. v-xxvii.

McCune, Marjorie W. 'The Danforths: Puritan Poets', Dissertation. Penn. State, 1969.

Murdock, Kenneth B. *Increase Mather, the Foremost American Puritan.* Cambridge, Mass., 1926.

Olsson, Karl A. 'Theology and Rhetoric in the Writings of Thomas Shepard', Dissertation. Chicago, 1949.

Sands, Alyce E. 'John Saffin, Seventeenth-Century American Citizen and Poet', Dissertation. Penn. State, 1965.

Scheick, William J. 'Anonymity and Art in [Increase Mather's] *The Life and Death of that Reverend Man of God, Mr. Richard Mather*', *American Literature*, XLII (1971), 457–67.

Strother, Bonnie L. 'The Imagery in the Sermons of Thomas Shepard', Dissertation. Tennessee, 1968.

Trimpey, John E. 'The Poetry of Four American Puritans: Edward Johnson, Peter Bulkeley II, Nicholas Noyes, and John Danforth', Dissertation. Ohio, 1968.

C. CONTINUITIES

A number of the works in the first section of this bibliography also deal, to some extent, with continuities. Each of the works listed below deals *mainly* with writers who came after the seventeenth century.

Ballinger, Martha. 'The Metaphysical Echo', *English Studies in Africa*, VIII (1965), 71–80.

Baritz, Loren. *City on a Hill: a History of Ideas and Myths in America.* New York, 1964.

Chmaj, Betty E. 'The Metaphors of Resurrection', *Universitas*, II (1964), 91–109.

Covey, Cyclone. *The American Pilgrimage.* New York, 1961.

De Jong, J. A. *As the Waters Cover the Earth: Millennial Expectations in the Rise of Anglo-American Missions, 1640–1810.* Amsterdam, 1970.

Feidelson, Charles, Jr. *Symbolism and American Literature.* Chicago, 1953.

Fritzell, Peter A. 'The Wilderness and the Garden: Metaphors for the American Landscape', *Forest History*, XII (1968), 16–22.

Heimert, Alan. *Religion and the American Mind: from the Great Awakening to the Revolution.* Cambridge, Mass., 1966.

Hills, Margaret T. 'The English Bible in America', *Bulletin of the New York Public Library*, LXV (1961), 277–88.

Kolodny, Annette. 'The Pastoral Impulse in American Writing, 1590–1850: Psychological Approach', Dissertation. Berkeley, 1969.

Lenhart, Charmenz S. *Musical Influences on American Poetry*. Athens, Ga., 1956.

Lynen, John F. *The Design of the Present: Essays on Time and Form in American Literature*. New Haven, 1969.

McAleer, John S. 'Biblical Symbols in American Literature: a Utilitarian Design', *English Studies*, XLVI (1965), 310–22.

Minnick, Wayne C. 'The New England Execution Sermons, 1639–1800', *Speech Monographs*, XXXV (1968), 77–89.

Minter, David. *The Interpreted Design as a Structural Principle in American Prose*. New Haven, 1969.

Otis, William B. *American Verse, 1625–1807: a History*. New York, 1909.

Pearce, Roy Harvey. *The Continuity of American Poetry*. Princeton, 1961.

Plumstead, A. W. 'Puritanism and Nineteenth Century American Literature', *Queen's Quarterly*, LXX (1963), 209–22.

Ruth, John M. 'English Hymn-Writing in America, 1640–1800', Dissertation. Harvard, 1968.

Sanford, Charles. *The Quest for Paradise: Europe and the American Moral Imagination*. Urbana, 1961.

Smith, Chard Powers. 'Plain Humor: New England Style', *New England Quarterly*, XLIII (1970), 465–72.

Stewart, Randall. 'Puritan Literature and the Flowering of New England', *William and Mary Quarterly*, III (1946), 319–42.

Tuveson, Ernest L. *Redeemer Nation: the Idea of America's Millennial Role*. Chicago, 1968.

Venčura, Zdeněk. 'Baroque Prose in America', *Studies in English of Charles University* [Czeckoslovakia], IV (1933), 39–58.

Waggoner, Hyatt H. *American Poets: from the Puritans to the Present*. Boston, 1968.

Warren, Austin. *The New England Conscience*. Ann Arbor, 1966.
  New England Saints. Ann Arbor, 1956.

Willett, Maurita. 'Salem Witchcraft in American Literature', Dissertation. Brandeis, 1959.

Williams, George H. *Wilderness and Paradise in Christian Thought: the Biblical Experience of the Desert in the History of Christianity and the Paradise Theme in the Theological Idea of the University*. New York, 1962.

Willson, Lawrence. 'The Puritan Tradition in American Literature', *Arizona Quarterly*, XIII (1957), 33–40.

Wright, Louis B. *The Cultural Life of the American Colonies*. New York, 1957.

Index

PUBLIC LIBRARY OF BROOKLINE

3 1712 00047 8233

JUN   1975

Public Library of Brookline

MAIN LIBRARY
361 Washington Street
Brookline, Mass. 02146

I M P O R T A N T

Leave cards in pocket

DEMCO